# Dominance,
# Self-Esteem,
# Self-Actualization:
# Germinal Papers of
# A. H. Maslow

**The A. H. Maslow Series**

Dominance, Self-Esteem, Self-Actualization:
Germinal Papers of A. H. Maslow
   *by the late A. H. Maslow and edited by Richard J. Lowry*
A. H. Maslow: An Intellectual Portrait
   *by Richard J. Lowry*
The Journals of A. H. Maslow
   *by the late A. H. Maslow and edited by Richard J. Lowry*
Abraham H. Maslow: A Memorial Volume

# Dominance, Self-Esteem, Self-Actualization: Germinal Papers of A. H. Maslow

*Edited by*
Richard J. Lowry
*Vassar College*

*For the*
International Study Project, Inc.

**Brooks/Cole Publishing Company**
**Monterey, California**
A Division of Wadsworth Publishing Company, Inc.

## Acknowledgments

*Journal of Genetic Psychology:* The role of dominance in the social and sexual behavior of infra-human primates: I. Observations at Vilas Park Zoo, 1936, **48,** 261–277; II. An experimental determination of the behavior syndrome of dominance, 1936, **48,** 278–309.

*Psychological Review:* Dominance-feeling, behavior, and status, 1937, **44,** 404–429; A theory of human motivation, 1943, **50,** 370–396.

*Journal of Social Psychology:* Dominance-feeling, personality, and social behavior in women, 1939, **10,** 3–39; Self-esteem (dominance-feeling) and sexuality in women, 1942, **16,** 259–294; The authoritarian character structure, 1943, **18,** 401–411.

Grune and Stratton, Inc., a division of Harcourt Brace Jovanovich: Self-actualizing people: A study of psychological health, in *Personality Symposia:* Symposium #1 on Values, 1950, pp. 11–34.

ISBN: 0-8185-0087-5
L.C. Cat. Card No.: 73-85044
Printed in the United States of America
1 2 3 4 5 6 7 8 9 10—77 76 75 74 73

*Production Editor: Micky Lawler*
*Interior & Cover Design: Linda Marcetti*
*Typesetting: Holmes Composition Service, San Jose, California*
*Printing & Binding: Kingsport Press, Kingsport, Tennessee*

# Preface

The papers presented in this book are diverse in both content and style, but at the same time they have a coherence that can scarcely be missed. They are, in fact, the high points of a connected series of papers that began with A. H. Maslow's early studies of primate "dominance," continued through his investigation of human (female) "dominance" and "self-esteem," and culminated in his proclamation of human "self-actualization." Certainly the last of these, self-actualization, is the most widely known and interesting of Maslow's psychologizings—and, if true, the most important. My hope is that this volume will bring the reader to a fuller understanding of the development of that notion. These papers do not, of course, tell the whole story of self-actualization, but they do tell a significant part of it, and in a way that cannot be duplicated by any second-hand account. Such a second-hand account is my book *A. H. Maslow: An Intellectual Portrait* (Brooks/Cole, 1973), of which the present volume is a fairly direct outgrowth. My purpose here is to extend that "portrait" by allowing the reader to follow the development of Maslow's psychological work—or at least a portion of it—at first hand. The period in question stretches from the early 1930s, when Maslow was still a graduate student in psychology, to the early 1950s, when he was fast approaching the height of his career.

I am most deeply indebted to Mrs. Bertha G. Maslow, who first enlisted my interest in this volume, then helped to arrange for its material support, and finally collaborated throughout in the selection of papers. She was especially valuable as a source of information about what her late husband himself would have considered most important and worthy of inclusion in a book such as this.

I am also very much indebted to Vassar College, which provided me with a year's leave during which I was able to work on this and other matters pertaining to Maslow, and to everyone associated with the International Study Project, Inc., of Menlo Park, California, which provided material support for the project—especially William Price Laughlin, William Crockett, and Mrs. Kay Pontius.

*Richard J. Lowry*

# Contents

# Dominance, Self-Esteem, Self-Actualization: Germinal Papers of A. H. Maslow

## Editor's Introduction
## to Papers 1 and 2

This first paper and the one that follows were the major portions of Maslow's Ph.D. thesis (University of Wisconsin, 1934), begun in the early 1930s and published in the *Journal of Genetic Psychology* in 1936. Harry F. Harlow, who supervised the research, has offered a charming description of the thesis and the events that surrounded it:

> [Maslow was looking] for a topic for an experimental Ph.D. thesis which would suit him. He had seen our monkey laboratory, which at that time was going through desperate neonatal growing pains, and our collection of monkeys involved one of each of perhaps a dozen species. Thus we had an animal collection that made it essentially impossible for anyone to do an adequate experimental Ph.D. thesis. This problem, which would have broken a weaker man, did not even phase Abe, and he accomplished mission impossible with purity and praise.
>
> The thesis which Abe chose was entirely his own, and I don't know where he got the inspiration. . . . It might be noted that no one had ever before studied dominance reactions in monkeys in a laboratory situation. With the help of an undergraduate whom he picked up as his chief research assistant, Abe completed a very effective doctoral dissertation in spite of the limitless handicaps which he faced. . . . Abe's most significant contribution was the finding that dominance was usually established by visual contact, without the need to fight. . . . Actually Dr. Maslow's data on dominance in monkeys was the final definitive research in this area for approximately 30 years, and to say that he was ahead of his time is an understatement of magnificent magnitude. . . .
>
> A year or so after Abe stopped his monkey study, we took apart the observation chamber which he had built. It was simply a chamber of plywood walls nailed together. When we took it apart, we found that the weight of the nails was greater than the weight of the walls, but Abe never made any great claims about being a carpenter. However, he built his apparatus himself, and this is more than most graduate students do now.*

These first two papers are good and interesting in their own right; but quite apart from that, they contain unmistakable anticipations of Maslow's later notion of self-actualization. Notice, for example, how his

*Reprinted by permission of Harry F. Harlow.

1

attitude toward his dominant primates often bordered on respect and admiration. He clearly believed that they were in some way superior creatures—and not just in physical size and strength. "The factors that seemed to determine dominance in our evenly matched animals," he wrote toward the end of the second paper, "seemed to be not so much size, physical strength, etc., as an attitude of . . . confidence." He might almost have said "strength of character" or, as he was later to put it, "self-esteem."

# 1

# The Role of Dominance in the Social and Sexual Behavior of Infra-Human Primates: I. Observations at Vilas Park Zoo[1]

*A. H. Maslow*

## I. General Introduction

The purpose of this series of papers is to investigate the role of dominance in social behavior. This principle of dominance is of fundamental importance in the study of all infra-human primate social relationships and furnishes an obvious and easily investigated nexus between the behavior of the individual and that of the group.

We shall attempt to emphasize the point that has so convincingly been made by Zuckerman (19), namely, that no adequate and valid primate sociology can be elaborated without constant reference to the principle of dominance.

Finally, we shall attempt to show that there are remarkably widespread correlations between various behavior categories that are seemingly discrete and unconnected. Sexual behavior, social behavior, feeding behavior, and aggression behavior will be found to be correlated rather than independently variable types of behavior.

From *Journal of Genetic Psychology*, 1936, **48**, 261–277. Reprinted by permission of The Journal Press.

[1]I wish to indicate here my thanks to Dr. H. F. Harlow for his very generous help in the determination of the form of this paper.

While several approaches to the elucidation of this principle are clearly possible, the stimulus given by Zuckerman's excellent study on infra-human primates has made these animals the most suitable ones for further investigation. In this work (19) is presented for the first time a clear indication of the importance of the dominance principle in primate sociology. Here also we find a preliminary mapping of the relationships holding between dominance and social and sexual behavior in these animals.[2]

While Zuckerman was the first to attack the problem of dominance in a systematic fashion, a number of other studies may also be found to be useful in this connection. These include the studies on the sexual life of infra-human primates by Kempf (9), Hamilton (6), and Bingham (4). Schjelderup-Ebbe (15) has also published some interesting observations on "pecking order" in hens, which may be interpreted as observations on dominance behavior.[3] Carpenter's (5) field study of the social relations of the howler monkey is particularly interesting. These papers will be discussed more fully in later papers in this series.

*Dominance Relationships in Monkeys.* Zuckerman (19, p. 224) has given us the best available description of the behavior of dominant and subordinate animals. He says:

> Every ape or monkey enjoys a position within a social group which is determined by the interrelation of its own dominant characteristics and those of its fellows. The degree of its dominance determines how far its bodily appetites will be satisfied. Dominance determines the number of females that a male may possess, and except on occasions when there is a superfluity of food, it also determines the amount of food a monkey eats. . . . Their dominance relationships . . . are conspicuous because they characterize every field of behavior.

Dominance relationships, he goes on to say, prevail also among the members of a family; they extend to material objects (such as gloves,

[2]See however (19) page 309, where Zuckerman reaches the conclusion that "social behavior—the inter-relations of individuals within a group—is determined by the mechanisms of reproductive physiology." This and many similar statements indicate that Zuckerman has missed the full significance of dominance as a determiner of social behavior.

[3]Yerkes' 1925 statement (17, p. 155) is worth quoting in full. "Dominance and subordination are evident in every group of primates. Apparently there is no such thing as equality of status and opportunity. Leadership, control, mastery are manifest. So in their relations with persons, the monkeys and apes merely exhibit their natural aptitudes and types of social behavior. Ordinarily there is aggressive leadership in cage, colony or family group. Domination may be by either sex, but dominance must be, and instead of a single leader associated with individuals of relative equality, there is likely to be serial subordination. So that each individual secures in its social group the degree of opportunity for control and self-expression to which its characteristics and stage of development entitle it."

See also Murchison's recent interesting papers on the mathematical analysis of a closed social system in chickens.

toys, and sticks); to punishment relationships, since monkeys usually hand down the punishment they receive; to desired privileges that are handed down by human beings (as petting, tickling, playing); to the determination of the frequency of sexual activity, to all the modes of behavior which have been called by Kempf (9) "prostitution behavior"; dominance relationships determine the fighting behavior of monkeys and baboons.

Thus Zuckerman describes the dominant animal as the one who gets the most females, gets the most food, acquires possession of any desirable material objects, who punishes other animals, who comes forward to be petted or played with, and who calls out "prostitution behavior" in other animals.

He describes the behavior of the subordinate animal as being typically the converse of the behavior of the dominant. Thus the subordinate animals get little or none of a limited food supply, and, if they are males, they do not achieve the normal sexual gratification available to the dominant male who "owns" his females. Common to all subordinate animals, says Zuckerman, are the "prostitution responses" consisting of the assumption of the female sexual position in a situation that is not inherently of sexual import.

These descriptions combined with our own researches give us a basis for clearly formulated though cautious definitions of our fundamental terms. *We shall define the dominant animal as one whose behavior patterns (sexual, feeding, aggressive, and social) are carried out without deference to the behavior patterns of his associates. The subordinate animal is one whose behavior patterns (sexual, feeding, aggressive, and social) are suggested, modified, limited, or inhibited by the behavior patterns of its more dominant associates.*

It may be noted that our terminology of dominance-subordination differs from the common terminology of ascendance-submission, used by Allport (2), Zuckerman (19), Harlow (7), and others. We believe the term "subordinate" to be superior to "submissive" for the following reasons:

1. The less dominant animal sometimes does not occupy his secondary position with any evidence of willingness or *submission*, but is forced to assume this attitude by the violence of his superiors. The dominance drive of the less dominant monkey is not lost but is merely submerged or overshadowed or expresses itself through other channels, and will continue to assert itself whenever the opportunity arises. In other words, the drive for dominance is continuous, and the mere fact that the more dominant animal attains permanent or temporary superiority does not imply submission by the less dominant animal. Such an implication would be as inaccurate as saying that a horse who had lost a hard-fought race had "submitted" to the winner.

2. The terms ascendance-submission trace back at least as far as McDougall's theory of social instincts. McDougall in explaining this principle suggested that there were two antithetical instincts and, as long as these terms are used, it is difficult to free oneself entirely from this prejudice. It seems to the writer to be more probable that *dominance is a single drive* that is present in all animals and that dominance and subordination are merely two degrees (or perhaps aspects) of a common impulse. The subordinate animal is merely one whose dominance has been overshadowed by greater dominance, and it is important that the terminology used imply this basic fact.

## II. Introduction

The following observations on the role of dominance in the social and sexual behavior of monkeys were carried out at the Vilas Park Zoo at Madison, Wisconsin. The purpose of this study was to obtain a description of dominance and subordination behavior in infra-human primates of varying species and to obtain evidence as to the relations of food, sex, aggression, and dominance attitude.

## III. Animals, Housing, and Care

*Subjects.* The animals used in this experiment were the series of infra-human primates housed in the monkey building at the Vilas Park Zoo at Madison, Wisconsin. In this colony, there were at any one time approximately 25 animals, housed in 13 cages. Deaths, acquisitions, and transfers made this a constantly but slowly shifting population. The larger proportion of the animals dealt with, however, were residents throughout the period of observation. Altogether, observations were made on about 35 infra-human primates of all kinds, ranging from Platyrrhine monkeys to chimpanzees.[4] Our animals ranged in age from new-born babies to senile animals.

Table 1 contains a list of the groups of animals used in this study. It should be kept in mind that these groups, in some instances, were not constant. This was true, particularly, for the groups of java monkeys and pigtail monkeys. Practically all the other groups remained constant throughout the experiment. Much was learned from the isolated animals

[4]We have not used the data for the pair of chimpanzees and the pair of cebus monkeys, since there are clear indications that dominance-subordination in these animals is not the same as it is in the Catarrhine monkeys. See Carpenter (5), Maslow (11).

TABLE 1. List of Groups Studied

| Group 1. | Sooty mangabey, female, adult. |
| | Mona guenon, adult male. |
| | Moustached guenon, prepubescent male. |
| Group 2. | Four java monkeys, all male prepubescents. |
| Group 3. | Two cebus capucinus, both adult males. |
| Group 4. | Four java monkeys, three male, one female, all prepubescent. |
| Group 5. | Three pigtail monkeys, two male, one female, all prepubescent. |
| Group 6. | Four macacus rhesus, three pubescent males, one prepubescent female. |
| Group 7. | Two chimpanzees, male (three and one-half years old); female (three years old). |
| Group 8. | Three macacus rhesus, one male, two females, all post-pubescent. |
| Group 9. | Three mandrills, one senile male, one prepubescent male, one prepubescent female. |
| Group 10. | Four pigtails, two males, two females, all prepubescent. |
| Group 11. | Mona guenon, adult male. |
| | Pigtail monkey, female pubescent. |
| | Coati mundi, adult male. |
| Group 12. | Sooty mangabey, adult female. |
| | Celebes macaque, adult male. |
| Group 13. | Two Hamadryas baboons, adult male and female. |
| Group 14. | Isolated yellow baboon, adult male. |
| Group 15. | Isolated white-handed gibbon, adult male. |

also. Their relations to the animals in neighboring cages and also to humans were instructive enough to warrant their inclusion in the list of animals used.

*Housing and Care.* The larger animals at Vilas Park were housed singly and the smaller ones in groups of from two to four in iron-barred cages 84 inches high, 72 inches wide, and either 72 or 144 inches long, one of these two longer cages being occupied by the white-handed gibbon, and the other by the pair of chimpanzees. Each cage communicated through an alleyway at its top with an outdoor cage of approximately the same size. These outdoor cages were used when weather permitted.

The animals were cared for by the attendants at the park. The cages were cleaned each morning at 8:30, and the animals were fed twice a day, at 9:00 A.M. and at 2:00 P.M., on the usual diet of fixed amounts of bread, carrot, apple, banana, and a few lettuce or cabbage leaves. The morning meal was very light. Water was available at all times.

## IV. Methods and Tests

*Observations.* The observations extended over a period of a year and a quarter from February, 1932 through May, 1933, with a gap of one month during the summer of 1932. Records were taken whenever relevant behavior occurred and were written on the spot. Only that behavior was recorded that was interesting from the point of view of correlations between dominance and social and sexual behavior.

Observations were made between the hours of eleven and one, three days a week. The length of observation at a single cage varied from about five minutes, for very stable groups in which behavior varied little from day to day, to an hour or more, for groups or pairs that exhibited atypical behavior. When the tests were being made, the experimenter travelled from cage to cage in order. At other times, he sat at a point where all the cages could be watched at the same time and records made as relevant behavior occurred in one cage or another.

*Tests of Dominance.* An experienced observer needs no objective test to determine the mere fact of dominance within a monkey group. This may be done by simple inspection, since the dominant animal is easily detected by his cocky, aggressive, and confident air. He struts whereas the subordinate animal slinks. He stares fixedly and ferociously at the other animals; they avoid his gaze. He comes to the front of the cage when favors are being handed out; the subordinate animals retire discreetly to the rear of the cage. He is generally the initiator of group action; the subordinate animal is the follower. Whenever dominance is fairly marked, these characteristics make its diagnosis very easy.

Simple observation may be supplemented and extended by the use of a simple test, that of throwing small bits of food singly into any cage. Since a dominant animal preempts all or most of a limited food supply if hungry (in our experiments the observations were carried out about three hours after the morning meal and the monkeys were almost always eager for food), this affords a ready objective check on other observations.

If one animal in the group gets practically all the bits of food thrown into the cage, his dominance is obvious. If a substantial percentage of the food bits is secured by more than one animal, diagnosis is less certain, although usually the degree of dominance is closely related to the amount of food obtained by each animal. Where dominance is very weak, the subordinate animals become progressively more daring and the food dominance may be partially obscured by other motivational factors.

Gradations of dominance may also be measured by a variation of the above test. Instead of dropping the food bits midway between two monkeys, the food may be placed closer to one than another. When dominance is slight, the subordinate animal will get progressively more food as it is brought relatively nearer to him and farther away from his more dominant partner. This method, therefore, affords a quantitative method of measuring dominance. In actual practice, its usefulness was limited by the fact that, in most cases, save where the difference in dominance was slight, when the food was dropped into the cage, the subordinate animal fled precipitately to a far corner of the cage and actually avoided the food even when the experimenter dropped it as close to him as possible. Of course, individual differences in hunger drive and appetite for the particular food used are uncontrolled variables in this test. Fortunately, however, they are usually completely nullified by the prepotent dominance behavior.

The following technique was also found to be useful in certain cases of dominance that was not very definite. In those cases in which several animals came to the front of the cage for food (thus indicating that dominance was not complete in the dominant animal or that there were large appetite differences), bits of food were given to all the animals at the front of the cage, even to those who were carefully avoiding the dominant overlord. In many cases this was enough to stimulate the latter animal to assert his dominance at once by driving away all the others. When he did not immediately do this, he was further teased by the experimenter's dangling the food bits just beyond his reach and then handing them directly to a subordinate animal. With several repetitions of this procedure, the dominant animal almost always became very angry, viciously attacking the subordinate animals and driving them away. The number of repetitions of this procedure necessary to call forth his angry attack could be considered an inverse measure of dominance. We shall hereafter refer to this procedure as the "teasing" technique.

*Social Behavior of Caged Animals.* It is possible to criticize experiments such as the following on the grounds that the behavior of the caged animals differs from the "normal." Although this is obviously true, such criticisms need not be taken too seriously, since, so far as we know, the behavior of the caged animals differs in no *fundamental* way from that of animals in a "normal" or wild environment. The behavior of the animals at the zoo or in the laboratory is not abnormal or perverted. What we have in the laboratory or at the zoo is, essentially, not so much the introduction of new factors as the exclusion of many variable and uncontrollable factors that are operative in large areas or in the wild. In any case, however, we shall consider that our results hold only for our conditions until they are proven to be more widely applicable.

The laboratory situation is, moreover, an effective way of concentrating temporally and spatially the behavior of the subordinate animal.

## V. Results

Limitations of space make it impossible to present all of the data accumulated during the course of the observations. We shall instead present them in summarized form according to topic. The data on sexual behavior seem interesting enough to warrant separate consideration in a later paper (12) and we shall include here only those observations that are strictly relevant to the thesis in hand.

1. *The Behavior Typical of Dominance and Subordination.* The typically dominant animal gets all or most of the food bits thrown into his cage. The subordinate animal gets few or none. In complete dominance, the subordinate animal will flee to a far corner of the cage when food is thrown in. If dominance is less complete, the dominant animal will have to drive the other animals away, and the amount of force necessary to do this will vary inversely with his dominance.

   *a.* The sexual behavior of the dominant animal will almost always be masculine (except under certain conditions which will be discussed later), *and this masculinity of behavior is independent of the sex (gender) of the dominant animal.* A dominant female will mount in the masculine fashion other animals in her cage, both male and female. The (typical) sexual behavior of the subordinate animal is female sexual behavior, *again regardless of gender.* Subordinate males will assume the female sexual position as often as subordinate females under similar circumstances. The dominant animal, on the other hand, whether male or female, will rarely assume the female sexual position, except if the dominant animal be a female in heat.

   *b.* The dominant animal will have the run of the cage. The behavior of the other animals will be oriented with respect to him. He will come and go as he pleases and they will get out of his way as he approaches. The subordinate animals in the typical group will usually be bunched as far away from the dominant animal as they can get. Various degrees of apprehension, fear, or actual terror will be displayed by these animals, varying with the degree and the kind of dominance displayed by the dominant animal. Any display of dominance by one of the relatively subordinate animals in the group against a still more subordinate animal is characterized by continual apprehensive looking at the dominant overlord of the cage. This display will cease if the latter approaches or stares severely at the less dominant animal. Any attacks or fights that may occur are usually initiated or caused by the dominant animal. The responses of the subordinate animal to aggressive display will vary with degree of subordination. He may fight back, he may assume a passive attitude, he may flee, or, in extreme subordination, he may lapse into a cataleptic rigidity, a waxy flexibility, or become completely limp.

   2. *Dominance in the Female.* The female may be dominant and, when she is, will behave exactly as does the dominant male. No differences have been observed in male and female dominance behavior.

   (The sooty mangabey in Group 1 and the two females in Group 8 were dominant in their groups. In Groups 5, 6, 9, and 10, a female was dominant over other animals in the cage, although they were at the same time dominated themselves by the overlord animal of the group. The female sooty mangabey in Group 12 was beginning to assume dominance over her mate when the observations came to an end.)

3. *Dominance and the Oestrous Cycle.* We have some (doubtful) evidence to indicate that a dominant female, when she is forced to assume the female position through the heightening of the sexual drive, will lose her dominance.[5] In other words, the dominance syndrome seems to change as a whole and not in parts. In the two cases observed, the assumption of the subordinate role in the sexual act was accompanied by the assumption of the subordinate role in the food dominance test, and in aggression behavior. This effect may possibly also be attributed to factors other than sexual, e.g., general malaise.

(In Group 8, after the early removal of a male overlord, female A was found to be completely dominant to both female B and the remaining male. The male was also dominated by female B. The behavior of all three animals was typical and needs no further description. Female A remained dominant until she came into heat. At the next observation period she was found to be completely subordinate to the male who mounted her continually, bullied and bit her, and allowed her to get no food. Her behavior attitudes were completely transformed. She had changed from a bullying, cocky, aggressive, and swaggering animal to a slinking, timid coward who showed terror whenever the male stared at her.

Female B now assumed the overlordship of the group, with the male second and the original overlord last. The new overlord behaved typically, until the time when she also came into heat. The phenomenon previously observed, of loss of dominance upon assumption of the female role, was repeated. The male became the overlord of the group, with female A second, and the erstwhile overlord last. The status of the group remained thus until the observations had to be cut short.)

These interesting happenings must be interpreted very cautiously and it is not the writer's intent to emphasize them.

4. *Age and Dominance.* The behavior syndromes characteristic of dominance and subordination seem to be less exactly marked in young animals. There is more blurring of the correlations between dominance and other forms of behavior, ordinarily very closely correlated with dominance. The subordinate animal will be seen to mount the dominant animal at times; the dominant animal will be seen to present more often.

(This was found to be true for both groups of pigtail monkeys in this study and for other young animals studied later.)

5. *The Incidence of Dominance.* In all of the groups studied here, with the possible exception of one, and in all other groups studied subsequently, there was found to be a hierarchy of dominance, and one

---

[5]This may possibly be a sudden accession of dominance in the male, brought on by new and potent stimuli, rather than loss of dominance in the female as a direct result of her physiological condition.

animal was always found to be overlord of the group. The one possible exception is Group 3, a pair of cebus monkeys, who were so timid that the test could not be used.

6. *Dominance and Play.* It was observed in several groups that the ordinary hierarchy of dominance obtaining in these groups was temporarily abrogated during periods of rather intense play. At such times subordinate animals mounted dominant ones and dominant ones presented to subordinate ones. No fear or timidity was observed in any of the animals during such periods nor was there any attempt on the part of the dominant animals to assert their dominance until the play period had come to an end and the normal social relationships of the group were resumed. This phenomenon was noted only in younger animals, and was never seen to occur in any of the older groups. In these latter groups, for that matter, almost no play at all was ever observed.

(In Group 10, one such abrogation of dominance was observed. At its height, it looked much like a group sexual orgy. All the animals were seen to present frequently and indiscriminately to any animal that happened to be nearby. Mounting always followed but it was merely nominal in the sense that it lasted for but a few seconds and was frequently followed by a reversal in role, the presenting animal now mounting. This procedure was repeated by all the animals for several minutes with much playful vocalization.

In Group 5, when the female was gone and only two males were left, the dominant animal was seen once to indulge in a similar kind of sexual play. He had very rarely allowed mounting by the subordinate animal but, in this instance, he began the game of presenting to the subordinate animal and then not allowing him to mount, either turning away or wrestling with his partner as soon as mounting was attempted. The subordinate animal was finally allowed to mount once or twice after this procedure had gone on for some time. This type of behavior was also seen four times in Group 6.)

7. *The Assumption of Dominance Role by a New Member of the Group.* A new member of a group usually took his position within the group at once and, ordinarily, this was done without any display of force. An animal that later turned out to be subordinate was subordinate at the very first moment, after the excitement incident to transfer had died down. A dominant animal seemed to become dominant at once and this could be seen in the immediate assumption of what might be called the dominance strut. The other animals in such cases behaved as if they tacitly acknowledged the dominance of this new member. In only one case was there any struggle when a new animal was introduced into Group 2. This new animal, we now know, after long experience with him, has an extremely strong urge to dominance in spite of the fact that he is

a small animal. He behaved in a dominant fashion when he entered the cage and remained so for a few minutes. But the overlord of the group, after a short interval, got to work and gradually beat the newcomer into a lesser role. This process took weeks of continual wrestling and fighting. This newcomer is to this day an extremely aggressive animal and in the several groups in which he has been since, has always had to be beaten into subordination, except in one case where he won dominance.

8. *"Prostitution" Behavior.* This concept (that is too susceptible to misinterpretation by inexperienced observers) was first used by Kempf (9) to describe sexual behavior that occurs in inherently nonsexual situations, usually to obtain some "economic" advantages, e.g., food, protection, immunity from attack. Such behavior usually consists in the assumption of the female sexual position by an animal that is being attacked, that wants to call forth an attack on a third animal, or that is being prevented from obtaining food, etc. It will be seen from our previous discussion that such an animal would usually be a subordinate one.

Such behavior undoubtedly does occur and we have numerous instances of it in our animals. Our interpretation of it would, naturally, be very different from that of Kempf and would resemble rather Zuckerman's interpretation. We should consider the act of presentation as a symbol of subordination (with some exceptions) and interpret it as a means whereby a subordinate animal indicates to the dominant animal that no challenge to dominance is offered. In situations where such behavior occurs, there is usually an implicit challenge to the dominance of the overlord. Such a situation usually calls forth assertion of dominance by the overlord and it is to ward off this threat that the subordinate animal will present. Of course, in this way, the subordinate animal will usually get what he wants, *but he does not get it by offering sexual favors,* as Kempf avers; he gets it rather by admitting social inferiority. In a good many cases, mounting does not take place and yet the dominant animal seems to be satisfied. Presentation must then frequently be interpreted as a social or subordination response, and not directly as a sexual response. A few examples will be sufficient to indicate this point.

A pan of food is thrown to the cage floor, enough for all. In many cases, the dominant overlord will threaten all the other animals as he gathers the food into his mouth and cheek pouches with both hands and both feet. The other animals will approach hesitantly, *half presenting all the time,* and in this way will reach the food and be allowed to partake. Any direct attack on the food by these subordinate animals would be likely to call forth the resentment of the overlord.

(In Group 8, after female A had lost her dominance, she gradually regained it. And it was during this period of resumption of dominance that she showed the following behavior. As the experimenter came to the cage bars, she always approached at the same time that the male did. She would be allowed to eat food that was handed to her directly. After a few repetitions of the teasing technique, he began to show dominance by staring at her or growling. She responded, usually by presenting to him in a purely nominal fashion, i.e., she would accept food but at the same time her hindquarters would be turned in his direction. In this position, she could continue to accept food if he were also given some. Her acceptance of food seemed no longer to constitute a challenge to his dominance, and he did not attack her.

The female mandrill in Group 9, an animal with a strong dominance drive, whenever she approached the old overlord, exhibited this same behavior of nominal presentation. The typical subordinate animal avoids the dominant animal fairly consistently but the female mandrill achieved a much greater freedom of action by this simple device of admitting subordination and thus warding off his dominance attacks. When she neglected this ceremony, she was frequently attacked or threatened. The old mandrill was never seen to mount the young female but he seemed nevertheless to be placated by the presenting behavior.)

9. *Permanence of Dominance Status.* The dominance hierarchy, once determined, continues unchanged unless other definite factors intervene. When the infrequent changes in dominance status do occur, it is usually possible to assign the cause for this change, which is often some change in the physiological status of the dominant animal, such as that occasioned by illness, accident, or change in oestrus cycle.

We have already spoken of the changes in dominance occurring in Group 8 when this change seemed to be correlated with change in phase of the oestrus cycle.

Change was also observed in Group 12. Toward the end of the observations, the sooty mangabey developed the habit of hanging and whirling on the chain that hung from the middle of the cage roof. Since this had a heavy wooden block attached to its lower end, it frequently struck the dominant male, who usually sat on the floor. After a good many futile attempts (she was a much faster animal), he gave up his efforts to catch her and punish her and, instead, retired to a corner or to the alleyway as soon as she started whirling the chain. Still later, his retirement began to be accompanied by squeals of fear, and it seemed obvious that the mangabey was now doing what she did with deliberate intent to annoy. About one month after this behavior had first begun, she seemed to become less and less subordinate and he less and less dominant. She began to get more food and was attacked less often. Finally, on two days just before the end of the observations, she was seen so to maneuver herself as to get into a semi-mounting position. Whenever he lay down or sat on the floor, she seized the opportunity to stand astride his body or to stand over him. This behavior had never been seen before. Soon after, observations ceased and we have no record of subsequent developments.

10. *Size and Dominance.* While we are not yet in a position to hazard guesses as to the factors determining dominance, we have some data on the influence of at least one of these factors, namely the size of the animals concerned.

It is fairly certain that marked differences in the size of a pair of animals will eventuate in the assumption of dominance by the larger animal. In every case where an animal was considerably larger than his partner or partners, he became the absolute overlord.

(Groups 1, 7, 9, 13, and also Group 8 at the beginning of observations, when an old male was a member of the group. Also, this same phenomenon has been observed in so many groups, since, that there is little doubt about the generality of this factor.)

When, however, the difference in size is not great, dominance may be determined, at least partially, by other factors. It is possible, then, that a somewhat smaller animal becomes the dominant animal. Superficially, it seems that such factors as confidence, cockiness, aggressiveness, greater strength of hunger and sex drives, and greater speed of reaction may overbalance a small difference in size. We cannot, unfortunately, give any exact data on these differences in size and it was impossible for us to weigh the animals. (In Groups 5, 6, and 11, a smaller dominated a larger animal.)

## VI. Summary of Conclusions

1. We need feel no hesitation about concluding that dominance is an extremely important determiner of social and sexual behavior in the monkey. To this extent, our observations constitute a confirmation of those made by Zuckerman. We may say with him that the animal's status in the dominance hierarchy determines to a very large extent the satisfaction of his bodily needs. Or, to express it in another way, we may say that there seems to be a high positive correlation between dominance and other types of behavior, especially feeding, sexual, and aggression behavior. We think, however, that Zuckerman has at times grossly underestimated the importance of the role of dominance in social behavior.

2. We found that the behavior syndrome characteristic of the dominant animal is as follows: he preempts all or most of a limited food supply; he displays practically all the aggressive behavior seen in his group; he plays the masculine role in sexual behavior, *regardless of gender*

(a dominant animal whether male or female will mount the subordinate animal); he himself is rarely or never mounted; and generally he expresses his drives in behavior without deference to those same drives in his subordinate partners.

3. The behavior syndrome characteristic of the subordinate animal is as follows: he gets little or none of a limited food supply; he responds to aggression by passivity, flight, and less often by fighting back; he rarely exhibits any aggressive behavior; he plays the female role in mounting behavior, whether male or female; and generally behaves with deference to the drives of his more dominant partner.

4. The female may be dominant over other females or over males, and, when she is dominant, her behavior differs in no observable way from that of the dominant male unless she comes into heat.

5. Some evidence is presented that seems to indicate that the assumption of the female role by a dominant female (due to coming into heat) leads to loss of dominance.

6. Dominance seems to be less marked in young than in older monkeys.

7. A dominant animal was found in every group studied (with the possible exception of one).

8. The dominance hierarchy may be temporarily abrogated during periods of intense play.

9. A new animal introduced into a group will assume his status in the dominance hierarchy of the group in a very short time.

10. The behavior called "prostitution" behavior by Kempf seems to be better interpreted as behavior motivated by the dominance drive, and is thus best thought of as subordination behavior rather than sexual behavior.

11. While dominance status is usually fairly permanent, it was observed to change in a few cases for assignable causes.

12. In a group or pair, the largest animal will almost certainly assume the role of dominant overlord, if he is much larger than the other animals. If, however, the difference in size is not very great, smaller animals may become dominant.

## References

1. Aaronivich, G. D., & Khotin, B. I. (The problem of imitation in monkeys.) *Novoye v Reflexologii i Fiziologii Nervnoy Systemi*, 1929, **3**, 378–390. Quoted from Murphy, G., and Murphy, L. B., *Experimental Social Psychology*. New York: Harper, 1931. P. 709.
2. Allport, F. H. Social psychology. Boston: Houghton Mifflin, 1924. Pp. xiv + 453.

3. Alverdes, F. Social life in the animal world. London: Kegan, Paul, 1927. P. 225.
4. Bingham, H. C. Sex development in apes. *Comp. Psychol. Monog.*, 1928, **5,** 1–45.
5. Carpenter, C. R. A field study of the behavior and social relations of howling monkeys. *Comp. Psychol. Monog.*, 1934, **10,** 1–168.
6. Hamilton, G. V. A study of sexual tendencies in monkeys and baboons. *J. Anim. Behav.*, 1914, **4,** 295–318.
7. Harlow, H. F., & Yudin, H. C. Social behavior of primates: I. Social facilitation of feeding in monkeys and its relation to attitudes of ascendance and submission. *J. Comp. Psychol.*, 1933, **16,** 171–185.
8. Kellogg, W. N., & Kellogg, L. A. The ape and the child. New York: McGraw-Hill, 1933. P. 341.
9. Kempf, E. J. The social and sexual behavior of infra-human primates, with some comparable facts in human behavior. *Psychoanal. Rev.*, 1917, **4,** 127–154.
10. Köhler, W. The mentality of apes. New York: Harcourt, Brace, 1925. Pp. viii + 342.
11. Maslow, A. H. The dominance drive as a determiner of social behavior in infra-human primates. (Abstract) *Psychol. Bull.*, 1935, **32,** 714–715.
12. ———. The role of dominance in the social and sexual behavior of infra-human primates: III. The sexual behavior of infra-human primates. *J. Genet. Psychol.*, 1936, **48,** 308–336.
13. ———. The social behavior of monkeys and apes. *Int. J. Indiv. Psychol.*, 1935, **1,** 4th quarter, 47–59.
14. Maslow, A. H., & Flanzbaum, S. The role of dominance in the social and sexual behavior of infra-human primates: II. An experimental determination of the behavior syndrome of dominance. *J. Genet. Psychol.*, 1936, **48,** 278–307.
15. Schjelderup-Ebbe, T. Social behavior of birds. In *A handbook of social psychology.* Ed. by Carl Murchison. Worcester, Mass.: Clark Univ. Press, 1935. Pp. 947–973.
16. Tinklepaugh, O. L. Sex behavior in infra-human primates as a substitute response following emotional disturbance. *Psychol. Bull.*, 1932, **29,** 666.
17. Yerkes, R. M. Almost human. New York: Century, 1925. Pp. xxi + 278.
18. Yerkes, R. M., & Yerkes, A. W. The great apes. New Haven: Yale Univ. Press, 1929. Pp. xix + 652.
19. Zuckerman, S. The social behavior of monkeys and apes. New York: Harcourt, Brace, 1932. Pp. xii + 356.

# 2

# The Role of Dominance in the Social and Sexual Behavior of Infra-Human Primates: II. An Experimental Determination of the Behavior Syndrome of Dominance[1]

*A. H. Maslow*
*Sydney Flanzbaum*

## I. Introduction

The purpose of this paper is twofold, namely, (1) to determine the behavior syndromes characteristic of dominant and subordinate monkeys under experimental conditions, and (2) to determine if possible the fundamental mechanisms and conditions underlying these behavior categories by the systematic control of as many variables as possible.

*The Animals; Their Housing and Care.* This experiment was carried out at the Primate Laboratory of the University of Wisconsin during the year 1933–1934 with 20 monkeys as subjects. Their names, classification, sex, weight, and approximate ages are found in Table 1.

From *Journal of Genetic Psychology*, 1936, **48**, 278–309. Reprinted by permission of The Journal Press.

[1]The authors' thanks are due to Dr. Harry F. Harlow, the director of the Laboratory, for his helpful cooperation throughout the experiment, and to the Wisconsin Alumni Research Foundation which contributed part of the funds that made the Laboratory a possibility.

TABLE 1. Physical Data, Names, and Classifications of Animals

| Familiar Name | Classification | | Sex | Age | Weight | |
|---|---|---|---|---|---|---|
| Pal | Macacus | nemestrinus | Male | Pubescent | 12 lb. | 8 oz. |
| Psyche | " | " | " | " | 11 " | 11 " |
| Icky | " | " | " | " | 11 " | 8 " |
| Percy | " | " | " | " | 11 " | 8 " |
| Growler | " | " | Female | " | 10 " | 6 " |
| Sappho | " | " | " | Prepubescent | 10 " | 0 " |
| Nira | " | rhesus | Male | " | 4 " | 2 " |
| Cwa | " | " | Female | " | 5 " | 5 " |
| Jack | " | " | Male | (Approx. 1 yr.) | 2 " | 0 " |
| Jill | " | " | Male | " | 1 " | 14 " |
| Glenny | " | mordax | " | Pubescent | 6 " | 14 " |
| Spitter | " | " | " | " | 6 " | 9 " |
| Java | " | " | " | " | 6 " | 11 " |
| Greeny | Cercopithecus sabaeus | | " | Prepubescent | 4 " | 7 " |
| Tim | " | " | " | " | 5 " | 8 " |
| Twit | Cebus capucinus | | " | Pubescent | 5 " | 5 " |
| Toughie | Macacus rhesus | | " | Prepubescent | 3 " | 15 " |
| Roughie | " | " | " | " | 4 " | 3 " |
| Min | " | " | Female | " | 4 " | 6 " |
| Bim | " | " | " | " | 4 " | 7 " |

These animals were housed in single living cages (30″ × 30″ × 33″), lined along the opposite sides of a long room. The cages were of wood construction, except for the front wall, which was made of three-eighths-inch iron bars, centered two inches apart.

The animals were fed once a day, immediately after the experimental period, on fixed amounts of bread, carrots, lettuce, milk, and cod liver oil.

## II. Apparatus and Procedure

*Controls.* The 20 animals were used in 12 pairings, four subjects being used in two pairings. In order to get at the conditions underlying dominance, the controls were so designed as to bring into especial focus those factors that had as yet received little or no consideration in the literature.

The animals in the pairings were equated as well as was possible for weight (to avoid the influence of great difference in size), sex, age, and species. With certain exceptions to be described later, they were studied in pairs to avoid the obscuring and complicating of the fundamental mechanisms of dominance by large groups of animals. Certain behavior will emerge when animals are paired that cannot be detected in a larger grouping (and vice versa). The experimental chamber was made large enough for the free behavior of two animals, but was so restricted in size that it concentrated spatially and temporally the behavior of the subordinate animal. Both hunger and appetite were controlled, hunger as has been described above, and appetite by using as an experimental food bits of apple, highly desirable, which the animals were fed at no other time (13). Only those animals were paired that had never before been together or had been separated for at least two months before the experiment, and the animals were isolated in single living cages at all times except during the experimental periods. In this way we were sure to obtain a complete record of *all* the social behavior occurring in a pair of animals from their very first meeting in this experiment.

*Scoring Sheets.* Scoring sheets were used to record, objectively, all significant behavior during the experimental period. The following items of behavior were listed and scored: (1) feeding, (2) genital inspection, (3) presentation, (4) dorso-ventral mounting, (5) ventro-ventral copulatory behavior, (6) attempts to mount, (7) bullying, (8) cringing, (9) passivity under aggression, (10) avoidance-escape or flight, (11) initiation of fighting, (12) anger (attack), (13) initiation of play, (14) grooming, (15) self-grooming, (16) general activity (exploration-curiosity), and (17) quiet sitting. Exact behavior definitions of these terms are included below. The data on grooming were gathered both because of possible relation to dominance and also because we considered this to be a good opportunity to attempt possible clarification of some of the questions raised by Dr. Yerkes in his interesting paper (20) on this behavior.

Each scoring sheet was divided into 20 parts, one for each minute of the experimental period. These sections were further subdivided into 15-second periods by light lines. A stop watch was started at the moment of the beginning of the experimental period and was kept running throughout, allowing continuous timing of all behavior. Duration of behavior was recorded by a continuous line which indicated when the behavior began and when it ended, with a margin of error of less than five seconds. A symbol above this line indicated which animal initiated the behavior. Notes were also made on the few bits of behavior not covered by our behavior rubrics, and also to call attention to particularly noteworthy or interesting behavior.

The maximum number of experimental periods for any pair of animals was 30. The actual number of periods for each pair was determined by its stability of behavior. When it seemed that no more could be learned from further experimentation, the experiment was concluded for that particular pairing.

The pairs of animals were evenly divided between the senior and junior author, each being completely responsible for his own pairs. In order to insure complete reliability of recording, all terms were carefully defined on an objective behavioral basis after mutual consultation and were then committed to memory. The first three experimental periods for each pair of animals were recorded by both experimenters sitting at independent tables. The resulting scoring sheets showed no significant differences, and indicated excellent reliability of scoring. The senior author is responsible for the form of this paper and the conclusions presented in it.

*Definition of Terms Used in Recording Sheet*

1. *Food* indicates the kind of food dropped into cage, when each piece was dropped, and which animal got it.

2. *Genital inspection* refers to genital inspection of a sexual nature only. Inspection may occur incidentally during grooming without having any sexual import. Visual, oral, manual, and olfactory inspection are included.

3. *Presentation* refers to assumption of the female sexual position. This may vary from a full sexual presentation, such as that displayed by a female in heat, to a barely perceptible and momentary twisting of the animal's hind quarters in the direction of the other animal. Between these two extremes occur all degrees of variation. Some degree of experience with monkeys is absolutely necessary before this behavior can be readily recognized and interpreted. Such behavior was recorded by us only when it was obvious and unmistakable.

4. *D-V* (Dorso-ventral mounting or "normal" copulation). This behavior varies so much that it is impossible to give an exact description of it. The essential component for our recording, however, was the mere mounting of an animal by another, whether or not functionally adequate. Notes indicated whether or not pelvic strokes ensued, or whether penetration took place (as nearly as we could make out) or whether the part mounted was the head, side, or rear. If the mounted animal remained in the sitting position (as often happened) this was also recorded in the notes.

5. *V-V* (Ventro-ventral copulation—face to face).

6. *Erection.* Whenever observed in meaningful situations, otherwise not recorded. Not always possible to observe this, so record on sheets is merely indication that it *did* occur at these times, but it may also have occurred at other times. These records will not be included in our charts and discussions for this reason.

7. *Attempts.* Attempts to mount for sexual behavior. Experience necessary to recognize this in some cases, although most of the time it is rather obvious. Behavior of other animal recorded in other columns (as anger, fighting, passivity). Also foreshortened mounting, of any unmistakable beginning of mounting.

8. *Bullying-teasing.* Plucking at another animal's fur, poking him roughly, biting, threatening with growls, taking food away from him roughly, pouncing upon him from above and mauling him. These called bullying only when other animal is more or less passive, or attempts to run away or otherwise avoid his aggressor. If persecuted animal protects himself by fighting back, this is recorded under fighting behavior. It may also turn into play behavior.

9. *Cringing.* An indication of extreme submissiveness. Very obvious and consists of curling up in ball with head hidden, sometimes accompanied by vocalizations indicative of extreme fear.

10. *Passive.* Covers all non-fighting reaction to aggression, not specifically included in rubrics. Often takes form of waxy flexibility. Usually less extreme; more or less apathetic acceptance of the aggression.

11. *Avoidance-flight* may range from precipitate flight to a constant but not marked avoidance, e.g., always being at opposite end of cage, being on shelf when other animal is on floor, and vice versa. Latter type not recorded. Thus, may be a reaction to a sudden aggression or else long-time submission behavior reaction to fairly well-marked dominance of other animal.

12. *Initiation of fighting.* If attacks of aggressor are resisted, fighting behavior ensues. Score indicates aggressor. In a few cases, difficult to distinguish from play or mock fighting. See *Play* for distinguishing characteristics.

13. *Anger* always refers to anger directed toward other animal, never experimenter or environmental objects. May be reaction to attempted mounting by other animal, bullying, etc. Vocalizations, gestures, postures were indicators of anger.

14. *Grooming.* Searching through fur of other animal or through his own fur. Letter indicates animal doing fur picking. Other animal almost always passive and frequently shows waxy flexibility and drowsiness. A passing interest in other animal's fur is often displayed. This is not recorded unless it continues for at least five seconds. Self grooming, mutual hetero-grooming, and other variations were all observed and recorded.

15. *Play* may be distinguished from fighting by presence of tumbling, frequent mock presentation, nipping instead of real biting, no damage ever done to other animal. No vicious growling or squeals of pain as in fighting. Very easily distracted by noise, food, etc. Many times initiator cannot be determined as they seem to begin simultaneously.

16. *Exploration-activity.* All preoccupation with physical surroundings. Also mere moving about, running, walking, nosing, and fingering of objects. Intended as rough measure of general activity.

17. *Quiet sitting.* This includes resting and watching other animals' behavior while sitting. Frequently, however, quiet sitting (in a subordinate animal) is marked by a submissive attitude, e.g., staring fixedly at floor, looking hesitantly at other animal out of corner of eyes, a minimum of movements and these very careful and slow when they do occur. No sudden, spontaneous movements or changes of position. In other words, less mere resting than a generalized, mild fear of the other animal. The animal's head, in such cases, is usually bowed over.

*Apparatus and Procedure.* Two techniques were used in this experiment. The technique for the first portion of the experiment was as follows. Each animal was housed in a cage that was directly opposite the cage of his experimental partner. For the experiment a runway (24" × 20" × 80") that fitted snugly between the two cage doors was lowered from the ceiling and the two cage doors were opened. Thus a continuous experimental observation chamber was formed by the two cages and the runway.

After four pairs had been run, this apparatus was changed to a separate experimental chamber (height 60", depth 40", width 35") in an adjoining room. The two animals to be used were led on a chain or ran of their own accord from the living cage into the experimental cage (after 5–15 days' familiarization with the procedure). Before the animals were used, they underwent a period of training or taming which minimized emotional reaction to the experiment.

All observing with this technique was done from behind a one-way screen which permitted clear vision to the experimenter and rendered him invisible to the animals.

A further change in the procedure was the more exact control of the factor of introduction of food into the dominance situation.

Twenty food bits (apple) of equal size were automatically dropped into the chamber during each experimental period, beginning with the sixth. A long tin tube, inclined at an angle of 45 degrees, led from behind the one-way screen into the chamber. After a warning signal (three clicks), a single sphere of apple was rolled down the tube into the chamber.

The following is a list of the pairings in chronological order. The name of the dominant member of the pair comes first. The asterisk indicates the animals tested by the first technique.

| Pal | with | Psyche* | Spitter | with | Glenny |
|---|---|---|---|---|---|
| Icky | " | Twit* | Java | " | Spitter |
| Growler | " | Sappho* | Nira | " | Greeny |
| Jill | " | Jack* | Cwa | " | Tim |
| Nira | " | Cwa | Min | " | Bim |
| Psyche | " | Percy | Roughie | " | Toughie |

## III. Results

The results for the 12 pairs of animals are presented in Tables 2–13. This type of table, which we shall henceforth call the ratio chart, is a convenient way of presenting, in a readily assimilable form, such data as we obtained.[2] It is constructed by scoring a plus for the animal who makes the larger score for any particular kind of behavior during any single experimental period. A minus is scored when he makes a smaller score than his partner during a single period. When there are no scores for either animal, the space is left blank. Such a table is easily interpreted and is particularly suited to our purposes because it will show at a glance just which kinds of behavior are consistent, how consistent they are, and will also show which kinds of behavior are positively or negatively correlated with dominance. These ratio charts are presented for the dominant animals only, since the same charts may be read for the subordinate animal by substituting a plus for the minus and vice versa.

[2]Our gross data charts for each pair of animals are not included for reasons of economy of space, and because they are too expensive to publish. They are, however, available for interested workers in a Ph.D. dissertation on file at the library of the University of Wisconsin.

TABLE 2. Ratio Chart for Icky and Twit; Record for Icky

| | 1 | 2 | 3 | 4 | 5 | 6 | 7 | 8 | 9 | 10 | 11 | 12 | 13 | 14 | 15 | 16 | 17 | 18 | 19 | 20 | 21 | 22 | 23 | 24 | 25 | 26 | 27 | 28 | 29 | 30 |
|---|---|---|---|---|---|---|---|---|---|---|---|---|---|---|---|---|---|---|---|---|---|---|---|---|---|---|---|---|---|---|
| Food | = | | | | | | | | | | | | | | | + | + | + | | | | | | | | | | | | |
| Genital inspection | + | + | + | + | | + | + | + | + | + | | + | | | | + | + | + | | | | | | | | | | | | |
| Presentation | | + | − | − | − | + | − | − | + | − | + | + | | + | | | | | | | | | | | | | | | | |
| Dorso-ventral mounting | + | + | + | + | + | + | + | + | + | + | + | + | + | + | + | + | + | | | | | | | | | | | | | |
| Ventro-ventral | | | | | | | | | | | | | | | | | | | | | | | | | | | | | | |
| Attempts to mount | + | + | | + | + | + | + | + | + | + | + | + | + | + | + | + | + | + | | | | | | | | | | | | |
| Bullying | + | + | + | + | + | + | + | + | + | + | | | + | + | + | + | + | + | | | | | | | | | | | | |
| Cringing | + | + | − | − | − | + | + | − | − | − | − | − | − | − | − | − | − | − | | | | | | | | | | | | |
| Passivity | | − | − | | | − | − | − | − | − | − | − | − | − | − | − | − | − | | | | | | | | | | | | |
| Avoidance, flight | − | − | − | − | | − | − | − | − | | | | − | − | | | | | | | | | | | | | | | | |
| Initiation of fighting | | | | | | | | | + | + | + | + | + | + | + | + | + | | | | | | | | | | | | | |
| Anger attack | | | | | | | | | | | | | | | | | | | | | | | | | | | | | | |
| Initiation of play | | | + | + | + | | − | | | | | − | | | | | | | | | | | | | | | | | | |
| Grooming | | | | | | | | | | | | | | | | | | | | | | | | | | | | | | |
| Self-grooming | + | + | + | + | + | + | + | + | = | = | = | + | + | + | = | − | = | = | | | | | | | | | | | | |
| Exploration activity | + | − | − | − | − | − | + | − | = | = | + | = | + | + | = | − | − | − | | | | | | | | | | | | |
| Quiet sitting | − | | | | | | | | | | | = | = | = | | | | | | | | | | | | | | | | |

(+) means a larger score for the dominant animal in that particular kind of behavior for that particular period.
(−) means a larger score for the recessive animal.
  A blank space indicates that no behavior occurred during that period in either animal.

TABLE 3. Ratio Chart for Jack and Jill; Record for Jill

| | 1 | 2 | 3 | 4 | 5 | 6 | 7 | 8 | 9 | 10 | 11 | 12 | 13 | 14 | 15 | 16 | 17 | 18 | 19 |
|---|---|---|---|---|---|---|---|---|---|---|---|---|---|---|---|---|---|---|---|
| Food | | | | | | | | | | | | | | | | − | − | + | + |
| Genital inspection | | | | | | | | | | | | | | | | | | | |
| Presentation | + | + | + | = | + | | + | − | − | | + | | − | − | + | + | | + | + |
| Dorso-ventral mounting | + | + | + | + | + | + | − | + | + | + | + | − | − | + | + | = | + | − | − |
| Ventro-ventral | | | | | | | | | | | | | | | | | | | |
| Attempts to mount | − | + | − | + | − | − | + | + | + | + | | | − | + | + | = | + | − | |
| Bullying | | | | | | | | | | | | | | | | | | | |
| Cringing | | | | | | | | | | | | | | | | | | | |
| Passivity | | | | | | | | | | | | | | | | | | | |
| Avoidance, flight | − | − | − | − | − | | − | − | | | | | | − | | | | | |
| Initiation of fighting | | | | | | | | | | | | | | | | | | | |
| Anger attack | | = | + | + | + | + | + | − | + | − | | + | − | | − | − | | | |
| Initiation of play | | | | | | | | | | | | | | | | | | − | |
| Grooming | | | | | | | | | | | | | − | − | − | | | + | |
| Self-grooming | | | | | | | | | | | | | | | | | | | |
| Exploration activity | = | − | − | − | − | + | − | = | = | − | − | − | − | − | − | − | − | = | − |
| Quiet sitting | + | + | + | + | + | + | = | | = | + | + | + | + | + | + | + | + | | = |

TABLE 4. Ratio Chart for Pal and Psyche; Record for Pal

| | 1 | 2 | 3 | 4 | 5 | 6 | 7 | 8 | 9 | 10 | 11 | 12 | 13 | 14 | 15 | 16 | 17 | 18 | 19 | 20 | 21 | 22 | 23 | 24 | 25 |
|---|---|---|---|---|---|---|---|---|---|---|---|---|---|---|---|---|---|---|---|---|---|---|---|---|---|
| Food | + | + | | + | + | | + | + | + | + | + | + | | + | + | | | | | | | | + | + | + |
| Genital inspection | | + | + | | + | | | | + | | | + | | | + | = | | | | | | + | | | |
| Presentation | | | − | | | | | | = | | | | | | + | = | − | + | | + | + | + | | | |
| Dorso-ventral mounting | + | + | + | + | + | − | + | + | + | + | + | + | + | + | + | + | + | + | | | | + | | | |
| Ventro-ventral | − | − | − | + | − | − | − | − | − | − | − | | + | + | − | = | + | + | − | − | = | − | − | − | − |
| Attempts to mount | + | | = | + | + | + | + | | + | + | + | + | + | − | + | + | − | + | + | + | | + | + | + | + |
| Bullying | | + | + | + | + | + | + | | | | | | | + | | | + | | | | | + | + | + | + |
| Cringing | | | | + | + | | | + | | + | + | + | + | + | | | | | | | | | + | | |
| Passivity | | | | − | − | | | | | | − | − | | | | | + | − | | | | | | | |
| Avoidance, flight | | − | − | − | − | − | − | − | − | − | − | − | − | | − | − | − | − | − | − | − | − | − | | − |
| Initiation of fighting | + | + | + | + | + | + | + | | | + | + | | | + | + | + | + | + | | + | + | + | | | |
| Anger attack | | | + | + | + | | | + | + | + | | | | | | | + | + | | + | + | + | | + | + |
| Initiation of play | | | | | | | | + | + | + | | | | | | | | | | | | | | + | + |
| Grooming | + | − | + | + | − | − | − | − | = | = | | + | + | − | | | + | | | | − | | | | |
| Self-grooming | | | = | | | | | | − | + | | | | | | | | | | | | | | | |
| Exploration activity | = | | = | | + | + | | | + | + | + | + | + | | + | + | + | + | + | = | | + | + | + | + |
| Quiet sitting | = | − | = | − | = | − | − | | − | − | − | | − | − | − | − | − | − | − | | | − | − | − | − |

TABLE 5. Ratio Chart for Growler and Sappho; Record for Growler

| | 1 | 2 | 3 | 4 | 5 | 6 | 7 | 8 | 9 | 10 | 11 | 12 | 13 | 14 | 15 | 16 | 17 |
|---|---|---|---|---|---|---|---|---|---|---|---|---|---|---|---|---|---|
| Food | | | | | | | | | | | | | | + | + | + | + |
| Genital inspection | | − | | | | | | | | | | | | | | | |
| Presentation | | − | | | | | + | − | | − | − | | | | | | − |
| Dorso-ventral mounting | | | | | | | | | | | | | | | | | |
| Ventro-ventral | | | | | | | | | | | | | | | | | |
| Attempts to mount | | | | | | | | | | | | | | | | | |
| Bullying | | | | | | | | | | | | | | | | | |
| Cringing | Sappho cringing continually | | | | | | | | | | | | | | | | |
| Passivity | | | | | | | | | | | | | | − | | | |
| Avoidance, flight | | − | | | | | | | | | | | | | − | − | |
| Initiation of fighting | | | | | | | | | | | | | | | | | |
| Anger attack | + | | | | | | | | | | | | | + | + | | |
| Initiation of play | | | | | | | | | | | | | | | | | |
| Grooming | − | − | | | | + | | − | − | − | − | − | − | − | − | − | − |
| Self-grooming | | | | | | | | | | | | | | | | | |
| Exploration activity | + | + | + | + | + | + | = | + | + | − | + | + | + | + | + | = | = |
| Quiet sitting | − | = | − | − | − | − | − | + | + | + | + | − | − | − | − | − | − |

TABLE 6. Ratio Chart for Psyche and Percy; Record for Psyche

| | 1 | 2 | 3 | 4 | 5 | 6 | 7 | 8 | 9 | 10 | 11 | 12 | 13 | 14 | 15 | 16 | 17 | 18 | 19 | 20 | 21 | 22 | 23 | 24 | 25 | 26 | 27 | 28 | 29 | 30 |
|---|---|---|---|---|---|---|---|---|---|---|---|---|---|---|---|---|---|---|---|---|---|---|---|---|---|---|---|---|---|---|
| Food | | | | | | + | + | + | + | + | + | + | + | + | + | + | + | + | + | + | + | + | + | + | + | + | + | + | + | + |
| Genital inspection | − | − | − | − | + | | | | | | | | | | | | | | | | | | | | | | | | + | − |
| Presentation | | | − | − | + | | + | + | + | + | + | + | + | + | + | − | + | + | | | − | | − | + | | + | − | + | + | − |
| Dorso-ventral mounting | + | + | + | + | + | + | + | + | + | + | + | + | + | + | + | + | + | + | + | + | + | | | + | + | + | + | + | + | |
| Ventro-ventral | | + | + | + | | | | | + | | | | | | | | + | | | | | + | + | | | | | + | + | |
| Attempts to mount | − | | | | | | | + | | | | | + | | | | | | | | | | | | | | | | | |
| Bullying | + | + | | | | + | + | + | + | + | + | | + | + | + | + | + | | | + | + | + | + | + | + | + | + | + | | |
| Cringing | − | − | − | − | − | + | + | − | + | − | + | − | − | − | + | + | − | | + | + | | + | + | + | + | + | + | − | | |
| Passivity | | − | | | | | − | − | − | − | − | − | | − | − | − | − | − | − | − | − | − | − | − | − | − | − | | − | − |
| Avoidance, flight | − | − | | − | | − | − | | | | | | | | | | | | | | | | | | | | | − | − | − |
| Initiation of fighting | + | + | | | | | | | | | | | | | + | | | | | | + | + | + | + | + | | | | | + |
| Anger attack | | + | + | + | | + | + | | | + | | + | | − | + | + | | | + | | + | + | + | + | + | + | | | | |
| Initiation of play | + | + | + | + | | | | | | | | | − | | | | | | + | | | | | + | + | + | − | + | − | |
| Grooming | + | − | + | − | + | − | + | − | − | − | − | − | − | − | − | − | + | − | + | = | + | = | − | + | + | + | + | + | − | − |
| Self-grooming | + | = | + | + | + | + | + | = | + | + | − | + | + | − | + | + | + | + | + | = | + | = | + | + | + | + | + | − | = | + |
| Exploration activity | + | | − | − | − | + | − | − | − | + | − | | + | − | − | + | + | − | − | + | − | + | + | + | + | + | + | + | = | − |
| Quiet sitting | − | − | − | − | − | + | − | − | − | − | − | − | − | − | − | − | − | − | + | + | − | + | + | − | − | − | − | + | = | − |

TABLE 7. Ratio Chart for Nira and Greeny; Record for Nira

| | 1 | 2 | 3 | 4 | 5 | 6 | 7 | 8 | 9 | 10 | 11 | 12 | 13 | 14 | 15 | 16 | 17 | 18 | 19 | 20 | 21 | 22 | 23 | 24 | 25 | 26 | 27 | 28 | 29 | 30 |
|---|---|---|---|---|---|---|---|---|---|---|---|---|---|---|---|---|---|---|---|---|---|---|---|---|---|---|---|---|---|---|
| Food | | | | | | + | = | − | − | − | − | = | − | − | + | − | − | + | − | − | − | − | − | − | = | + | = | + | − | − |
| Genital inspection | | | | | | | | | | | | | | | | | | | | | | | | | | | | | | |
| Presentation | | | | | | | | + | + | | − | − | − | | | + | | | | | | | | | | | | | | |
| Dorso-ventral mounting | | | | + | | | | | | | | | | | | | | | | + | + | | | | | | | | | |
| Ventro-ventral | | | | | | | | + | + | | | | | | | − | | | | | | | | | | | | | | |
| Attempts to mount | | + | + | | | | | | + | + | − | + | − | = | = | + | | | − | + | + | + | + | + | + | + | = | + | + | + |
| Bullying | | + | + | | | | | | + | + | + | + | | + | + | + | | + | + | + | + | + | | + | + | + | + | + | + | + |
| Cringing | | − | − | − | | | | | − | | − | | | | | + | | | | | − | | | | − | | − | − | − | |
| Passivity | − | − | − | | | | | | | − | − | − | − | − | − | | | | | | | | | | | | | | | − |
| Avoidance, flight | | + | − | − | | | | | | − | − | − | − | − | + | | | − | − | − | − | + | + | | | − | + | − | − | − |
| Initiation of fighting | | + | + | + | | | | | | + | | + | | + | + | + | | | + | | + | + | + | | | − | + | − | + | + |
| Anger attack | | | | | | | | | | | | | | | − | | | | = | | | | | | | | | | | |
| Initiation of play | | + | + | | | | | | | | | | | | | | | | | + | | | | + | = | | | | | |
| Grooming | + | + | + | | | + | + | + | + | + | + | + | − | + | − | − | − | + | + | + | − | + | − | + | = | + | + | + | + | + |
| Self-grooming | + | + | + | + | | + | + | + | + | + | + | + | − | + | + | + | + | + | + | + | + | + | + | + | + | + | + | + | + | + |
| Exploration activity | + | + | + | + | = | + | + | + | + | + | + | = | + | + | + | + | + | + | + | + | + | + | + | + | + | + | + | + | − | + |
| Quiet sitting | − | − | − | − | = | − | − | − | − | − | − | = | − | + | + | + | + | + | + | + | + | + | + | | + | + | + | + | + | + |

TABLE 8. Ratio Chart for Nira and Cwa; Record for Nira

| | 1 | 2 | 3 | 4 | 5 | 6 | 7 | 8 | 9 | 10 | 11 | 12 | 13 | 14 | 15 | 16 | 17 | 18 | 19 | 20 | 21 | 22 | 23 | 24 | 25 | 26 | 27 | 28 | 29 | 30 |
|---|---|---|---|---|---|---|---|---|---|---|---|---|---|---|---|---|---|---|---|---|---|---|---|---|---|---|---|---|---|---|
| Food | | + | + | + | + | + | − | + | + | + | + | + | + | + | + | + | + | + | + | + | + | − | + | = | + | + | = | + | + | + |
| Genital inspection | | | | | | | | | | | | | | | | | + | | | | | | | | | | | | | |
| Presentation | − | + | | + | + | | + | | | | | | | | − | | | | | | | | | | | − | − | + | − | + |
| Dorso-ventral | | + | + | + | + | | + | | + | + | + | + | + | + | + | + | + | + | + | + | + | + | + | | + | + | + | + | + | + |
| Ventro-ventral | | | | | | | | | | | | | | | | | | | | | | | | | | | | | | + |
| Attempts to mount | | | | | | | + | | | − | | | | | | | | | | | | | = | − | − | | | | | |
| Bullying | | | | | | | | | | | | + | | + | | + | | + | + | + | + | + | = | + | + | + | + | + | + | + |
| Cringing | − | | | | | | | | | | | | | | | | | | | | | | | | | | | | | − |
| Passivity | | | | | − | − | | | − | | − | − | − | − | − | − | − | − | − | − | − | − | − | | − | − | − | − | − | − |
| Avoidance, escape | | | | | | | | | | | | | | | | | | | | | | − | | | | | | | | − |
| Initiation of fighting | | | | | | | | | | | | | | | | | − | | | | | | − | | | | | | | |
| Anger attack | | | | | | | | | | | | | | + | | | | | | | | | + | | + | + | | | + | + |
| Grooming | + | + | + | + | + | + | + | + | + | + | + | + | + | + | + | + | + | + | + | + | + | + | + | + | + | + | + | + | + | + |
| Self-grooming | − | − | − | − | − | − | = | | | − | − | − | − | − | − | − | − | − | − | − | − | − | − | + | + | + | − | + | + | + |
| Initiation of play | | | | | | | | | | | | | | | | | | | | | | | | + | + | + | + | | | |
| Exploration activity | + | + | + | + | + | + | + | + | + | + | + | + | + | + | + | + | + | + | + | + | = | = | + | = | + | + | + | + | + | + |
| Quiet sitting | − | − | − | − | + | − | = | = | − | − | − | − | − | − | − | − | − | − | − | − | − | = | − | − | − | − | − | − | − | − |

TABLE 9. Ratio Chart for Spitter and Glenny; Record for Spitter

| | 1 | 2 | 3 | 4 | 5 | 6 | 7 | 8 | 9 | 10 | 11 | 12 | 13 | 14 | 15 | 16 | 17 | 18 | 19 | 20 | 21 | 22 | 23 | 24 | 25 | 26 | 27 | 28 | 29 | 30 |
|---|---|---|---|---|---|---|---|---|---|---|---|---|---|---|---|---|---|---|---|---|---|---|---|---|---|---|---|---|---|---|
| Food | | | | | | + | + | + | + | + | + | + | + | + | + | + | + | + | + | + | + | + | + | + | + | + | + | + | + | + |
| Genital inspection | | − | | | | | | | | | | | | | − | | | | | | | | | | | | | | | |
| Presentation | | | | | | | | − | − | | | | | | | | | | | | | | | | | | | | | |
| Dorso-ventral mounting | | + | | | + | + | + | + | + | + | + | + | | | + | + | | + | + | | + | + | + | + | + | | + | + | + | + |
| Ventro-ventral mounting | | − | | + | − | | | | | | | | + | | − | | | + | + | | | + | | | | | − | | | + |
| Attempts to mount | − | | | | + | | + | + | + | | | | | | | | | | | | | | | | | + | | | | − |
| Bullying | | + | | | | − | + | + | | | | | | | | | | | | | | | | | | | | | | |
| Cringing | | | | | | + | − | | | | | | | | | | | | | | | | | | | | − | | | |
| Passivity | | − | | | − | − | − | − | | | − | + | | | − | − | − | | | | − | | − | − | − | | − | − | − | − |
| Avoidance, flight | | | − | | | | − | | − | − | | | | | | | | | | − | | | | | | | | | | |
| Initiation of fighting | − | − | | | | + | + | | − | | | | | | + | | | + | + | | + | | | | + | + | | | | + |
| Anger attack | + | − | | | | + | + | | | | | | | | | | | + | | | | + | | | | | | | | |
| Initiation of play | | | | | | | − | | − | − | − | | | | − | | − | | | − | | | | | | | | | | |
| Grooming | | − | + | + | + | + | + | + | + | + | + | + | + | + | − | + | + | + | + | + | + | + | + | + | + | + | + | + | + | − |
| Self-grooming | | | | | | | | | + | | | | | | − | | | + | | + | + | + | | + | + | + | + | + | + | |
| Exploration activity | | = | − | + | − | = | = | = | − | = | − | − | | | − | | | − | − | − | = | = | | − | − | | | = | − | + |
| Quiet sitting | + | = | − | − | + | = | = | + | − | | = | = | | | − | + | | + | + | + | = | = | + | | | | | | − | + |

TABLE 10. Ratio Chart for Spitter and Java; Record for Java

| | 1 | 2 | 3 | 4 | 5 | 6 | 7 | 8 | 9 | 10 | 11 | 12 | 13 | 14 | 15 | 16 | 17 | 18 | 19 | 20 | 21 |
|---|---|---|---|---|---|---|---|---|---|---|---|---|---|---|---|---|---|---|---|---|---|
| Food | | | | | | + | + | + | + | + | + | + | + | + | + | + | + | + | + | + | + |
| Genital inspection | | | | − | | | | | | | | | | | | | | | | | |
| Presentation | | | | | | | | | | | | | | | | | | | | | |
| Dorso-ventral mounting | − | | | | | | | | | | | | | | | | | | | | |
| Ventro-ventral | | | | | | | | | | | | | | | | | | | | | |
| Attempts to mount | | | | | | | | | | | | | | | | | | | | | |
| Bullying | | | | | | | | | | | | | | | | | | | | | |
| Cringing | | | | | | − | | | | | | | | | | | | | | | |
| Passivity | | | | | | | | | | | | | | | | | | | | | |
| Avoidance, flight | | | | | | − | − | | | | | | | | | | | | | | |
| Initiation of fighting | | | | | | | | | | | | | | | | | | | | | |
| Anger attack | | | | | | | | | | | | | | | | | | | | | |
| Initiation of play | | | | | | | | | | | | | | | | | | | | | |
| Grooming | − | − | − | − | − | − | − | − | − | − | − | − | − | − | − | − | − | − | − | − | − |
| Self-grooming | − | | + | + | + | + | + | + | + | + | + | + | + | + | + | + | + | + | + | + | = |
| Exploration activity | − | = | + | + | + | + | + | + | + | − | = | | + | | − | | + | − | + | + | |
| Quiet sitting | + | − | | − | | − | − | − | | − | | − | − | + | | | = | | = | − | |

TABLE 11. Ratio Chart for Cwa and Tim; Record for Cwa

| | 1 | 2 | 3 | 4 | 5 | 6 | 7 | 8 | 9 | 10 | 11 | 12 | 13 | 14 | 15 | 16 | 17 | 18 | 19 | 20 | 21 | 22 | 23 | 24 | 25 | 26 |
|---|---|---|---|---|---|---|---|---|---|---|---|---|---|---|---|---|---|---|---|---|---|---|---|---|---|---|
| Food | | | | | | + | + | + | + | − | − | − | − | + | − | − | − | − | − | − | − | − | − | − | + | + |
| Genital inspection | | | + | + | + | + | | | | + | + | | | | | | − | + | + | | + | + | | − | | + |
| Presentation | | | | | | | | | | | | | | | | | | | | | | + | | | | |
| Dorso-ventral mounting | | | + | + | + | + | + | | + | | | | | | | | + | | | | + | | | | | + |
| Ventro-ventral | | | | | | | | | | | | | | | | | | | | | | | | | | |
| Attempts to mount | | | | | | | | | + | | + | | | | | | | | | | | | | | | |
| Bullying | | | + | + + | + + | + + | + + | + | + | | + + | + | | + + | + + | + | | | | + | | + | + | + + | + | + + |
| Cringing | | | − | − | − | − | − | | − | | − | | | | | | | | | | − | − | − | − | − | − |
| Passivity | | | | | | | | | | | | | | | | | + | | | − | | | | | | − |
| Avoidance, flight | | | − | − | | | | | | | | | − | | | | | | | − | | | | | | |
| Initiation of fighting | | | + + | | + + | + + | + + | | + + | | | + + | + | | | | | | | | | | | | | + |
| Anger attack | | | | | | | | | + | | | | | | | | | | | + | | | | + | + | + |
| Initiation of play | | | | | | | | | | | | | | | | | | | | | | | | | | |
| Grooming | | + + | + | + + | | | | + + | | | + + | | | + + | + + | + | + + | − | + + | + | + + | + | + | + | + | + + |
| Self-grooming | + | + | + | + | + | + | + | + | + | + | + | + | + | + | + | + | + | | + | + | + | + | + | + | + | + |
| Exploration activity | − | − | − | − | − | − | − | − | − | − | − | − | − | − | − | − | − | − | − | − | − | − | − | − | − | + |
| Quiet sitting | + | + | + | + | + | + | + | + | + | + | + | + | + | + | + | + | + | + | + | + | − | + | + | − | + | − |

TABLE 12. Ratio Chart for Roughie and Toughie; Record for Roughie

| | 1 | 2 | 3 | 4 | 5 | 6 | 7 | 8 | 9 | 10 | 11 |
|---|---|---|---|---|---|---|---|---|---|---|---|
| Food | | | | | | + | + | + | + | + | + |
| Genital inspection | | | | | | | | | | | |
| Presentation | | | | | | − | | | | | |
| D-V | | | | | | | | | | | |
| V-V | | − | − | | | − | | | | | |
| Attempts to mount | | | | | | + | | | | | |
| Bullying | + | | | | + | + | + | | | + | |
| Cringing | | | | | | | | | | | |
| Passivity | | | | | | − | − | | | | |
| Avoidance, flight | − | − | | | | = | − | | | − | − |
| Initiation of fighting | | | | | | − | + | | − | | |
| Anger | | | | | − | | | | | | |
| Initiation of play | | | | | | | | | | | |
| Grooming | + | + | + | + | + | + | + | + | + | + | + |
| Self-grooming | + | | = | − | | + | + | + | + | | |
| Exploration activity | − | = | | − | | − | − | − | − | = | + |
| Quiet sitting | = | + | = | + | | + | + | + | + | | − |

TABLE 13. Ratio Chart for Min and Bim; Record for Min

| | 1 | 2 | 3 | 4 | 5 | 6 | 7 |
|---|---|---|---|---|---|---|---|
| Food | | | | | + | + | + |
| Genital inspection | | | | | | | |
| Presentation | | | | | | | |
| D-V | | | | | + | | |
| V-V | | | | | | | |
| Attempts to mount | | | | | | | |
| Bullying | | | | | + | | |
| Cringing | | | | | − | | |
| Passivity | | | | | − | | |
| Avoidance, flight | | | | | − | − | − |
| Initiation of fighting | | | | | | | |
| Anger | | | | | + | | |
| Initiation of play | | | | | | | |
| Grooming | + | − | + | + | + | + | + |
| Self-grooming | = | + | | | + | | + |
| Exploration activity | + | − | − | − | − | − | − |
| Quiet sitting | − | | + | − | + | + | + |

*Summary of Results.* The data for all our pairs are presented in Table 14 in summarized form. Only those types of behavior are included that seem to have some significance for our main purpose. The data for genital inspection, erection, attempts to mount, anger, self-grooming, and quiet sitting were not included either because of obvious lack of correlation with dominance, or because of paucity of data, or, as in the case of quiet sitting, because we already had an inverse measure of the same behavior. Ventro-ventral copulatory behavior was omitted because these data did not lend themselves to statistical treatment, but seemed, instead,

TABLE 14. Summary of Data

| | Pal Psyche | Icky Twit | Growler Sappho | Jill Jack | Nira Cwa | Psyche Percy | Spitter Glenny | Java Spitter | Nira Greeny | Cwa Tim | Min Bim | Roughie Toughie |
|---|---|---|---|---|---|---|---|---|---|---|---|---|
| Food | 13 | 7 | 4 | 2 | 20 | 25 | 25 | 16 | 5 | 7 | 3 | 6 |
| Presentation | 17 | 17 | 14 | 36 | 8 | 21 | 0 | 0 | 17 | 17 | 0 | 1 |
| Dorso-ventral mounting | 140 | 104 | 0 | 190 | 77 | 195 | 61 | 0 | 6 | 24 | 1 | 1 |
| Bullying | 121 | 77 | 0 | 119 | 41 | 37 | 7 | 1 | 47 | 43 | 2 | 11 |
| Cringing | 0 | 61 | S. cring. contin. | 0 | 0 | 0 | 0 | 2 | 2 | 0 | 1 | 1 |
| Passivity under aggression | 23 | 81 | 3 | not recor. | 83 | 202 | 44 | 0 | 36 | 52 | 1 | 4 |
| Flight, escape | 147 | 114 | 9 | 18 | 16 | 69 | 28 | 4 | 33 | 16 | 17 | 9 |
| Initiation of fighting | 153 | 51 | 7 | 40 | 14 | 14 | 32 | 0 | 37 | 15 | 0 | 3 |
| Grooming | 4 | 3 | 13 | 25 | 28 | 8 | 16 | 21 | 21 | 10 | 11 | 6 |
| Exploration activity | 16 | 12 | 1 | 14 | 26 | 22 | 19 | 11 | 13 | 25 | 6 | 1 |
| Initiation of play | 2 | 0 | 0 | 11 | 8 | 1 | 11 | 0 | 6 | 1 | 0 | 0 |

to need individual treatment. In spite of the fact that the data on presentation showed little correlation with dominance, they were included because of the importance they have assumed in the literature on the subject of monkey behavior [see Kempf (11) and Zuckerman (21)]. All other categories of behavior that were included in this table are considered to be correlated with dominance to a greater or lesser degree.

The figures listed under food, grooming, and general activity represent not raw data, but the total number of plus signs scored in the ratio charts for each animal. Using the raw data would have given us near-astronomical figures to contend with. All the other figures are totals of the raw data for the whole experiment, e.g., the number of times Pal mounted Psyche throughout all their 25 periods together, the number of times Nira bullied Cwa during all their 30 periods together, etc.

The pairings are listed at the top of the table with the name of the dominant animal above the name of the subordinate animal of the pair. The same is true for the scores in each box.

A summary of the lumped data for all the animals is presented in Table 15. Each figure represents the total number of times the behavior occurred throughout the experiment for the dominant or the subordinate animal, as the case may be, except for the food-getting activity and grooming, where each figure represents the total number of plus signs obtained in the ratio charts.

Certain of the pairs of monkeys, however, may be considered as atypical. In the case of the two inter-species pairs (Nira-Greeny and Cwa-Tim), the green monkeys were more agile and speedy than their dominant rhesus partners with the result that the obtained scores on food getting and activity differ from those obtained in intra-species pairings.[3]

In two pairs of animals dominance was not complete (Jill-Jack and Pal-Psyche) with the result that the behavior for the members of these pairs is atypical in many of the scored behavior traits.[4]

A more accurate picture of dominance and subordination can be obtained by omitting from the corrected summary the scores made by Nira-Greeny and Cwa-Tim (inter-species pairs) in food getting and activity, which were particularly affected by difference in speed, and by omitting the scores made by Jill-Jack and Pal-Psyche in all the other behavior categories. Thus we shall have data for ten pairs. This corrected summary of results is given in Table 16, and we shall base our discussions of results upon it rather than on the uncorrected data.

[3]See discussion in first paper (14). The two green monkeys are excellent illustrations of our contention that the drive to dominance is continually active, even in subordinate animals, and will express itself in behavior when external social inhibitions are such that they may be neglected with impunity or else circumvented.

[4]Nira and Cwa showed a change in dominance toward the end of the experiment with Cwa beginning to behave in a dominant fashion. We shall not correct for this factor because it is impossible to select any one point at which dominance was reversed.

TABLE 15. Summary of Results of 12 Pairs

|  | Dominant Animals | Subordinate Animals |
|---|---|---|
| Food getting | 133 | 35 |
| Presentation | 97 | 87 |
| D-V mounting | 798 | 187 |
| Bullying | 386 | 2 |
| Cringing | 0 | 93 |
| Passivity under aggression | 16 | 529 |
| Flight | 9 | 580 |
| Initiation of fighting | 366 | 61 |
| Initiation of play | 54 | 40 |
| Activity | 117 | 96 |
| Grooming | 119 | 89 |

TABLE 16. Corrected Summary of Results of Ten Pairs

|  | Dominant Animals | | Subordinate Animals | |
|---|---|---|---|---|
| Food getting | 121 | (97%) | 4 | (3%) |
| Presentation | 44 | (43%) | 59 | (57%) |
| D-V mounting | 468 | (98%) | 10 | (2%) |
| Bullying | 265 | (99%) | 2 | (1%) |
| Cringing | 0 | (0%) | 70 | (100%) |
| Passivity under aggression | 6 | (1%) | 506 | (99%) |
| Flight | 3 | (1%) | 415 | (99%) |
| Initiation of fighting | 173 | (85%) | 30 | (15%) |
| Initiation of play | 51 | (65%) | 27 | (35%) |
| Activity | 103 | (65%) | 55 | (35%) |
| Grooming | 114 | (62%) | 70 | (38%) |

This summary, we believe, gives a more typical picture of dominance and subordination behavior than does the uncorrected summary, and henceforth we shall refer to it rather than to the previous summary.

## IV. Discussion

The types of behavior which are most closely correlated with dominance or subordination and which should, therefore, be included in a description of their behavior syndromes, may now be listed.

For dominance, these are:

1. The ability to preempt all or most of a limited food supply.
2. The assumption of the above or masculine position in copulatory behavior, regardless of the sex of either animal.
3. The assumption of the bullying role.
4. The initiation of most of the fights that occur between the pair of animals.
5. The initiation of (roughly) twice as much play as is initiated by the subordinate animal.

6. A tendency to greater activity and freer exploration.
7. A tendency (perhaps) to groom rather than be groomed.

The types of behavior most closely correlated with subordination are:

1. Cringing.
2. Passivity under aggression and sexual attempts.
3. Flight from aggression or danger of aggression.

If we use these two lists of traits that are correlated with dominance or subordination to construct the behavior syndromes of dominant and subordinate animals, we get the following:
The dominant animal:

1. Preempts all or most of a limited food supply (97%).
2. Assumes the above or masculine position in copulatory behavior (regardless of gender) (98%).
3. Does practically all the bullying (99%) observed in a pair, and is rarely or never bullied by the subordinate animal.
4. Initiates most of the fights (85%) that occur in the cage and is, of course, the victor in practically all of them.
5. Initiates (roughly) twice as much play (65%) as his subordinate associate.
6. Shows a tendency to greater activity (65%) and freer exploration of his environment than his partner.
7. Shows (perhaps) a tendency to groom rather than to be groomed (62%).
8. Is rarely passive under sexual aggression (1%), never cringes and never flees from the subordinate animal.

The subordinate animal:

1. Gets little or none of a limited food supply.
2. Always, or nearly always, assumes the below or feminine position in copulatory behavior (regardless of gender), but almost never plays the masculine role in such behavior.
3. Is very rarely the aggressor, almost never bullies the dominant animal but is usually bullied.
4. Initiates few of the fights that occur in the cage.
5. Responds to bullying or sexual aggression by passivity, cringing, or flight.
6. Initiates less play than the dominant animal.
7. Shows tendency to be less active and less free in exploration.
8. Shows (perhaps) a tendency to be groomed rather than to groom.

For reasons already discussed, we may discard several types of behavior that have not proved to be valuable in the construction of the behavior syndromes of dominance and subordination. These are (1) genital inspection, (2) presentation, (3) ventro-ventral copulatory behavior, (4) erection, (5) attempts to mount, (6) anger, and (7) quiet sitting. We do not wish to imply that these may not have significance with relation to dominance. Indeed we suspect that several of the behavior types are exceedingly interesting from just such a point of view. These data were, however, inadequate for proper evaluation.

We wish to call especial attention to the data on presentation. This behavior has been given high importance by Kempf (11) and Zuckerman (21), the latter regarding it as an important way in which a subordinate animal adjusts himself to a system based on dominance. A similar interpretation may be read into Kempf's paper. He considers this behavior to be the chief manifestation of "prostitution." The implication that it is a necessary or unique characteristic of subordinate behavior is obviously exaggerated. The dominant animal presents almost as often as the subordinate animal and the subordinate animal often fails completely to show this behavior.

It is quite true that in many cases of presentation the only motivation in the presenting animal is a subordinate attempt to adjust to a system of dominance. But it is just as true that there are other situations in which this behavior occurs that are not directly dominance situations. The most important of these is play; another is curiosity; another is the attempt to lure an enemy within striking distance.

One form of behavior that we have not included in our table is ventro-ventral copulatory behavior. This behavior may have a very interesting relationship to dominance and will be discussed more fully in the next paper in the series (15).

Our data on grooming are equivocal and conclusions may not be drawn before more data are gathered. The corrected summary shows that the dominant group groomed 53 per cent more than the subordinate group (114 plus scores for ten dominant animals and 70 for ten subordinate animals). Three of the ten subordinate animals, however, groomed more than their dominant partners, and in some cases the dominant animal did not groom at all.

We are inclined to interpret our data as a resultant of two facts. First, there are strong individual differences in grooming, some animals being predominantly groomers and others, groomees; second, the dominant animal that is a groomer can force the subordinate animal to be groomed but the dominant animal that is a groomee cannot force his subordinate partner to be a groomer if the latter animal is not so inclined.

The data are particularly interesting in view of Yerkes' recent paper on grooming behavior (19). He presents in this paper the interesting hypothesis that "grooming, as typified by chimpanzee, represents an important pattern of primate social response from which have evolved varied and highly significant kinds of social service" (p. 5). Our data

show grooming to be an important form of social behavior in the catarrhine monkey, but they do not permit us to call this behavior a kind of social service, if we mean by this phrase altruistic, unselfish behavior in which the motivation is the securing of good or pleasure to another animal. Grooming in catarrhine monkeys may well be a progenitor of social service, an evolutionary fore-runner from which altruism may eventually develop, but in our animals this behavior both in the groomer and the groomee was what we must call "selfish."

No other construction can be put upon the behavior of the dominant animals who forced their partners, willy-nilly, to submit to being groomed. There were also other dominant animals, who generally preferred being groomed to grooming, who persistently presented to the subordinate animals for grooming. Very frequently, when the subordinate animal refused to groom and turned away, he was viciously attacked by the dominant monkey. It would seem then that altruism or social service (at least in grooming) cannot be said to begin until we get to the chimpanzee.

While it is extremely difficult to make definite statements about this aspect of grooming behavior without anthropomorphizing, the grooming behavior of our monkeys (while showing more mutuality of participation than any other type of behavior) exhibited less mutuality and more dominance-subordination than is ascribed to the chimpanzee by Yerkes. A young pair of chimpanzees observed by us in our previous study (14) also showed far more cooperative and altruistic behavior than we have ever seen in any monkeys or baboons, and it is probable that the differences that exist between chimpanzees and monkeys with respect to grooming are a reflection of this general difference between apes and sub-anthropoid primates.

The data that we have, of course, permit no generalizations beyond the catarrhine monkeys. The general picture, however, of dominant-subordinate behavior within this group would appear to be clearly defined since all of our work is in substantial agreement with that of Zuckerman on the baboon and with the historical data that he presents.

Carpenter's excellent monograph on the behavior of howler monkeys in the wild (6) clearly shows that these animals have a different kind of dominance-subordination relationship. It seems fair to say that dominance and subordination are found in the social relationships of these animals, especially in juveniles, but that they exist in a much more tenuous and diffuse form than is found in the catarrhine monkey.

The differences are due, certainly, to some extent, to the differences in environmental conditions in the wild and in the laboratory. Abundance of food makes competition unnecessary for the howler monkey. Our data show that when competition for food is made necessary by a limited supply, the struggle for dominance is heightened and made more evident. In at least one of our pairs, dominance status was not clearly established until the factor of competition for food was introduced into the experimental situation. Carpenter also says (p. 37), "Were conditions such as to bring about keen competition for food, social facilitation and inhibition of feeding would be more pronounced than it is in the communal groups of howlers."

Generally instances of competition in howler monkeys are rare. From Carpenter's description, it would seem that dominance relationships emerge from the play of juvenile animals and are most evident during such play. He says (p. 81), "Young howlers apparently compete with each other during playful activity. Individuals which show much facility in the playing activity control the course of action to a greater degree than others. Viewed objectively, play may function to establish among young animals a dominance scale, similar in kind but far less in degree than the dominance so thoroughly described by Zuckerman for the baboon."

It seems to be at least a possibility that the cebus monkey will also, upon closer study, be found to exhibit dominance-subordination behavior of a non-catarrhine type. The fact that solitary females of this species have been found in the wild indicates this possibility (21).

We are now in a position to bring up for discussion several other more general questions with relation to dominance that should not be overlooked.

1. *When Was Dominance Established?* If we take as our criterion the first emergence of *scorable* dominance behavior, we find that in ten out of our twelve pairs, dominance was established before the fourth period. In six pairs, it was established in the very first period, and in one other pair, during the second period. Dominance seems, therefore, to be a relatively immediate status into which, most of the time, both animals fall at once. It would be fairly accurate to say that one animal seemed, in most cases, to assume at once that he was dominant, and that the other animal seemed, just as naturally, to admit that he was subordinate. Attitudes, gestures, and other *nonscorable* dominance behavior in some cases appeared before scorable behavior was observed. A trench-worn sergeant, during the war, described a similar situation when he said, "You go over the top, pick your heinie, look him in the eye, and one of you is a dead man before you start fighting."

Some animals, of course, assumed subordinate status with but ill grace. They seemed to be "naturally" dominant animals and had to be pushed into an inferior role by sheer force of arms. This happened in two of our pairs (Java-Spitter and Spitter-Glenny).

2. *What Is the Nature of Dominance?* It is possible to envisage dominance as a drive or motive to behavior. If it be a drive it would seem furthermore to be one which is separable from the feeding drive or the sexual drive, although highly correlated with them. We are reminded here, very forcefully, of the analogous mechanisms that have been discussed for man: Adler's ego or superiority drive, MacDougall's instinct of self-assertion (and also his instinct of self-abasement, corresponding to subordination), Allport's ascendance and submission, etc. If dominance is a drive, it is very different from others in several important respects that would necessitate an overhauling of the general concept of "drive," e.g., it is continuous and not cyclic, it has two aspects, dominance and subordination, it is not known to be directly a function of simple glandular or physiological mechanism, it expresses itself through many indirect channels such as food, sex, pugnacity, that are themselves direct functions of simple drives.

3. *What Factors Determine Dominance?* Zuckerman suggests, tentatively, size, better canines, and better fighting ability. He discards size alone as a determining factor because of the fact that smaller animals are often dominant over larger animals. We also have found this to be true. The other two factors suggested by Zuckerman imply that dominance is always a result of fighting. In our animals, this was not found to be the case, although it may be true for the Hamadryas baboon. Any valid explanation would have to take account of the fact that in most cases dominance is established without any physical violence at all.

It is just as possible also to envisage dominance as an "attitude," to the determination of which a dominance drive core (physiological in nature) would contribute, but which is also a delicate balance or resultant of the effects of this putative drive, the immediate social situation, the previous experience of the animal, his physiological state of hunger, thirst, etc., the physiological state of the partner animal, etc.

Our suggestion would be that dominance is determined by or actually is a composite of social attitudes, attitudes of aggressiveness, confidence or cockiness that are at times challenged, and which must then, of course, be backed up by physical prowess. A very apparent "sizing-up" process goes on during the first moments of meeting, and it is during these moments and during this process that dominance seems to be established. A later paper will discuss this question more fully.

4. *What Role Does the Struggle for Food Play in the Determination of Dominance?* In 10 of our 12 pairs and possibly in an eleventh, dominance was established before the struggle for food became a factor in the situation. This is not to say that the introduction of this factor is of no importance. In many of our pairs it seemed to be a sharpening factor, bringing the respective behavior syndromes to a sharp focus.

Generally then we must consider our data to be a disproof of the hypothesis advanced by Harlow and Yudin (9) on the basis of their ingenious experiments on social facilitation of feeding.

5. *Is an Animal that Has Been Subordinate in One Pairing Necessarily Subordinate in Other Pairings?* Four of our animals were used in two pairings. Three of these animals, who had been subordinate in the first pairings, were dominant in the second. The other animal was dominant in both pairings.

6. *How Permanent Is Dominance, Once Established?* In 11 of our 12 pairs, dominance, once established, remained constant throughout the experiment. In one pair, it seemed to be changing in the last periods. This finding may be due to the comparatively short extent of the experimentation with any one pair. Changes in dominance were observed somewhat more frequently at the Vilas Park Zoo (14), where observations of a group sometimes extended over a period of a year and a half.

7. *Is the Drive for Dominance Determined Predominantly by Innate Rather than by Environmental Factors?* The previous discussions would seem to indicate a preponderance of hereditary influence in the determination of the dominance drive but we do not feel at all certain of this. We feel that the data that we have gathered and those available in the literature are inadequate with respect to this question. It is probable that the question cannot be attacked until our experiments can be repeated with animals that have been born in a laboratory.

8. *Is There a "General" Dominance Factor or Are There Specific Food Dominance, Sex Dominance, and Aggression Dominance Drives?* We must again plead inadequacy of data in attempting to discuss this question. Our data show in general that there is high correlation between sex, feeding, and aggression behavior, but there are several exceptions to this general finding, indicating that these behavior types are separable, practically as well as logically. The fact that we have not obtained perfect correlations between dominance behavior, feeding behavior, and sexual behavior indicates that they are independent drives that are highly correlated with each other but are far from being identical.

9. *Is Dominance Necessarily a Masculine Characteristic?* We have already expressed ourselves on this point in our previous paper (14), but we wish to reemphasize the fact that a female animal may be dominant, and that when she is, her behavior will differ in no way from that of a dominant male. Cwa, a female, was dominant over Tim, a male, and had begun to assume dominance over Nira, also a male, at the end of the experiment. She behaved in the typical dominant fashion.

## V. Summary and Conclusions

Two experimental techniques were used with 12 pairs of monkeys in an effort to achieve a quantitative determination of the behavior syndromes characteristic of dominance and subordination. The factors of age, weight, sex, species, introduction of food, and previous experiences were controlled as well as was possible. The animals were scored for almost all known types of social and sexual behavior.

Several of these types of behavior were found either to occur too infrequently or else to be unrelated to dominance and were, therefore, not included in the description of the behavior syndromes of dominance and subordination. These were (1) genital inspection, (2) presentation, (3) erection, (4) attempts to mount, (5) anger, (6) quiet sitting, and (7) ventro-ventral copulatory behavior. The sixth was discarded because in "general activity" we had an inverse score of the same behavior. The seventh was discarded, in spite of the fact that it seems to be very significant behavior, because of the paucity of data. It is a type of behavior that clearly calls for further investigation.

Other types of behavior were found to be closely related to dominance and subordination, and the following behavior syndromes seem to be characteristic of dominance and subordination.

The dominant animal typically:

1. Preempts all or most of a limited food supply (97%).
2. Frequently mounts the subordinate animal, irregardless of the gender of either the mounting or mounted animal (98%).
3. Is rarely or never thus mounted by the subordinate animal (2%).
4. Frequently bullies the subordinate animal (99%), but
5. Is almost never thus bullied by the subordinate animal (1%).
6. Initiates most of the fighting that occurs in the pair (85%).
7. *Never* cringes under aggression (0%).
8. Is rarely passive under aggression (1%).
9. Almost never flees from the subordinate animal (1%).
10. Is likely to be more active than his subordinate partner (65% of all scores).
11. Is likely to do more grooming than his subordinate partner (?), (62% of all scores).
12. Is likely to initiate more play than his subordinate partner (65% of all scores).

The negative of each of these 12 behavior characteristics gives the behavior syndrome for the subordinate animal.

Dominance may be envisaged either as a drive to behavior or as a social "attitude." If the former, it would then be a unique kind of drive, differing in several fundamental respects from such drives as hunger, thirst, etc. In the laboratory situation that we have canvassed, dominance is very often established at the very first meeting of the pair. Dominance was observable in one member of every pair we studied, although it varied in degree.

The factors that seemed to determine dominance in our evenly matched animals seemed to be not so much size, physical strength, etc., as an attitude of aggression or confidence. It was infrequently the outcome of a physical struggle. Neither does it seem to depend very frequently on struggle for food, for, in at least 10 of our 12 pairs, dominance was established before food was introduced into the situation.

Dominance status may change, although this was infrequent in our experimental set-up, being observed in only one of our 12 pairs.

An animal subordinate to one animal may be dominant over another.

## References

1. Aaronovich, G. D., & Khotin, B. I. (The problem of imitation in monkeys). *Novoye v Reflexologii i Fiziologii Nervnoy Systemi,* 1929, **3,** 378–390. Quoted from Murphy, G., and Murphy, L. B., *Experimental Social Psychology.* New York: Harper, 1931. P. 709.
2. Adler, A. The neurotic constitution. New York: Moffat, Yard, 1917. Pp. xxiii +456.
3. Allport, F. H. Social psychology. Boston: Houghton Mifflin, 1924. Pp. xiv +453.
4. Alverdes, F. Social life in the animal world. London: Kegan, Paul, 1927. P. 225.
5. Bingham, H. C. Sex development in apes. *Comp. Psychol. Monog.,* 1928, **5,** 1–45.
6. Carpenter, C. R. A field study of the behavior and social relations of howling monkeys. *Comp. Psychol. Monog.,* 1934, **10,** 1–168.
7. Fox, H. The birth of two anthropoid apes. *J. Mammal.,* 1929, **10,** 37–51.
8. Hamilton, G. V. A study of sexual tendencies in monkeys and baboons. *J. Anim. Behav.,* 1914, **4,** 295–318.
9. Harlow, H. F., & Yudin, H. C. Social behavior of primates. I. Social facilitation of feeding in monkeys and its relation to attitudes of ascendance and submission. *J. Comp. Psychol.,* 1933, **16,** 171–185.
10. Kellogg, W. N., & Kellogg, L. A. The ape and the child. New York: McGraw-Hill, 1933. P. 341.
11. Kempf, E. J. The social and sexual behavior of infra-human primates, with some comparable facts in human behavior. *Psychoanal. Rev.,* 1917, **4,** 127–154.
12. Köhler, W. The mentality of apes. New York: Harcourt, Brace, 1925. Pp. viii + 342.
13. Maslow, A. H. Hunger and appetites in animal motivation. *J. Comp. Psychol.,* 1935, **20,** 75–83.
14. ———. The role of dominance in the social and sexual behavior of infra-human primates: I. Observations at Vilas Park Zoo. *J. Genet. Psychol.,* 1936, **48,** 261–277.

15. ———. The role of dominance in the social and sexual behavior of infra-human primates: III. A theory of sexual behavior of infra-human primates. *J. Genet. Psychol.*, 1936, **48**, 310–338.

16. ———. The social behavior of monkeys and apes. *Int. J. Indiv. Psychol.*, 1935, **1**, 4th quarter, 47–59.

17. Schjelderup-Ebbe, T. Social behavior of birds. In *A handbook of social psychology*, ed. by C. Murchison. Worcester, Mass.: Clark Univ. Press, 1935. Pp. 947–973.

18. Tinklepaugh, O. L. Sex behavior in infra-human primates as a substitute response following emotional disturbance. *Psychol. Bull.*, 1932, **29**, 666.

19. Yerkes, R. M. Genetic aspects of grooming, a socially important primate behavior pattern. *J. Soc. Psychol.*, 1933, **4**, 3–25.

20. Yerkes, R. M., & Yerkes, A. W. The great apes. New Haven: Yale Univ. Press, 1929. Pp. xix+652.

21. Zuckerman, S. The social behavior of monkeys and apes. New York: Harcourt, Brace, 1932. Pp. xii+356.

## Editor's Introduction
## to Paper 3

Harry F. Harlow has written that, when Maslow left the University of Wisconsin in 1935, "he indicated that he was going to work strictly with people, and I was saddened because I thought that a fine monkey man had gone down the drain. However, I was not surprised, since I knew all along that Abe's interests surpassed the simians." The following paper, published in 1937 in the *Psychological Review*, was one of Maslow's first postdoctoral attempts to do just that—surpass the simians. Especially to be noticed are the distinctions drawn here among dominance-feeling, dominance behavior, and dominance status. Maslow took great care to point out that, although these three items might sometimes go together, they do not do so necessarily. Thus a person may display much dominance behavior and yet be relatively low in dominance-feeling and dominance status, or he may have high dominance-status in the relative absence of dominance-feeling, and so on. Although Maslow did not spell it out in just these words, it is clear that he was beginning to see "dominance-feeling" as the essential ingredient of authentic "dominance" (as distinguished from mere "domineeringness, with antagonism to others, willfulness, impoliteness, aggressiveness, tyrannizing, etc.").

# 3

# Dominance-Feeling, Behavior, and Status[1]

## A. H. Maslow

This paper has several purposes. (1) It will present briefly the
heuristic system of definitions and concepts relative to dominance in
human beings that has arisen as a product of experimental researches
in dominance in human beings and infra-human primates.[2] It appears
to the writer that this conceptual framework is more useful than other
discussions of will-to-power, dominance, power drive, etc., and has the
inestimable advantage of being an *experimental* product of work with normal subjects rather than a clinical or philosophical one. Neither is it a
product of any urge to system-building. It is therefore less apt to be distorted factually by the sort of esthetic architectonic that hates inconsistencies or unsolved problems and attempts to fit them to the Procrustean
bed of an *a priori*, prearranged theoretical scheme.

From *Psychological Review*, 1937, **44**, 404–429. Copyright 1937 by the American
Psychological Association, and reproduced by permission.

[1]I wish to express my thanks to Drs. E. L. Thorndike, G. Murphy, L. B. Murphy,
S. Asch, Miss Neva Lowman, and Miss Ruth Ritzman for useful suggestions and criticisms.
This study is one item in a program of research supported by a grant from the Carnegie
Corporation.

[2]In a series of papers on dominance in monkeys, (12), (13), (14), (15), (16), the
interested reader may trace for himself the struggle to approach some useful definition
of dominance. The definitions employed here, however, could not have come from work
with either humans or animals alone, but were made with reference to the comparative
facts in both. While fuller reports of the work with humans will be published in the future,
it may be well to give a very brief indication of the technique used. About 100 women
and 15 men, most of college age and intellectual calibre, were studied very carefully by
means of long, intensive interviews that attempted (1) to understand the whole personality
of the subject, and (2) to understand the role that dominance played in this personality
picture.

(2) It will present discursively some of the broader conclusions arrived at as a result of these researches.

It has been found necessary to distinguish between the following and to treat them as separate psychological data: dominance-feeling, dominance behavior, dominance status, craving or desire for dominance, feelings of inferiority and superiority, matter-of-fact superiority and inferiority, and compensatory dominance behavior. This paper will be built around the discussion of these concepts and the demonstration of the interrelations between them.

## I. Dominance Status and Dominance-Feeling

*Dominance Status.* It may be readily observed in pairs of human beings that, in a good many cases, one member of the pair will dominate the other. He will lead, suggest, order or inhibit the behavior of the subordinate one. The latter will often defer to the wishes of the dominant one, and respect him more than the dominant one respects *him*. In a marriage, for instance, in which the wife definitely and strongly dominates the husband, her opinion will usually prevail whenever there is any conflict; she will be more forceful and direct in the expression of her opinions than he will. In their social relationship, she is more confident in her behavior, gets what she wants more often than does the husband, feels superior to him, generally feels herself to be stronger than he is, and respects herself more than she does him. Her behavior, depending on the kind of dominance, is apt to express either (1) condescension, contempt, impatience, irritability, (2) pity, tenderness, protectiveness or good-natured toleration, or (3) aloofness and superiority.

The husband's behavior will express inferiority, deference, child-parent attitude, respect, "looking up to," willingness to concede. He *asks* rather than *tells* in his conversation and is apt to change his opinion if his dominant partner questions it.

If, however, we examine the further social relations of these two people, we find that she may stand in exactly the same relationship to certain other people as her husband stands to her, that is, other people may dominate her. Also we shall inevitably find that there are some people to whom the husband stands in a dominant relationship. He will now behave and feel in these relationships, approximately the same as his wife behaves and feels with respect to him.

It is this kind of relationship to which the terms "dominance status" and "subordinate status" refer. They may be more exactly defined as follows: *in a social relationship between two people, in which one dominates the other either overtly in behavior, or implicitly in feeling, the one who dominates is said to be in, or to have, dominance status. The other is said to be in, or to have, subordinate status.* While this kind of relationship does not *always* obtain in social pairings, it is very common in our culture. (See below for equality status, "split dominance," etc.)

Dominance status is then a relative thing. It refers to the particular relationship between two particular people.[3]

It is necessary to go behind these facts to another very interesting fact, namely, that some individuals dominate practically all the people they meet, and that other individuals are dominated by practically all the individuals they meet (feel subordinate to them). If now, as the writer has done, one subjects many individuals of both these groups to long, careful individual study, by means of lengthy, intensive interviews, hypnosis, dream interpretation, questionnaire studies, observation of behavior, and the subject's own reports of his behavior, we find that we can distinguish types of a sort; we can speak of high-dominance people, low-dominance people and middle-dominance people. For each of these we can observe fairly definite syndromes of behavior and feeling that are generally characteristic of these people in most of the affairs of daily life. We have discovered that the differences in feeling and attitude are more important and characteristic than the differences in behavior (that is to say, much more can be predicted from a knowledge of dominance-feeling). We shall therefore refer chiefly to differences in

[3]There are at least two broad types of dominance status. Further sub-distinctions might be made, but for our purposes these two are most useful. The first is the kind we find in infra-human primates in which all those factors called "cultural" play little or no part. This is the face-to-face, man-to-man situation in which two personalities are weighed on their own merits, without any superficial cultural advantages accruing to one or the other because of wealth, money, social position, economic position, etc. Our description would hold mostly for this kind of determination of status in which simply strength of character decides the outcome of the sizing-up process.

However, we must also deal with cultural, social and economic status if we wish to complete the picture. There is no doubt that, in most of the instances in which human beings meet each other in the ordinary framework of society, such considerations are as important in determining the status relationship that will emerge as are fundamental strength of personality, forcefulness of character, etc. The man who has a distinguished title or who is known as a very wealthy man or as a man who employs many men and women—such a man has a tremendous advantage over a person who is his employee or one who is looking for a job with this man. The first type we might call "face-to-face" dominance status, the latter, "cultural" dominance status. In general, dominance-feeling will correlate highly with "face-to-face" dominance-subordination status. It is likely to correlate less closely with "cultural" status.

Another determining factor in the "sizing-up" process is admitted by some subjects, namely, the *use* that this person can be to the subject in achieving his purposes. In other words, the perception of a person as a means to any of the subject's ends may influence the eventual determination of status. For instance, a person with high dominance-feeling meeting a person with low dominance-feeling may modify his dominance behavior considerably because this latter individual may have a father from whom a desired position might be obtained through his son's intervention.

It must be remembered that, as a result of the "sizing-up" process, status is sometimes "given," sometimes "taken," and sometimes both, as is also the case with monkeys. We know also that being a stranger lowers the chances of achieving dominance status. This is true for animals and for humans.

dominance-feeling rather than differences in dominance-behavior when we speak of high- or low-dominance people.

*Dominance-Feeling.* It is at the moment impossible to define succinctly what is meant by the feeling of dominance or subordination.[4] Various near-synonyms are possible. Together with a list of sub-aspects of the feeling, these almost-synonyms can at least give a working idea of what the feeling consists introspectively. These are (1) self-confidence, (2) self-esteem, (3) high self-respect and evaluation of self, (4) consciousness or feeling of "superiority" in a very general sense, (5) forcefulness of personality, (6) strength of character, (7) a feeling of sureness with respect to other people, (8) a feeling of being able to handle other people, (9) a feeling of masterfulness and of mastery, (10) a feeling that others do and ought to admire and respect one, (11) a feeling of general capability, (12) an absence of shyness, timidity, self-consciousness, or embarrassment, (13) a feeling of pride. These are the words and phrases which dominant people themselves have used when asked to describe their own feelings about themselves.[5]

Low-dominance feeling generally consists of either the absence or opposite of these feelings, as well as of certain positive and unique characteristics. Very often a low-dominance person will describe his feelings about himself in negative fashion. "I lack self-confidence." "I feel inferior with most people." "I guess I don't think much of myself." "I think I'd rather be like someone else if I could." The feelings of persons of this type are of uncertainty, lack of confidence, general inferiority, shame or lack of pride, weakness, general admiration and respect for others rather than for themselves, a feeling of being, in a very metaphorical sense, "below" others, of being looked down upon, of wanting to be like someone else rather than oneself, of being dominated by others,

[4]Operationally defined, "feeling" is what subjects say in the interview about their implicit, affective, and attitudinal responses. "Behavior" is what we can see from the outside. Thus we may observe that a subject is rather aloof and snobbish in her *behavior* at a party; later, in response to questioning, she may say that she *felt* shy and unwanted. "Feeling," so defined, is of course entirely on a conscious level. No interpretation or symbolic analysis is involved. What the subject *says* is the psychological datum used, that is, of course, if good rapport has been established.

[5]It is necessary at this point to insist as strenuously as possible that dominance-feeling not be confused with domineeringness, with antagonism to others, willfulness, impoliteness, selfishness, aggressiveness, tyrannizing, etc. If the reader finds himself prone to think of a high-dominance person as rather a nasty person, one who would push him out of line or punch him in the face, let him substitute "self-confidence" for "high-dominance feeling" and "lack of confidence" for "low-dominance feeling." They are not synonymous, but at least the substitutes bring less misunderstanding in this direction. The writer uses the word 'dominance' because, even after much thought, he has not been able to find one that is not misunderstood, and at least our phrase makes the animal work continuous with work for children and adult human beings. Another possible substitute is high or low ego-level.

of lack of faith in oneself and in one's abilities. They often feel shy, inhibited, timid, unworthy, self-conscious and embarrassed. Generally they cannot be said to be satisfied with themselves. This is further illustrated by the presence of inferiority feelings as an important and primary part of the personality picture in low-dominance people (which is only infrequently the case in high-dominance people).[6] Generally, in low-dominance people we do not see the ease, the calm, the natural assurance, the lack of restraint and "tension," the lack of fearfulness, that impresses us in high-dominance people.

One question that frequently comes up in the mind of the person not thoroughly acquainted with the various concepts of dominance is the variability with mood. He is apt to think that at one time a person feels very dominant and at another time very subordinate. Of course this opinion is partly due to the confusion between dominance-feeling and status. It is perfectly true that status can vary widely with a situation and that the general mood is, to some extent, a reflection of the status, but it is the writer's impression that, as a usual thing, dominance-feeling fluctuates (because of mood) only within a small range of the total range of dominance. Introspectively, of course, any one person knows only his own range of dominance-feeling and is apt to regard it as a very wide one. With increased knowledge of the total range for the general population, realization of the comparatively minor size of his own individual fluctuation is sure to ensue.

There is no doubt that a long series of successes or failures, shocks, traumata, continual subjection to one kind of status rather than another will all have their effect on general dominance-feeling—that is to say, there may be a slow long-time lowering or raising with long-time success or failure. Feeling, however, is a relatively stable thing. It can change, but it needs major impacts and many of them for this change to occur.

If we were forced to choose a single synonym or definition for dominance-feeling, we should say that it was chiefly the evaluation of, or confidence in, the personality (self-confidence). High-dominants evaluate their personalities or selves highly; the self of the low-dominant is given a low evaluation by the subject himself.[7] Between the two extremes described, there are all degrees of intermediate strengths of

[6]This list of at least partially disparate feelings and attitudes would indicate that dominance-feeling is not a unitary thing, that it is more heterogeneous than homogeneous. It is probably more cautious to proceed on the basis of such an assumption, since unitariness of all these aspects of dominance-feeling has not yet been proved. It is the writer's belief and impression, however, that dominance-feeling is ultimately a simplex, rather than a complex.

[7]This means evaluation of the *whole* personality, rather than just one part of it. A person may evaluate his intelligence very highly indeed and still be low in dominance-feeling.

evaluation of, or confidence in, the self, and the whole forms a smooth continuum on a single dimension, in which it is possible to place almost any single person. It is obvious that, since this dominance-feeling varies in degree, it is susceptible to treatment by the usual statistical and experimental methods that have been used, for instance, with such great success in the consideration of intelligence. Such a phrasing, it seems to the writer, is a far more useful one to the *science* of psychology than the clinical, psychotherapeutic, qualitative treatment accorded it by the psychological physicians (even though we have probably oversimplified).

## II. The Relationship between Dominance-Feeling and Dominance Status

Feeling and status of dominance are at least partially circular in their relationship. Feeling, to a large extent, determines status, and status (to a lesser extent) also determines feeling.

When two people come together in a face-to-face relationship, a conscious or unconscious sizing-up process ensues, that looks much like what we see in infra-human primates (14). This process, of course, is infinitely more subtle than it is in animals. It is much more influenced by the immediate psycho-social situation, and by such cultural elements as clothes, wealth, reputation, social position, etc. Also, in meetings of unlike-sex pairs, the generally inferior position of women in our culture puts her at a further disadvantage.[8]

It is still possible and valid, however, to point out that the main elements at work in this sizing-up process are the levels of dominance-feeling in the two members of the pair. Each has a certain opinion of himself, of his own strength and forcefulness, of his capabilities and shortcomings, of his own place in the generality of people whom he has met and whom he will meet. It is this evaluation of the self that is com-

---

[8]It is interesting to compare with these statements the conclusions and speculations of the writer on the establishment of dominance status in pairs of monkeys meeting for the first time. "Our suggestion would be that dominance (status) is determined by, or actually is a composite of social attitudes, attitudes of aggressiveness, confidence or cockiness.... A very apparent 'sizing-up' process goes on during the first few moments of meeting, and it is during these moments and during this process that dominance (status) seems to be established" (14, p. 305). In these animals difference in size was very important in this sizing-up process. This is much less true for humans, although still a factor. In retrospect, it is at least possible to read for 'social attitudes, attitudes of aggressiveness, confidence or cockiness,' simply 'dominance-feeling,' with the one amendment that aggressiveness is not a necessary or even usual component of dominance status in human beings. In humans, as in animals, the first meeting is usually far more important in determining dominance status than any single subsequent meeting.

pared with the evaluation of the self (expressed overtly) before him, and it is from the unconscious perception or realization of the comparative status of the two personalities that the dominance-subordination relationship of the particular social group emerges, in some cases immediately, if the relative status of dominance-feeling is very obvious to both members of the pair, in other cases slowly and with much feeling-out and unconscious "sparring." In still other cases, there need be no emergence of a relationship of dominance-subordination; instead we may have a perception of equality, friendship, and mutual respect, with a consequent status of equality for the two members of the pair.[9] To some extent, also, in such pair relationships, it is possible to have "split dominance status." That is to say, one of the pair may be by far the better of the two in intellectual equipment and capabilities, whereas the other may be recognized as the undoubted superior in social abilities and equipment.

This latter relationship of "split dominance" is met less frequently than most people think. For one thing, people usually have few voluntary contacts with those who are very different from themselves in any important respects. The person who values intellect very highly is not so apt to come in close and sustained contact with persons who do not value intellect highly. In the second place, the more usual rule is that all the capabilities, strengths and weaknesses of the personality are thrown together into a unit and it is this *unit* that is the basis of comparison with others. The usual person thinks of himself as a whole and not as

[9]Dr. Max Wertheimer, in private conversation, has brought up the following very interesting point. Dominance-feeling is to some extent connected with being "high." This can mean (1) higher than others, better than they are, or (2) "high" in the sense of being adequate to the task or problem in hand, without reference to comparison with other men. That is to say, there are those artists, physicians, or scientists who wish only to express themselves as adequately as possible—to help, to serve, to fulfill their obligations to society, and to express themselves to the best of their abilities. What others might do in a similar situation has nothing to do with the self-evaluation. An artist who has painted a portrait may think in either of two ways: "Is this better than the products of my rivals?" or "Does this satisfy me; is it the best I can do; does it express my original conception satisfactorily?" Some artists need the admiration of audiences and the stimulus of rivalry, but some artists do *not*. These evaluate themselves only by an internal and personal scale of values rather than by a social, competitive criterion.

I agree that, even though people of this latter type are rare, they should be considered, since their rarity is not so much a reflection of fundamental emphasis in human nature as it is a product of the dominant trends of rivalry, competition, urge-for-power-over-others which characterize our culture. Presumably, in a cooperative culture such personalities would be the rule rather than the exception.

In this same connection we may mention also Dr. Wertheimer's insistence on other determiners of dominance behavior, for instance, sheer *need* for dominance behavior because of the situation; *e.g.*, a father who sees his child assaulted by a bully may behave in a way that has no reference whatsoever to his dominance-feeling. Another possible source of dominance behavior is being right or correct when others are not. Still another determiner of behavior that might look like dominance is hyper-energy.

a melange of separate and discrete superiorities or inferiorities.[10] It is true that the psychologist, from the outside, may diagnose Case L. M. B. to be one of high dominance-feeling, which seems to be built mostly upon an undoubted attractiveness to, and success with, men. L. M. B. herself, however, does not diagnose herself so. To herself, she is simply a superior person in a very general sense. It is even truer to say that she does not diagnose herself at all; she simply feels superior.

We have already described above the general syndrome of behavior and mutual attitude for the dominance-subordination status relationship. To some extent such syndromes must remain a generalized abstraction or averaging of the realities of behavior, since there are several different ways of expressing dominance, any one of which may be used by an individual (either monkey or man). Some dominants are protectors, others are tyrants, others are "individualists" in the sense that they do not readily express dominance in behavior so long as others do not try to dominate them.[11] To be more accurate, we should describe at least three syndromes of dominance-subordination status behavior, corresponding to these three kinds of dominant people.

One further amendment must be made to the generalized description of status behavior that we have outlined. If either person in the relationship is at either extreme of the distribution of dominance-feeling, modification of status behavior is likely to result. For one thing, the person

[10]Dr. E. Duffy and Dr. G. Murphy have pointed out that sheer dominance-feeling or feeling of general inner strength seem to some extent to vary independently of evaluations of some sub-abilities or sub-sections of the personality. In empirical terms, this has meant in our study that we have had subjects who were low or middle in general dominance-feeling at the same time that they were superior and felt superior in (1) intellectual ability, (2) social ability or intelligence (girls who come from "best families" and who have recognized social status), and (3) mechanical ability. There are probably more, but these are the only ones we have ourselves observed. We have also observed cases in which complete inferiority in any one of these respects was taken calmly and matter-of-factly without any repercussions on general dominance-feeling. For example, one man with high dominance-feeling seemed to be completely untouched by the fact of his inferiority in mechanical abilities, and there was even detectable in him a slightly condescending attitude toward people who were interested in such things. It is the degree of importance assigned to a particular ability by the subject himself that will determine its importance as a builder of dominance-feeling. An intellectual's level of dominance-feeling is pinned far more closely to his superiority or inferiority in intelligence than would be the case, for example, in a professional athlete. It is the writer's experience that social inadequacy is less apt to vary independently of dominance-feeling than either intellectual or mechanical inadequacy. That is to say, it is easy to find cases of people of low dominance-feeling who are confident in their ability to handle tea-cups, introductions, and matters of etiquette correctly, but cases of people who are high in dominance-feeling and who at the same time lack the superficial social attainments are much more rare, although they can be found.

[11]We have observed at least these three qualities of dominance expression in three species of infra-human primates. The dominant macacus rhesus is typically a tyrant and a bully, the chimpanzee a friend and a protector, and the cebus monkey an "individualist" in the above sense. See (12). See also Bühler (4) for descriptions of three types of social personality in children.

high in dominance-feeling is apt to be very restive in subordinate status, especially if the person in dominant status is arrogant, tyrannical, silly, bullying, or if in general he is felt not to be worthy of dominance status. Further it is the writer's impression, although he has too few observations bearing on this point, that persons very low in dominance-feeling may never or rarely behave in a dominant fashion even when in dominance status, especially if the person or persons in subordinate status are felt to be higher in dominance-feeling. (This may be the case, for instance, in some such instance as the housewife, low in dominance-feeling, who is mistress of several servants.)

Aside from these and similar considerations, the dominance-feelings of the members of this pair or group are apt to have surprisingly little influence on status behavior, after relative status has once been determined. In rhesus monkeys it was found possible to study many separate interpairings of animals and then to treat one animal with dominance status as equivalent to any other animal with dominance status. One could do the same for all (rhesus) monkeys in subordinate status. One dominant animal, by and large, behaves like any other dominant status animal, and a subordinate status animal behaves like any other animal in this same status. And in our experiments this held true *even when we paired and interpaired a small group of six animals*. This same animal A, who was dominant over B and subordinate to C, behaved like any other dominant animal with B, and like any other subordinate animal with C.

It may be assumed that these animals differed in dominance-feeling but, once social status was determined, it was impossible to diagnose the level of dominance-feeling of the individuals concerned except in extreme cases. See, for instance, the behavior of Kathryn (16), a strong dominance animal, who occupied subordinate status in the pairings because of her youth and small size.

In other words, for these rhesus monkeys there seem to be only two kinds of status, dominance and subordination, and within each status we have found relatively little range of individual differences determined by dominance-feeling. (This is much less true for chimpanzees and cebus monkeys.)

In humans we find some likenesses and some differences. Generally we find more similarity between pairs (*e.g.*, married couples) than we might have suspected. We may find in one married couple that the husband is dominant to the wife but that both are very high in individual dominance-feeling. In another couple we may find the same status of wife and husband but find them both *low* in individual dominance-feeling. In these two pairs we shall find much community of behavior. The same seems to be true (although our evidence is limited) where the status is reversed, *i.e.*, the wife is dominant over the husband.

True, the level of dominance-feeling in the individual will determine broad differences (chiefly in attitude toward sexual behavior) from one pair to the other, and we shall find the dominance-feeling of the individuals determining relationship to outside people in the expected way, but the married relationships *qua* relationship in the two married couples are similar in their broad outlines, *e.g.*, one determines, the other concedes, one tends to withdraw before the anger of the other, respect flows more in one direction than in the other, one is more "powerful" than the other, etc.

As in the monkeys, we find at the extremes of the range of dominance-feeling some determination of differential behavior in subordinate status. A woman with very high dominance-feeling, who is nevertheless in subordinate status to her husband, tends to criticize, to quarrel and to resent her status, and sometimes attempts to change it.

It has been found that this fact of little range of behavior within a status has extensive implications for the methodology of studying dominance in humans. The experimenter who attempts to determine dominance rating by inspection or short interview will inevitably find that he underrates the dominance-feeling of many people who stand in a subordinate status with respect to him, and to overrate many people who stand in a dominant relation to him. This follows naturally from our discussion above. All people in subordinate status to him will look spuriously alike in their general social behavior (with respect to the experimenter); all people who dominate the experimenter will look more similar to each other than they really are. To a giant all dwarfs look equally small and to a dwarf, giants look equally tall.[12]

### III. Dominance Behavior: Compensation

Dominance behavior is almost always social, almost always with respect to another person or persons. If it were possible to observe single isolated human beings in such a way that they were not aware of being observed, it is doubtful whether we could distinguish easily between

[12]It follows that the interviewer must be very careful in several respects: (1) He must know where he himself stands in the scale of dominance-feeling; (2) he must not judge the dominance-feeling of a subject merely from the relationship obtaining in the interviewing room; (3) he must judge and rate the subject by the latter's behavior and feeling with respect to the *general* population, and not to one or two people; (4) if ratings of the subject are to be obtained, it is best that these be average ratings by several people who stand in a close relationship to him (as peers, *not* as parents, teachers, employers, etc.); (5) it follows also that, theoretically, the best single ratings in an experiment on the general population can be obtained from a rater who stands at the middle of the scale for dominance-feeling; (6) he must be careful to appreciate completely the influence of his own cultural status, *e.g.*, being a teacher, physician, older person, etc.

even the most and the least dominant subjects on the basis of their behavior with respect to inanimate objects alone.

In social situations, however, it is usually possible to make at least a very rough rating of dominance-feeling of the subjects involved on the basis of their behavior alone. As the situation in which observations are made becomes more experimental, *i.e.*, constant psychologically from subject to subject, quantitatively scorable, etc., as for instance, in the experiments of Jack (10) and Page (18), the rating or score becomes more and more reliable and valid. This rating, if it hopes to measure dominance-feeling rather than mere dominance status, must be a composite of the behavior of the subject with respect to *many*, rather than one or two other subjects. When one attempts to rate the dominance-feeling of a subject on the basis of his behavior with respect to *one* other person, results are sure to be very inexact, for reasons that we have discussed above.

It must be remembered that dominance behavior may not be expressed by a woman as freely as by a man. The very definite training that most women in our culture get in being "lady-like" (non-dominant) exerts its effect forever afterwards. The dominant woman may differ little or not at all in her dominance behavior from the median dominance woman, at least in the ordinary daily social routine. In any case, she at least knows *how* to be, as one subject phrased it, "innocent and girlish and sweet sixteen," and can put on this appearance at will, especially in dealing with people of the older generation. For instance, it seems, from all that can be gathered from the subjects of this study, that the ordinary college Dean of Women *never* sees any kind of behavior but this.[13]

A few kinds of dominance behavior are to some extent independent of status, being instead almost purely functions of level of dominance-feeling. That is to say, a person with high dominance-feeling may show a degree of constancy in certain behaviors regardless of his status at the moment. The same is true for the low-dominance person to a lesser extent. For instance, the high-dominance woman in subor-

[13]Inhibition of dominance behavior differs in various parts of the country, and it differs in different ways for the two sexes. For instance, the writer has been told by a psychologist who was born and raised in the South that she was taught never to express dominance behavior openly with respect to men, at least marriageable men. It seemed to be permissible to attempt domination *after* marriage, but even this was to be done subtly by coaxing, wheedling, pleading, etc., rather than by any "unladylike" and open forcefulness of behavior. As nearly as the writer can determine, open and at times cruel domination of Negroes is permitted for either sex, but even this differs with different classes of the population, and for different "kinds" of Negroes. Various kinds of dominance behavior are treated differentially in other parts of the country, also. In completely different cultures, we may of course see even more marked discrepancies between dominance-feeling and behavior. For instance, among the Japanese, subordination behavior has become institutionalized as the *only* way to behave politely.

dinate status—say, in an office—will not blush or be embarrassed or self-conscious even when she speaks to her boss (although other behavior *will* reflect the influence of her subordinate status, *e.g.*, deference, respectful behavior, etc.). Carriage, mien, demeanor of a certain type seem also to be constant characteristics of high-dominance women, regardless of status. For instance, it seems to the writer, although he has no more specific evidence than impression, that the high-dominance person stands more erectly and has better carriage, has a firm handshake, gazes steadily into the eye of the person to whom he or she is speaking, walks with a freer swing of the body, is less apt to hesitate or stammer in speaking, etc.[14]

There is, however, still another reason why dominance behavior alone is a weak reed to rest on if the desideratum is a rating of dominance-feeling; namely, the fact that some people compensate for a feeling of weakness (low dominance-feeling) by behaving in a very dominant fashion.

*Compensation may be diagnosed when the behavior of the subject is rated higher in dominance than in dominance-feeling.* Such subjects feel weak but wish to appear strong. In order to achieve this end it is necessary for them to put about them a cloak of dominance behavior that, in a sense, is not "natural" to them. Such people protect or defend themselves psychologically, and with only superficial observation of behavior to rely on, it is very easy to confuse these cases with genuine cases of high dominance-feeling.

If, however, we observe cases of *over*-compensation closely, certain characteristics of behavior may in some instances enable it to be distinguished from dominance behavior that flows from high dominance-feeling. In the first place, it is apt to give the observer the impression of being strained and unnatural. It is more aggressive and louder than seems to be appropriate to the situation. It is, in some cases, apt to be even somewhat vulgar, and may sometimes also give the observer the impression of expressing defiance or a chip-on-the-shoulder attitude, rather than calm assurance. Such people are apt to be more "flip" than the average, to be hyper-critical, to be "wise-crackers," to be ultra-sophisticated in a manner that indicates an eager desire to impress others with this quality. In several cases, feelings of conflict and ambivalence toward sex went with very free, even loose, talk about sex. In other instances the compensatory behavior took the form of apparent snobbishness with haughty, cold, aloof behavior. All the above is less true for compensating (rather than *over*-compensating) cases.

[14]A careful, extensive study of dominance-feeling and expressive movements, now being made by P. Eisenberg, will furnish a check-up on these and other hypotheses about dominance-feeling and behavior (6).

The compensating subjects turned out to be located around the middle of the distribution for dominance-feeling, both by interview rating and scores obtained in the author's "Social Personality Inventory," a test for dominance-feeling now in process of standardization. Of the relatively few subjects with low dominance-feeling that we have been able to study, there was no case of compensation.[15]

Very little can as yet be said about the etiology of the tendency to compensate, if we confine ourselves to our own results.[16] Of interest, however, is the fact that, of twelve clear cases of compensation, eight were Jewish women, whereas Jewish women were only 20 per cent of the total group studied. The research lead here is obvious. The writer's "hunch" is that at least one fruitful hypothesis about compensatory dominance behavior might be to consider it, for research purposes, the reaction of a minority cultural group to its feeling of not being quite at home in the larger cultural milieu, of not being completely wanted or respected. This hypothesis is borne out by the fact that behavior with family, with close friends, with the husband, etc., is *not* of the compensatory type. It occurs only when *defense* is felt to be necessary.[17]

Compensatory dominance behavior may be taken as one example of a larger concept; namely, discrepancy in general between feeling and behavior. We have already demonstrated that the correlation between feeling and behavior is not close in many instances. We should also mention the fact that in many instances in our own culture and in other cultures behavior is *less* dominant than feeling. The direction of the discrepancy would, to some extent, seem to be determined by the basic emphases of the culture in question. In aggressive, competitive, or rivalrous groups, high dominance behavior would be more desirable socially; and in such cultures we should expect to find much compensation and

[15]There was no difficulty in getting women in the middle of the distribution and above to submit themselves to fairly embarrassing interviews concerning their private lives. It was practically impossible to get as subjects women at the lower end of the distribution. The few that were obtained were students of science and felt that it was their duty to submit themselves, especially in view of the almost tearful pleadings of the by now distraught experimenter. Low-dominance women find it extremely difficult and distasteful to reveal their psychological "innards," even for the sake of science. We do not care to make this a generalization, since of sixty women studied, only four were definitely low in dominance, and even in these there were some isolated instances of "putting on a front" for psychological self-defense.

[16]We owe the invention of the concept of compensation to Alfred Adler (2), and his works should be consulted for extensive discussions of the role of compensation in the personality. We have deliberately restricted ourselves here to drawing conclusions *only* from our own data.

[17]One subject, a case of compensatory dominance behavior, said of a certain man who was conversing with her, "He was so dominant, I relaxed completely." Another girl, obviously compensatory, said she could not relax except in the company of very close friends or someone who was very dominant. In the company of one man, who dominated her completely, she always relaxed completely.

over-compensation in one sense. In Japan behavior is usually non-dominant, while feeling, on the other hand, is, so far as we can tell, more or less "normally" distributed. There is cultural repression of overt dominance behavior in this instance.

In the case of the early Christians the stress again was on lack of dominance behavior with respect to one's fellows. It is true that there was just as much stress on lack of dominance-feeling, and that the whole trend of thought was in the direction of humility and meekness, but it is easy to see that the cultural stress would have been far more efficient in stamping out dominance behavior than in stamping out dominance-feeling.

Dr. Wertheimer has suggested[18] the term "psychological lying" for such discrepancy between feeling and behavior—since dominance behavior may give a completely false index to the immediate inner state that motivates it or is associated with it.

### IV. Matter-of-Fact Superiority and Inferiority

Dodge and Kahn (5) have made the distinction between *feelings* of inferiority or superiority on the one hand and matter-of-fact superiority or inferiority on the other. In our work this distinction has turned out to be a very fruitful one, being extremely important particularly in the consideration of the self-evaluation of the non-dominant woman. Our finding is that matter-of-fact superiority and inferiority are clearly and fairly objectively recognized and understood by the more dominant woman. In her, however, we do not find many *feelings* of inferiority (in a psychopathological sense). There may be feelings of superiority but they again are not in any sense psychopathological. They are rather calm, objective recognition of facts that exist.

In the non-dominant woman on the other hand, we find a very different state of affairs. Far greater stress is laid in the psychic life upon matter-of-fact inferiority, little stress upon matter-of-fact superiority, much as we should think that the opposite would be the case. Further, it has been found that regardless of matter-of-fact superiority or inferiority, a predominant role in the personality picture of non-dominance women is played by feelings of inferiority. These feelings in many cases have no bases in fact. That is to say, the outside world may recognize such a woman to be very intelligent, but she is very apt to have feelings of inferiority about her intelligence in spite of this. Where the opinion of the outside world about matter-of-fact superiority has finally been

[18]In conversation.

impressed upon and accepted by the non-dominant subject (as in the case of one woman who was outstandingly lovely), in no cases has the writer found that such recognition gives rise to feelings of superiority. Rather such recognition of matter-of-fact superiority is pushed into the background and is not used as one might expect in the building up of self-evaluation. It seems unimportant and has little influence in the personality picture of such women, whereas, on the other hand, the slightest matter-of-fact inferiority is selected out, magnified and concentrated upon. A dozen assurances of, for example, high intelligence, are outweighed by one statement or hint of the contrary. This seems much more important in the total personality than one would ever expect.

In summary, then, we may say in a very general fashion, that dominant women have few "feelings" of inferiority, but that non-dominant women do have many such feelings of inferiority and in both cases the presence or absence of these feelings is not plainly determined by matter-of-fact inferiorities or superiorities.

## V. The Craving for Dominance

It is very easy to confuse the craving or desire for dominance with the other concepts that have been presented above. They should be clearly distinguished. It is not, for instance, the same as dominance-feeling. Our tentative finding about the relationship between the two is that some people high in dominance-feeling do have the craving for dominance status, and others do not. This seems to go with the degree of presence of the independent variable of activity or aggressiveness. The dominant person who is high in aggressiveness or activity (in the Adlerian sense) is the extremely ambitious person who craves recognition of superiority by others or, in other words, dominance status (face-to-face). The dominant person who is not active in this sense is quite content to feel superior without attempting to force recognition of this superiority upon others. In other words, he is quite content to feel superior whether or not others recognize this superiority.

Obviously the cases we have described as compensatory may be said to have great craving for dominance status. They also have a desire to *feel* dominant. "I wish I could be calm and self-assured." No person high in dominance-feeling ever makes such a statement.

It is difficult to discuss the place of craving for dominance in the low dominance-feeling case, because of the small number of subjects. It is the writer's impression that there is a certain distrust of their own ability to maintain and be successful in dominance status. They do not wish to be bosses or executives or leaders simply because they think they would not be successful in such roles. But it is definitely true for the cases studied that they *do* crave higher dominance-feeling. They wish to be other than they are, in that they hate their feeling of inadequacy, of weakness and lack of forcefulness. They would wish not to be shy, bashful and timid. Their self-consciousness tortures them and they would like to be rid of it.

Another way of looking at the craving for dominance is to attempt to understand its place in our culture. If we consider the total range of dominance-feeling and of dominance behavior, it is obvious that in our society the upper ends of these distributions are the more socially approved ones. What we interpret as the craving for dominance may then be a direct expression of the fact that most of us are creatures of our culture and desire what it desires. If the cultural stress is upon high dominance-feeling and high dominance behavior, then these are what we wish or crave.

Finally, it is possible that the most parsimonious way of treating this concept is to think of it in specific, rather than general, terms. It may be possible and even desirable to speak *not* of craving for dominance, but of craving for health *per se*, or for an automobile (not for what it symbolizes psychologically, but simply for its own sake). Or one may crave to be free of timidity, not because of an attempt to increase self-evaluation, but simply for vocational efficiency; *e.g.*, in order to be a better teacher or a more efficient physician.

## VI. The Role of Dominance in the Total Personality

In our dealings with subjects as total personalities, we found, as an observational fact, that some high-dominance people were active and aggressive, and that others, equally high in dominance-feeling, were calm, quiet, and non-aggressive; some were sociable and some were not; some were highly sexed (in a sheerly physiological sense) and some were not. Of these four traits of dominance, activity, sociability, and sexual drive, any combination seemed to be possible. For instance, a single individual might be high in all traits, or high in any one and low in the others, or high in two and low in two, and so on.

No claim is made that these four traits analyze the personality definitively into a perfect and inclusive system.[19] There are many aspects

---

[19]Or better, *three* traits, since sheer physiological sexual drive has surprisingly little influence on personality, or for that matter, even on sexual behavior. The proofs for this statement will be presented in a forthcoming paper. Another possible dimension of personality is "ego-security."

of personality that were not considered because of the techniques used or because of the limitation of the research purpose. Nor is it necessarily true that these are fundamental and homogeneous. It may be that they are cross-cut, superficial, resultant products of other personality traits. These conclusions are presented merely as a set of variables that are independent from the point of view of a researcher interested in knowing how much can be predicted from a knowledge of dominance and in the hope that they may be suggestive. It is our experience that at least two general kinds of behavior that *cannot* be so predicted (within our framework of definition and method) are activity and sociability (also sexual drive). If it be conceded that one task of the experimentally oriented psychologist is to analyze the personality into the fewest possible number of mutually exclusive traits, whose measure would give us the optimum picture of the personality attainable by quantitative methods, then the particular system of proposed independent variables of personality presented here is a start in the right direction.

All three qualities taken together give a very nicely rounded and fairly complete picture of a particular individual. Knowing the subject's rating for them, we should be able to predict a good deal of his social behavior, of his relationships to specific kinds of people, of his interests, likes and dislikes, vocational aptitudes, etc.

It is interesting to note that factor analysis studies to some extent support the primary importance of the qualities we have mentioned (excluding sexuality which is not and cannot now be studied scientifically because of cultural restrictions). Flanagan's (7) well-known factor analysis of the four Bernreuter personality scales led him to the conclusion that these four (neuroticism, introversion-extroversion, self-sufficiency and dominance) were cross-cuts of two main variables which he named *self-confidence* and *sociability*. Flanagan's self-confidence comes close to our conception of dominance-feeling, and for the moment we may assume it to be an equivalent.

Williams (19) also made a factor analysis of some data on social behavior of children. Thirty traits were observed and rated separately. Analysis showed that two factors accounted for almost all these traits of behavior, ascendance-submission and what Williams calls approach-withdrawal. Examination of his data leads us to believe that this latter "factor" is a combination of our two factors of sociability and activity.

A study by Dr. H. C. McCloy (17) of mutual character ratings by a group of intimately associated college men has given approximately similar results. The first two factors in McCloy's analysis are strikingly similar to Williams' two factors. The factor which he calls "social qualities" again seems to be a complex of what we are calling activity and sociability.

A recent study by Guilford and Guilford (9) again gives similar results. Factor analysis of the results from a test of introversion-extroversion brings to light five factors of which one seems to be comparable to dominance in one restricted sense, and another one to sociability.

While the validity and usefulness of the factor-analysis technique are still being discussed and being called into question, such similarity in four different studies using various kinds of material is surely suggestive.

It is as yet too early to say which of the various maps of the personality offered to us is best and most useful. We wish only to stress here that an empirical approach to this problem is possible. In the actual contact with many personalities we can find out, at least in a preliminary fashion, (1) which are the most important fundamental aspects of personality, (2) what is the most parsimonious way of analyzing the total personality into conveniently handled aspects, (3) which of these aspects of personality are related to each other and which are independently variable, and (4) what behavior is connected with each of these aspects.

*The Relationship of Behavior to Inner State.* We have already demonstrated, in the field of sexual expression, that a single kind of behavior may be a product of (or may be correlated with) different inner states in animals. In monkeys, sexual behavior may be an expression of impulse to dominate, or it may be a direct product of physiological sexual tensions. There are also indications that the same thing is partially true for humans also.

We wish now to call attention to the fact that a single inner state may give rise to various different forms of behavior. This, of course, is nothing new, for Freud has long since pointed out (8) that a state of conflict and repression may result in expression through any one of the so-called "Freudian mechanisms," *e.g.,* sublimation, hysterical symptoms, rationalization, etc. We have pointed out above a few of the various possible relationships between dominance behavior and dominance-feeling and have, we think, demonstrated the lack of invariable relationship between them.

A start has been made in the analysis of seemingly similar behaviors that are, however, correlated with different inner states. For monkeys, see (15). We have attempted in this paper to indicate how compensatory dominance behavior and "true" dominance behavior may be distinguished. In the early stages of his work, the experimenter was unable to see any differences at all between them, just as at first he could see no overt differences between dominance-sexual behavior and hormone-sexual behavior in monkeys. Close observation and analysis gave at least partial success in both instances. It may be that the same will be the case in other similar problems.

## VII. Culture, Personality and Dominance[20]

We wish to emphasize that the picture we have presented is drawn for *our culture alone*. And even then there are many indications that there exist many broad sectional-cultural differences of real significance within the United States alone. What is more, there are within the two places where most of this research was prosecuted (Madison, Wisconsin, and New York City) significant class, race, religious, educational and socio-economic differences in determination of dominance-feeling and behavior.

It may be that there will be found, in the future, innate bases of one sort or another for individual differences in dominance-feeling within a particular cultural frame of reference. On *a priori* grounds, there would seem to be good reason to believe that differences in hormone balance which are independent of culture should have something to do with predisposing one individual to greater or lesser aggressiveness, for instance. At the moment, however, we cannot emphasize too strongly that, while such biochemical determiners have not yet been demonstrated conclusively, we are even now sure of some cultural determination of dominance-feeling, behavior and status.

The writer has made a study of some of the ethnological literature in the hope of finding broad common human characteristics in connection with dominance. Little that is certain was carried away from this study beyond the fact that in most of the cultures which were studied, there seemed to be discernible relationships (of a kind) of dominance-subordination as between individuals. That is to say, there seem to be found in most cultural groups some individuals who are considered to be "inferior" persons, and these judgments of relative value of personalities seem to be as important in determining dominance status as they are in our culture. *But*, and this should be kept firmly in mind, the bases for a person considering himself "superior" in cultures A, B, C and D may be widely different, and also the strength, ubiquity and nature of such relationships differ very widely from culture to culture.[21]

In some cultures, it seemed to the writer that (at least on the basis of the psychologically inadequate data usually presented by the social anthropologist) no distinction could be made between "face-to-face" and "cultural" dominance-subordination status. Or perhaps it might be better to say that in some cultures no evidence is given for

[20]I wish to thank Dr. Ruth Benedict for suggestions given in dealing with this subject.

[21]Among such cultures as the Zuñi, we find many forms that can be interpreted only as a stamping-out by the group of the impulse to dominate (3).

the existence of the former. In very rigidly stratified and structural groups (caste system of India) most status relationships follow reflexly and without any lability from cultural status determined before the birth of either individual in any pair.

In other cultures with little structuring (*e.g.*, Eskimo), relationships of dominance-subordination are more often determined by such animal qualities as strength, size, agility, cunning, etc. See also Linton (11) on "status personality."

With few exceptions the behaviors characteristic of dominance-subordination feeling or status are local, cultural accidents. It follows, therefore, that the problem of understanding why particular behavioral ways of expressing dominance-feeling came to be *connected* with this feeling, is not so much a psychological as a cultural-historical study.

It is interesting to note the indications of a few universal (so far as we can tell) ways of expressing dominance and subordination in behavior. For instance, so far as our study has taken us, we have found no group any place in the world where kneeling, bowing or prostrating oneself before another person is an expression of dominance. These and similar forms of behavior express *only* subordination in all those cases in which they have any social-personal meaning at all. It may be the fact that the writer has found this same tendency in monkeys (for the dominant animal to be physically above the subordinate animal) that causes him to suspect a deeper significance in this trend than would appear on the surface.

Another instance of similarity between the infra-human and the human primate is the expression of dominance by sexual aggression. Wherever we find rape or forced marriage to exist in a recognizable form in primitives or in the history of civilized nations we find that it is the females of the conquered peoples who are its object. And it is just this act that is the last bitter sign of complete submission and humiliation for the men of the conquered people. On purely *a priori* grounds there seems to be no reason why the case should not have been quite otherwise, *i.e.*, that the women of the conquering peoples should not have forced the conquered men to sexual connection or marriage. But this seems never to have been the case (except for certain kinds of individuals in special circumstances which will be discussed in another paper).

Other possible instances of such universal dominance behavior are the infliction of death, and the expression of superior strength (we know of no instance of strength-competition in which to be the weaker one is to be the more dominant). We are not aware, furthermore, of any group in which inferior height is regarded as a dominant characteristic over greater height (within "normal" limits). Again in no case (in the few cultures for which this behavior is described) is a less sexually potent man regarded as dominant over the more potent and virile man. Quite as interesting as this is the fact that this is *not* true for women.

However, these few instances of possible universality of dominance behavior (throughout the Primate order) are far outnumbered by the multitudes of local, cultural, dominance behaviors.

.

## Bibliography

1. Adler, A., The neurotic constitution, New York: Moffat, Yard, 1917, pp. xxiii + 456.
2. ———, Organic inferiority and its psychical compensation, New York: Nervous and Mental Diseases Publishing Co., 1917, pp. x + 86.
3. Benedict, R., Patterns of culture, New York: Houghton Mifflin, 1934, pp. xii + 290.
4. Bühler, C., The social behavior of the child, in "A Handbook of Child Psychology" (Ed. C. Murchison), Worcester: Clark University Press, 1931, p. 392.
5. Dodge, R. and Kahn, E., The craving for superiority, New Haven: Yale Univ. Press, 1931, pp. vii + 69.
6. Eisenberg, P., Dominance and expressive movements, *Arch. of Psychol.* (to be published).
7. Flanagan, J. C., Factor analysis in the study of personality, Stanford Univ. Press, 1935, pp. ix + 103.
8. Freud, S., General introduction to psychoanalysis, New York: Boni and Liveright, 1920, pp. x + 406.
9. Guilford, J. P. and Guilford, R. B., Personality factors S, E and M, and their measurement, *J. of Psychol.*, 1936, **2**, 109–127.
10. Jack, L. M., An experimental study of ascendant behavior in pre-school children, *Univ. Iowa Studies: Studies in Child Welfare*, 1934, **9**, No. 3.
11. Linton, R., The study of man; an introduction, New York: D. Appleton-Century, 1936, pp. viii + 503.
12. Maslow, A. H., The dominance drive as a determiner of social behavior in infra-human primates (abstract), *Psychol. Bull.*, 1935, **29**, 117–118.
13. ———, The role of dominance in the social and sexual behavior of infra-human primates: I. Observations at Vilas Park Zoo, *J. Genet. Psychol.*, 1936, **48**, 261–277.
14. ——— and Flanzbaum, S., II. The experimental determination of the dominance behavior syndrome, *J. Genet. Psychol.*, 1936, **48**, 278–309.
15. ———, III. A theory of sexual behavior of infra-human primates, *J. Genet. Psychol.*, 1936, **48**, 310–338.
16. ———, IV. The determination of hierarchy in pairs and in a group. *J. Genet. Psychol.*, 1936, **49**, 161–198.
17. McCloy, H. C., A factor analysis of personality traits to underlie character education, *J. Educ. Psychol.*, 1936, **27**, 375–388.

18. Page, M. L., The modification of ascendant behavior in preschool children, *Univ. of Iowa Studies: Studies in Child Welfare*, 1936, **12,** No. 3.
19. Williams, H. M., A factor analysis of Berne's "Social behavior patterns in young children," *J. Exper. Educ.*, 1935, **4,** 142–146.

# Editor's Introduction
## to Papers 4 and 5

Maslow had a keen interest in female psychology that dated back at least as far as his graduate-student days. The next two papers report research that he conducted in that area in the late 1930s and early 1940s. The first was published in 1939 and the second in 1942, both in the *Journal of Social Psychology*. Take special note here of how Maslow is beginning to suspect that "dominance-feeling" (spoken of in the first paper as "ego-level" and in the second as "self-esteem") is somehow intimately related to psychological health.

# 4

# Dominance, Personality, and Social Behavior in Women*

## A. H. Maslow

### A. Introduction

This paper is a report of results obtained in a clinical-experimental research on the interrelations between dominance-feeling (ego-level) and various other attributes of personality, social behavior, and sexual behavior. The sexual data will be presented in another paper (14) and will not be discussed further here.

More specifically, the attributes of personality that we have related to dominance-feeling, and which we will discuss here, are such characteristics as feelings of shyness, timidity, embarrassability, self-confidence, self-consciousness, inhibition, conventionality, modesty, fearfulness, poise, inferiority feelings, social ease, and the like. A previous paper has dealt with the general concepts involved in the research, definitions of the terms involved, and a general description of the main trends in the data, together with some of their implications (16). We shall repeat here only what is necessary for clarity.

#### 1. Definitions

a. *Dominance-feeling (or ego-level)* is an evaluation of the self; operationally defined, it is what the subject says about herself in an intensive

From *Journal of Social Psychology*, 1939, **10,** 3–39. Reprinted by permission of The Journal Press.

*This study is one item in a program of research supported, under the direction of Dr. E. L. Thorndike, by a grant from the Carnegie Corporation.

interview, after a good rapport has been established. High dominance-feeling empirically involves good self-confidence, self-assurance, high evaluation of the self, feelings of general capability or superiority, and lack of shyness, timidity, self-consciousness, or embarrassment. Low dominance-feeling is seen as lack of self-confidence, self-assurance, and self-esteem; instead there are extensive feelings of general and specific inferiority, shyness, timidity, fearfulness, self-consciousness. Such people are easily embarrassed, blush frequently, are generally silent, and tend to be incapable of normal, easy, outgoing social relationships or forward behavior.

b. *Dominance status* is a social relationship; it is an expression of social position with respect to another person, and is always relative to this other person. A person is in dominance status with respect to another when he dominates this other person either overtly in behavior or implicitly in feeling. The dominated person is said to be in subordinate status.

c. *Dominance behavior* is sharply differentiated from dominance-feeling, since there is rarely a one-to-one relationship between them. Dominance-feeling is only one of the determiners of dominance behavior. Other determiners are dominance status, compensatory efforts, specific training, the specific situation, and cultural pressures, both local and general. Diagnosis of dominance-feeling from dominance behavior alone is apt to be inexact. Examples of dominance behavior are bursts of temper, aggressive behavior, insistence on one's rights, free expression of resentment or hostility, openly overriding rules and conventions, arguing freely, etc.

### 2. General Purposes of the Research

Originally, our preoccupation with dominance in human beings was a comparative study, in which the attempt was to discover how much of the data found in infra-human primates (9–13) could also be found in human beings, and what similarities and differences there were. Careful analysis of our data, particularly those on sexuality, has convinced us that this comparative study has a more important purpose, namely, to study, in a semi-experimental fashion, the influence of the addition of important cultural determiners to our primate heritage. That is, our data may be set up in such a fashion as to make the presence or absence of culture (interiorized) the independent variable. This is a far cry from the original interest which motivated the study of dominance in monkeys, namely to test some aspects of the Adlerian and Freudian psychology.

In our struggles with new methodologies, new questions and purposes have arisen. As we found ourselves studying the age-old problem of the interrelations of culture and personality from a comparative viewpoint, much new light was thrown on various theoretical and practical problems of personality, and new discoveries were made in the field of sexuality, an aspect which in the beginning was quite incidental.

Another purpose motivating this research and its particular methods derives from the author's dissatisfaction with several psychoanalytic beliefs. Analysts have usually been unable to see any halfway point between their highly individual, clinical, interpretive technique and those of scientific psychology. The same is also usually true in academic circles. The writer has felt for some time also that neurotics and normal people might be qualitatively as well as quantitatively different. This impression derived mainly from his observation that many of the Freudian mechanisms could be seen overtly and superficially in well adjusted people, in spite of the fact that Freud describes them as unconscious, repressed, and hidden. Such well adjusted people seemed to be almost completely understandable without any reference to the concept of "unconscious." On the other hand, the writer's experience with neurotics convinced him just as completely that such people could be understood *only* with the aid of Freudian concepts.

Our research was designed therefore so as (a) to eschew interpretation, (b) to use lay concepts, (c) to use "normal" subjects, and (d) to ignore the concept of the unconscious. We have taken as our data the subjects' own statements, *not* our opinion or interpretation of them. Presumably, other investigators would come to the same conclusion if stenographic records were available. Contrast this with the interpretation of a dream, in which different results must usually be obtained by different interpreters. As to the normality of our subjects, we imply only that they are fairly competent to meet the ordinary problems of life, they have no functional physical symptoms, and that they have no incapacitating compulsions, manias, phobias, or anxieties.

### B. Method

The main method used in the research was what may be called the "intensive interview" or "personality investigation by conversational probing." Since this procedure differs in many ways from what is ordinarily understood by "interview," it may be well to describe it in some detail.

In the first place, questioning, or, rather, conversation, was started only after satisfactory rapport had been established. This meant mostly a frank, trusting, friendly relationship, resembling somewhat the transference of the psychoanalysts.

In the second place, the investigator subordinated objectively and standardized procedure to the necessities of the separate situations presented by each individual subject. Each one was treated as a unique individual to be understood and handled in a different way. The investigator attempted always to be sensitive and adaptable to these widely varying situations. He conceived his first task to be the understanding of the person before him *as an individual*, and only then to attempt to follow through the specific demands of the research. The technique, then, is something of a fusion of the experimental and clinical approaches.

The third difference was the extreme flexibility of the interview itself. In the beginning stages of the investigation, the interview was entirely exploratory. The only consideration that determined the choice of question and guided the lines of investigation were the facts and hypotheses that had been obtained in previous experiments with infra-human primates, which we have already reported. With each subject more was learned and lists of questions began to be possible. These lists expanded as the number of subjects grew, even though questions found to be fruitless were dropped from time to time.

These "questions" were, in any case, no more than a list of cues for the conversation. For instance, the word "self-consciousness" served as a reminder to find out all that was possible about this feeling in the particular subject. No set questions were asked, but the procedure followed was the one that at the moment gave promise of best success with the individual being talked with at the time. The particular procedure used depended on the particular situation, the particular subject, her level of dominance, her social background, her cooperation, her loquacity, etc.

As a result, our data are not quite comparable for all subjects, not in the sense that they do not mean the same thing when we do have data, but rather that we do not have complete data for all subjects.

In addition, a good deal of our knowledge of low-dominance people was obtained in a somewhat scrappy form. We have described in a previous paper the great difficulty we experienced in obtaining low-dominance women for our interviews. We supplemented the data we obtained from our subjects, in every way possible, forming friendships, observing behavior, questioning their families and friends, etc.

Such interviewing must always to some extent remain an art. One must acquire a sensitivity to unspoken attitudes, to hidden resentments, to slight antagonisms, and one must be able to sense the exact moment when trust changes to suspicion. Some subjects resent being treated coolly and objectively like guinea pigs; others will permit no other kind of relationship. Each one must be felt out and understood separately before work begins, and it must be understood that this is a two-way process, for the subject wishes to know the investigator is trustworthy. He is put into a position of power and dominance and must be felt by the subject to be worthy of it, or else her data are useless if, indeed, she does not break off the whole procedure at once.

### 1. Subjects

About 130 women and 15 men were used. Of the latter we shall not speak, since the work with men is still in process. Practically all of these women were college women of college intelligence, between the ages of 20 and 28, of middle class urban background. About three out of four were married. About 75 per cent were of Protestant, 20 per cent of Jewish, and 5 per cent of Catholic parentage. This is, then, a study of a fairly homogeneous group and must be considered a *highly selected* portion of the general population. *Our data are presumed to be true only for this group, except where the contrary is specifically stated.* We have found important differences when studying different sections of the population.

## C. Results

### 1. Self-Consciousness

There is a negative correlation between dominance-feeling and self-consciousness. This is perhaps one of the clearest relationships we have found. The most important problem for subjects low in dominance-feeling is themselves. On the other hand, for our high cases, the most important problem tends to be an external one. All of our low-dominance cases, men and women, were completely preoccupied with the shortcomings of their own personalities and described themselves as self-conscious in a general sense. This was also true to a lesser degree for about 30–50 per cent of the middle-dominance cases, and for perhaps 10 per cent of the upper-dominance cases. In the latter group where it did occur, it was for very different reasons, which will be discussed below. As we went up the range of dominance-feeling, this self-consciousness tended to be restricted to fewer and fewer situations, whereas at the bottom of the scale, the cases were self-conscious in practically *all* social situations and, in some situations, even when they were alone.

This spread of self-consciousness may be envisaged in terms of "social radius." If the center of the social circle is the "Self," the immediate family may be thought of as the smallest "social radius," other relatives as a somewhat larger radius, friends as still larger, and acquaintances, neighbors, strangers, and strangers with dominance status as increasingly larger. We can say, then, that, in general, self-consciousness, timidity, and bashfulness increase in all our subjects with social radius. Also, however, we find that the effective psychological social radius grows smaller as we go lower and lower in the scale of dominance-feeling or ego-level. That is, as the social radius increases, the point at which self-consciousness begins depends on the dominance-feeling. Thus a low case may feel at ease and be able to be normally outgoing and expressive with her mother and sister only. Her brother and father and of course everyone else in her social sphere may arouse self-consciousness. For a middle case, self-consciousness may not be present when with any of the members of the immediate family or when with close relatives or a few close friends. For the high case, it may never be present, except when confronting a large critical group of strangers or in making a speech.

### 2. Embarrassability

Generally low-dominance people are more easily and often embarrassed; high-dominance cases are rarely embarrassed except in extreme situations. Two or three of our high cases claimed that, so far as they could remember, they had never felt embarrassed and could not think of any situations in which they would react in this fashion. As we go up the scale, we find again what we found with self-consciousness; that it increases with social radius, and also that the psychologically effective point in the social radius is a function of dominance-feeling. Furthermore, if we were to construct a scale of embarrassing situations in terms of their "extremeness," we should find that, as we go up the dominance distribution, it takes more and more "extreme" situations to embarrass.

It should be emphasized that we refer here to the *feeling* of embarrassment as known to the subject herself. Often this feeling was not accompanied by obvious embarrassment behavior. By obvious embarrassment behavior we mean blushing, stammering, turning the eyes away, observable tremor, unsuitable verbalization, obvious disorganization of verbalizations, obvious change of subject of conversation, etc. Indirect embarrassment behavior might be laughing or giggling hysterically or uneasily, saying something silly or inapropos, or any one of dozens of other individual behaviors which are usually known only to the subject herself as a behavior accompaniment of embarrassment feeling. Sometimes the subject is certain that there is no behavior consequence whatsoever. In many cases the writer could observe no such behavior, even though assured later that the subject felt embarrassed.

### 3. Shyness, Timidity

Our findings need not be described in detail, since they were in general exactly like our findings for self-consciousness and embarrassability both for feeling and behavior. It is our impression, however, that if we were to categorize people as either shy or not (neglecting the fact that in actuality it is quantitatively graded), we should find the breaking point in the dominance distribution to be somewhat lower than for self-consciousness or embarrassability. That is, few cases, and those almost entirely low, were willing to describe themselves as, in general, shy or timid people.

### 4. Fearfulness

Our subjects differentiated timidity from fear in a crude fashion, the former seeming more often to be applied to social situations, the latter to the outside world. Also, they were timid when they knew no harm could come to them, fearful when physical harm might be involved. There is a crude tendency for fearfulness to correlate negatively with dominance-feeling. That is, low-dominance people are afraid of more things and situations than high-dominance people, and are more intensely afraid than high-dominance people when the same stimulus is involved.

There seems also to be a fairly clear tendency for them to be afraid of more things that do not seem objectively to be fear-arousing—that is, to have "unreasonable" fears. Horney (5) has differentiated between fear and anxiety on a similar basis. Fears for her are commensurate with the objective situation; anxieties are not, but seem unreasonable and out of proportion to the objective danger of the stimulus or situation. If we accept these definitions, we can say that low-dominance cases tend to have somewhat more anxieties as well as more fears.

The correlations with dominance-feeling are not as distinct or as high as is the case with self-consciousness or shyness. We find fears throughout the whole distribution of dominance-feeling, sometimes even in our highest cases. Such few fears as do exist in our high cases seem to be quite specific and unrelated to the general personality and remind us inevitably of the behavioristic explanation for fear, namely as a specific conditioning which is related only to the intensity of the original conditioning situation. On the other hand, the main trend in our data would indicate that to explain all fearfulness in such simple terms would be highly naive. Undoubtedly we have found in the fact of individual differences in dominance-feeling at least a partial explanation of the fact that, of many people going through an objectively similar conditioning situation (e.g., war), some will be conditioned, others not. In any of the cases of phobia described in literature, we may be sure that the original situation, assigned as the sole cause of the phobia, has in many other cases been inadequate to have permanent effect. Low-dominance people ("fearful" people) carry within themselves greater possibilities for fear conditioning than do high-dominance people. This hypothesis is offered here as one that can very easily be put to experimental test.

### 5. Self-Confidence

Taken as a general quality, we find more and more self-confidence as we go higher and higher in the dominance distribution. At the extremes of the distribution we find that *all* high-dominance cases describe themselves as self-confident; *all* low-dominance cases describe themselves as lacking in general self-confidence.

We must realize, however, that it is necessary to differentiate between self-confidence as a generalized personality characteristic, and self-confidence in specific abilities, tasks, or situations. The same person who describes herself as completely lacking in what she may call "self-confidence in general" will describe herself as self-confident in her home, cooking, sewing, or being a mother. The intellectual may be relatively self-confident in her writing or teaching, and lack this quality in all other aspects of her life.

This is not to say, however, that the two aspects of self-confidence are completely independent. This is not the case. Our conclusion is that the general level of self-confidence (which may be called confidence in the self or in the personality) pervades and alters the specific self-confidence (which may be called confidence in an ability). The low-dominance case almost always underestimates to a greater or lesser degree her specific abilities and endowments; the high-dominance person usually gauges her abilities accurately and realistically, or else in a few cases tends to overestimate. This statement is true for the high-dominance case only when her attention is called to the problem. Usually she does not think about her abilities or lack of them; she is more apt to think of the task in hand rather than of herself.

To put this hypothesis in a form that may be checked experimentally, we are willing to hazard the prediction that, given equal intelligence in a low-dominance and in a high-dominance subject, the former will have less confidence in her intellectual ability, her level of intellectual aspiration will be lower, and it is even possible that the intellectual achievement will be lower also. Another possible experimental check at another level would be as follows: if high-and low-dominance cases are rated objectively for facial beauty or attractiveness to men, and are then asked to rate themselves, we are willing to predict that the low cases will estimate themselves as less beautiful and less attractive than the high-dominance group, even when the groups are equated on the basis of the objective ratings.

## 6. Poise, Self-Possession

Low-dominance people feel that they lack poise and self-possession; high-dominance people do not ordinarily feel this. This feeling of lack of poise is not necessarily reflected in the externally observable behavior in ordinary situations. That is, the objective observer may observe no such lack. In a fair number of low-dominance cases, they themselves tended to realize or almost realized that this was true (that they looked well poised even if they did not feel so), but this realization had less effect than might be expected on their feeling lack of poise.

Even in terms of behavior, more low-dominance cases than high-dominance cases will be judged by the observer to lack poise. As might be expected, this becomes even more true when the situation is more "extreme." In our interviews, which are often extremely embarrassing for some subjects, this discrepancy in poise became very obvious.

## 7. Feelings of Inferiority[1]

We have discussed these data in another paper (16) in some detail, and it is not necessary to give more than a brief sketch here. It was our finding that fewer and fewer inferiority feelings are found as we go higher and higher in the dominance scale. It was found furthermore that these inferiority feelings have little relation to matter-of-fact inferiority and superiority. That is, a low-dominance case may think of herself as homely even if she is judged by five men, who know her, to be very pretty. Our high-dominance cases had no feelings of inferiorities. That is, a low-dominance girl who has to wear spectacles is apt to think of herself as repulsive in her appearance and to worry a good deal about it; a high-dominance case will recognize that she has weak eyes, and that her spectacles are not apt to improve her appearance, but she does not worry about it, nor will she feel inferior because she has to wear them.

Another illustration is a low-middle dominance case who felt inferior because she had red hair and felt that no man would ever love

---

[1]See also in this connection Sears' excellent paper (20), which has just come to hand. His tests on *Ideas of Reference and Self-Criticism* are essentially tests of low dominance-feeling. As we would expect, they show high correlation (r = .644). Our phrasing of this correlation is that it is high because it measures two aspects of the same thing, i.e., low dominance-feeling. Sears also confirms our finding that there is little relationship between feelings of inferiority (self-criticism) and matter-of-fact inferiorities.

her because of it. She rated herself very low in beauty and attractiveness to men. Four men who knew her rated her as above average in beauty and about average in attractiveness. A high-dominance subject was found who had about the same shade of red hair. When asked how she felt about its effect on her attractiveness, she thought that it was very attractive to some men and not at all to others—"just like blonde, or black hair," she said, and added, "anyway, it doesn't matter to anyone with any sense."

### 8. Conventionality, Morality, Rules

Our high-dominance people are less conventional than our low-dominance people. This holds true for any aspect of conventionality, whether it concerns conventional morality or day-to-day etiquette. The former are apt to make their own etiquette, and to pay no attention to what they call "silly," e.g., man giving seat to them, standing up when girl comes into room, walking on outside. Indeed, they are apt to despise a conventional person, man or woman, as making an important matter out of what they consider essentially unimportant. Such women prefer to be treated "like a person, not like a woman." They prefer to be independent, stand on their own feet, and generally do not care for concessions that imply they are inferior, weak, or that they need special attention and cannot take care of themselves.

This is not to imply that they cannot behave conventionally. They do when it is necessary or desirable for any reason, but they do not take the ordinary conventions seriously. A common phrase is "I can be as nice and sweet and clinging-vine as anyone else, but my tongue is in my cheek."

Of course, there are other variables that enter into the determination of this behavior. Women from the South are generally more conventional both in behavior and in inner conviction. Behavior with strangers is apt to be more conventional than behavior with friends. Behavior with older people "who wouldn't understand" is more conventional than behavior with friends of like age. Catholics are more conventional than non-Catholics. All these determiners are, to some extent at least, independent of dominance-feeling, so that correlation with conventionality is apt to be low except in homogeneous groups.

Our very highest cases have sometimes said that they had no code of morals or ethics. They felt they could do *anything* if necessary, even to the extent of killing without a qualm. They felt their own ends to be very important and were willing to override all sorts of opposition. This feeling did not often appear in behavior, however. Another way of illustrating what is meant here is to point out that people in our highest bracket of dominance-feeling often could not remember a single thing that they felt guilty about, or that had bothered their conscience. "If I did it, it was all right." In the paper on sexuality, it is pointed out that, among the cases in this highest bracket, promiscuity, masturbation, homosexual experiences, and perversions of all sorts were often found. Not one of these women had guilty feelings about any of these. Some of them recognized that some of their behavior was objectively bad or undesirable, but there was no affective reaction of self-castigation or shame. A typical comment was "I guess that was a pretty slimy thing to do, and I guess I won't do it again, but I've never thought about it since, and it doesn't bother me a bit." This was in connection with seducing a very young boy.

Rules per se generally mean nothing to these women. It is only when they approve of the rules and can see and approve of the purpose behind them that they will obey them. This is not to say that they live anarchic lives. This is very far from being the case, for they are strong, purposeful, and *do* live by rules, but these rules are autonomous and personally arrived at. It is not that they lack codes of decency, friendship, obligation, or duty, but that these codes are apt not to be "conventional." Nor do they *like* to break rules simply for the sake of breaking them. They simply weigh them and tend to pay no attention to them if they are found wanting.

Low-dominance women are different. They are apt to be very moral, ethical, and usually do not dare to break rules, even when they (rarely) disapprove of them. Their morality and ethics are usually entirely conventional. That is, they do what they have been taught to do by their parents, their teachers, or their religion. The dictum of authority is usually not questioned openly, and they are more apt to approve of the status quo in every field of life, religious, economic, educational, and political. For instance, it is our general impression (not yet checked) that they show somewhat the tendency to be political conservatives, while our higher-dominance cases tend to be liberal or radical.[2]

A higher percentage of high-dominance women smoke and drink. It is the compensating person who deliberately breaks rules just for the sake of breaking them and who is aggressively unconventional. Low-dominance women also seem to be more honest in the ordinary day-to-day sense, e.g., money, keeping promises, not stealing, etc. The evidence for this is, however, not adequate.

[2]It might be well to stress the highly selected character of our subjects by pointing out that high-dominance women in the business world tended definitely to political conservatism and to the attitude of "the race is to the strong, and the devil take the (weak) hindmost."

## 9. Introversion, Extroversion

Our results indicate that the dimension of introversion-extroversion is not as fundamental as has been thought in personality; nor is it as useful as has been claimed. Undoubtedly deeper-lying classifications of the fundamental dimensions of personality will cross-cut it and make it unnecessary.

With relation to dominance-feeling, introversion must be split into at least two aspects. First, it seems to be, in lower-dominance women, a product of failure or rebuff in early social life. It is an adjustment on an inward basis because of failure of non-acceptance of the more fundamental tendency that can be found in many of them to turn outward in the social adjustment. We have, for instance, a case in which the most extreme introversion, which was interpreted as psychological defense or guard against being hurt socially, was turned to a fair degree of extroversion by a series of successes. Another subject, asked why she did not try to get some fun from her social life, said that all her hurt had been from people, and she had learned that a good defense against further damage was to make her inward world more important. She was able to trace back in some detail the beginnings of her introversion in a bad family situation.

Another aspect or kind of introversion seems to be independent of dominance-feeling, or fortuitous social history, seeming instead to be an unchangeable, deeply characteristic facet of the personality in which it occurs. It may occur in high-dominance people. While it is impossible to describe in satisfactory detail, we may say it seems to be partially related to the independent variable of sociability that we have already discussed (16). These are the people who find within themselves many delights that are equal or superior in attractiveness to what can be found outside. Their own introspective experience is often poignantly beautiful and important to them at the same time that it may be quite undescribable. There is some indication that it is to be expected more often in the aesthetically endowed.

In such people, it is not to be interpreted as a psychological defense, for when it occurs in high-dominance people, it may go along with excellent social facility and ease, with a wide circle of friends, and with perfect behavior in the social sphere. Social life is undoubtedly enjoyed by these people a good deal of the time, but it is apt to be thought of as an obligation, something which is demanded by others. Such people will treasure and look forward to the moments when they can be alone, and are apt to sigh with relief when this is possible. Such "introversion" is not defensive.

Even if we neglect this distinction, we should still expect to find a fair correlation between a test for dominance-feeling and a test for extroversion, since the latter type is found much less often than the former.

*10. Happiness*

No clear clinical relationship of ego-level with happiness was found. Cases at any part of the scale are apt to be happy or unhappy, and it is our tentative conclusion that happiness is more closely related with ego-security than with ego-level. If anything, somewhat more of the low-dominance people are on the unhappy side, but the difference is small enough to make us unsure. A very important difference is found, however, between the *causes* of unhappiness. The unhappiness of the low- or middle-dominance woman is far more apt to be caused by worry over the personality and its shortcomings, inferiority feelings, lack of boy friends, lack of social adjustment, etc. The unhappiness of the high-dominance woman is more apt to be caused by external problems, a career, an unsatisfactory husband, conflict with family, economic worries, etc.

We see here again an instance of the general tendency to outgoingness that comes with higher dominance-feeling, as opposed to the preoccupation with self and defensive inward-turning that we tend to find in low dominance-feeling. This is probably also a partial product of the fact that has already been discussed (16), namely, the generalized cultural approval of higher-than-average dominance-feeling in women. The ideal personality extant in the cultural tradition will help to determine one's own evaluation of one's personality. Being close to the ideal will validate one's good self-opinion; differing markedly from it will cause feelings of difference and probably also self-depreciation. This is to some extent true of the women who are higher in dominance-feeling than the ideal range, but is much more marked in those who are definitely lower than the ideal.

*11. Brooding, Worrying, Moodiness*

No very clear relation with dominance-feeling has been found, to our surprise. There seems to be only a slight tendency for the low cases to worry and brood more than the higher-dominance cases. Again we find, however, that the subject of the worry is different. The lower cases tend to worry about personality and social adjustment; the higher ones about more external things. To some extent also the low cases tend to worry about little things, and to think about them for a longer period.

It is perhaps necessary to appeal for fuller explanations to some such variable as emotional cyclicity, which would seem to be independently variable for ego-level. An alternative independent variable may be one that we have called very vaguely "ego-security" and which we understand only to a slight extent. This will be discussed below.

### 12. Religious Feeling

We have found a fairly definite tendency for low-dominance women to be more religious than high-dominance women. Generally our subjects have not been a very religious group, but practically all who called themselves religious were at the middle of the distribution or below. This finding calls to mind the distinction that William James made between the "tender-minded" and the "tough-minded." It is the tender-minded person who *needs* religion. In our work we found that religious faith is a definite support for our low-dominance women. In some cases, it is even difficult to think what they would do without it. Two low cases who were only vaguely religious were definitely suicidal in their fantasies. *None* of the religious ones were. Probably the best way to describe our low cases who were devoutly religious is to call them "secure." This suggests, as a simple experiment with therapy, an attempt at religious exhortation with low cases who are not "secure."

Our high cases were practically none of them religious except sometimes in a very vague sense; where it was found, it tended to be intellectualized and social-ethical rather than dogmatic and submissive. A good many scoffed at the idea, in spite of the fact that very few of our cases did not receive religious training of some sort. They did not seem to *need* religion in the same way as the low cases did. Generally they tended to be "tough-minded" about it, especially in the higher levels of the distribution. The low percentage of religiousness in our subjects makes it necessary to emphasize the fact that we have been dealing with a very specially selected sample of the population, and therefore cannot vouch for the more general validity of the data.

### 13. Masculinity-Femininity

We shall adduce reasons in a forthcoming paper for our dissatisfaction with this concept as a dimension of personality. Suffice it to say, in advance of presentation of complete evidence, that it is our finding that, from a psychological point of view, a high-dominance woman is more like a high-dominance man than she is like a low-dominance woman. This of course is not true for (a) anatomical and physiological makeup, and (b) the external details of social conventionality, e.g., clothes, training, etc. If we speak of inner personality, however (see below), we must conclude that it is better either (a) to describe as masculine both high-dominance men and women, and as feminine low-dominance men and women; or (b) to drop the terms altogether because they are so misleading.

Our high-dominance women feel more akin to men than to women in tastes, attitudes, prejudices, aptitudes, philosophy, and inner personality in general. They are apt to consider women in general to be small, mean, catty, petty, trivial, etc. They ordinarily get along better with men in general than with women in general. Completely aside from sexual considerations, they prefer the company of men to that of women. Many of the qualities that are considered in our culture to be "manly" are seen in them to a high degree, e.g., leadership, strength of character, strong social purpose, emancipation from trivialities, lack of fear, shyness, etc. They do not ordinarily care to be housewives or cooks alone, but wish to combine marriage with a career. Often they do this with the intention of maintaining their independence and self-respect in their own eyes. Their salary may come to no more than the salary of a housekeeper, but they feel other work to be more important than sewing, cooking, etc. They tend to like gambling, drinking, smoking, and dangerous sports.

### 14. Modesty

As we might now expect, the lower the dominance-feeling, the more modesty we find in both feeling and behavior. This was rated more specifically by determining the attitude toward nudity in various situations. For instance, none of the low cases would find it possible to go to a nudist camp. On the contrary, some of them undressed not even in front of their mothers or sisters. A physical examination by a physician, even if female, was thought of as excruciatingly embarrassing and to be avoided if at all possible. On the other hand, the high cases had a much wider "social radius" for nudity, and in some cases definitely liked the idea of a nudist camp. Examination by a physician meant nothing to them, and even hypothetical nudity in various possible embarrassing situations did not bother them, at least to think about. A good many of them reported remembered situations in which they were nude but unembarrassed, even though they thought other women might be.

It was interesting to notice that this difference in feeling of modesty reflected itself in the clothes worn by the subjects, the way they sat and moved about, the manner of speech and its content, etc. For instance, a check showed, after this was first noticed, that low cases rarely sat with their knees showing, nor with their legs crossed or stretched out or spread apart. All of these were noticed frequently in higher-dominance cases.

No low cases ever cursed or blasphemed or used "smutty words" or expressions, while this was fairly common among the high cases. One can also construct a series of scaled attitudes toward risqué stories and find such attitudes to be fairly closely correlated with dominance level. Low-dominance women hate such stories; middle-dominance women tolerate them but do not like them except within a very limited social radius; high-dominance women are apt to like listening to them as well as telling them.

In general we have found that it is practically impossible for low cases to discuss any aspect of sex without discomfort, embarrassment, or suspicion of the investigator's motives. It is a subject always highly charged with emotion, one in which objectivity becomes impossible. It is not too uncommon to find in such women a deliberate eschewing of all discussion and reading about sex. Some literally wish to know nothing about it, feeling it to be a dangerous, nasty, besmirching topic, against which the only defense is ignorance. As we go up the scale of dominance-feeling, objectivity becomes more and more evident. A simple way of testing these observations experimentally would be to correlate ego-level with attitude scores toward any of the institutions or issues connected with sex, e.g., contraception, companionate marriage, double standard, monogamy, etc. Our prediction is that a significant positive correlation would be found between dominance-feeling and unconventional or "liberal" attitudes.

What is true for sexual topics also is true for the general eliminative processes. Low-dominance women will never talk about them unless absolutely necessary. For instance, one woman reports that, in a gathering, she suffered severe discomfort because she was afraid or too shy to stand up and go to the toilet since everybody would notice her leaving. Such women will always use the "bathroom" rather than the toilet, often explaining that they wish to wash their hands. They slink into stores carefully selected because they have lady attendants in order to get necessary but embarrassing sanitary supplies. They are never or rarely willing to use any of the words connected with elimination or menstruation. They are often willing to undergo physical and mental torture rather than go to a physician who might embarrass them by examinations or cross-questioning.

In contrast with these attitudes are those of the high-dominance women which we approach gradually as we go higher and higher in the scale of dominance. All natural processes are discussed when necessary, with the same lack of emotion and embarrassment they would show in a discussion of eating. Circumlocutions are less and less used; menstruation is menstruation and not "being sick," urination is urination and not "washing my hands," sexual organs are spoken of by their scientific names, not as "down there." In some, a certain amount of ribald joking and slang words of a Rabelaisian sort center about sex, elimination, and menstruation.

### 15. Crying, Nail Biting, "Nervousness," Tics

We found little or no relationship between ego-level and amount of weeping, to our surprise. The women in our highest brackets of dominance-feeling do not cry, but crying may be found with approximately equal frequency anyplace else on the scale. There is also more tendency-to-weep in low cases. As we might expect, however, the effective stimulus for weeping differs at least a little in different parts of our population. The woman with middle or somewhat higher dominance is more apt to cry from anger than from hurt. Generally it is our feeling that we must again have recourse to some factor of "security" rather than to dominance-feeling as an explanation for weeping. It is probably more accurate to say that the insecure person tends to weep than it is to say that the low-dominance person tends to weep.

We found even less relationship between ego-level and nervous habits. Probably there is no relationship at all. These too are probably more closely related to ego-security as well as to more specific emotion factors.

### 16. Self-Evaluation, Self-Esteem

We have already indicated the relationship between inferiority feelings and ego-level. An increasing tendency is found as we go down in the dominance scale, to self-depreciation, self-distrust, and low self-evaluation. The ramifications of this fact in behavior are tremendously extensive. For instance, an opinion held by someone else is far more apt to be held valid than one's own opinion if one is low in dominance-feeling. Others are felt to be more intelligent, more attractive, more healthy, better dressed, more wise, more poised, more *everything*. This attitude will be involved in such widely diverse activities as picking a new hat, a college course, a political opinion, or even a husband. This low self-evaluation seems to be basic to the general increased social suggestibility of lower-dominance women.

Higher-dominance women usually say "I'm as good as anybody else." Low-dominance women more usually say "I wish I were more like Mary" or "I should like to have some of Jane's self-confidence." General self-esteem increases as dominance-feeling increases. Low-dominance women usually admire and respect others more than they do themselves.

## 17. Envy, Jealousy, Suspicion, Resentment, Distrust

These reactions are found more typically in lower-dominance women as a consequence of several other factors that we have already mentioned, namely, low self-evaluation, inferiority feelings, modesty, lack of self-respect, low self-confidence, etc. For instance, low-dominance women cannot "take" compliments in spite of the fact of their need and hunger for them. This is because they are apt at once to discount the compliment as untrue and seek suspiciously for other motives. Often, for example, they may think the compliment is making fun of them, holding them up to ridicule, or else trying to get something out of them. For a suitor to convince such a woman that he loves her takes a very long time, and often his sincerity is doubted even after marriage. In a few cases, the reaction has been observed, "Something must be wrong with him that I don't know about if he loves (poor) me."

The experimenter, during the course of some interviews, attempted a simple experiment in therapy. It consisted simply of assuring such people that they weren't as bad as they thought they were, that they were underestimating themselves, etc. In almost all cases he had to stop because he found that such attempts were regarded either as subtle ridicule, or else it was being said "Just because you're a psychologist and I guess that's your job." Several such subjects came back to the experimenter some time after the interviews had ceased to find out if it was possible that John or Dick could really be in love with them. Such doubts are rarely or never entertained by higher-dominance women, who take it as part of the natural course of things that they should be admired and loved by some at least.

It is fair to say that as we go down in the dominance distribution, that we find somewhat increased hostility, suspicion, and distrust, not as overtly observable phenomena, but in fantasy, unexpressed attitudes, dreams, and as deductions from behavior otherwise unexplainable. It is probable that investigation of the deeper layers of the personality would show this far more clearly (psychoanalysis), but it is apparent even without such deep analysis.

It may seem superficially that these findings are not consistent with the tremendous respect shown for authority, with idolization and imitation of others, with the complete "voluntary" subordination to others, and in general with the great respect for others. Actually they can be consistent. These latter attitudes are overt; the former (envy, distrust, etc.) are covert. Then, too, they tend to be alternating points of view in the same person. That is, an idol will be worshipped for a time, and this may give way to hatred and resentment for a time for some reason, to be again replaced by over-respect and idolatry at a later time.

Undoubtedly these reactions also involve a second source, insecurity. Which of the two, dominance-feeling or insecurity, is more important or more closely related, we cannot say. Generally these feelings when they come to the surface, are explained by the subject as resentment because she is controlled so much by other people while she controls them not at all; that their opinions matter so much and hers not at all; that she is so "considerate" and gives in so frequently while they rarely do; that she is not consulted or respected; that she should not give in so often because it is "unhealthy" or not "well balanced"; that other people take advantage of her; that she ought to be "stronger" than she actually is. Such attempts to be stronger and more forceful are, however, rare and are usually abortive, being then replaced by the more customary behavior. Undoubtedly cultural pressures and evaluations are involved in such revolts. Such people realize eventually, or the realization is forced upon them by the comments and criticisms of others, that they are not behaving "as they should," that they are weak and easily exploited (that they are deviants from the cultural ideal), and the resulting self-castigation and lowering of self-esteem sometimes leads to sporadic efforts to "improve."

### 18. Quietness, Neatness, Temper, Politeness

Increase in all these qualities except for "temper" is found with decrease in dominance-feeling. We are not able to see why low-dominance women should tend (somewhat) to be more neat than high-dominance women, but the other qualities are easily related to other characteristics of low dominance-feeling. The low-dominance woman generally finds it difficult to say "No." A strong request is usually acceded to, even if it may be completely undesirable and unwanted.[3] Also she usually finds it quite impossible to express hostile feelings. It is possible for another person to find out indirectly after years of supposed friendship that she was hated and resented all the time (this in spite of the fact that the low-dominance woman might have behaved beautifully during all this time). Bursts of temper are possible only within the most restricted social radius, being in some cases completely unthinkable outside this radius. Such women express envy and admiration for those who have

[3]A onetime subject, low in dominance-feeling, had offered to help me with some stenographic work. She was seen later and asked if she were still willing to help. She said that she was. I was by now aware of her characteristic inability to refuse and urged her to be sure not to accept if it was even slightly inconvenient, but she seemed quite eager to help. Some weeks later I found that my request came just before an intensive examination period, that she had to stay up for whole nights to do what I asked, and that she hated me violently during every minute that she did work, upbraiding herself for not having been strong enough to refuse.

"nerve" enough to say what they think, and courage enough to show anger when it is necessary.

Quietness is a concomitant of shyness, inferiority feelings, and a general feeling that anything they could say would be stupid and would be laughed at. General conventionality also is at the bottom of a good deal of the low-dominance politeness and good temper.

### 19. Sense of Humor

The relationship between sense of humor and dominance-feeling is not a simple one, or a direct one. Still, no picture of the character of the low-dominance woman would be complete without a consideration of the way in which her sense of humor is affected by her personality position. Her sensitivity and readiness to feel that she is being made fun of make it impossible for her to be the butt of jokes; she is too easily hurt, too apt to go home and weep because nobody likes her and everybody makes fun of her. This is true even when the jokes are mild and made in the best of humor and without malice. As for herself, she is most often not daring enough to make jokes or tell stories that will focus the attention of the group upon her for the moment. Her sense of humor is apt to be turned inward, to become delicate, whimsical, and private, rather than coarse, bawdy, or even hearty. It is interesting to notice that typically she cannot laugh heartily, easily, and without restraint or self-consciousness. If she has been dragged or forced into a party (she is apt not to go otherwise), she prefers to sit back in a corner and not be seen or heard. She *cannot* take part in the fun. At the same time such an experience is apt to be a rather harrowing or saddening one, since her sense of isolation is sharpened by "being out of it." Weeping privately in bed at night is too often the result.

### 20. Sociability, Friendliness

So far as the *feeling* of sociability goes, it seems that this is unrelated to dominance-feeling. Most people, whatever their personality position may be, have turned out to want friends. The few who prefer isolation for its own sake at times, and who live the most important part of their lives privately, have been scattered through the whole dominance distribution.

So far as *behavior* and actual overt sociability and friendliness are concerned, there is a very definite relationship with ego-level. Generally we find the *ability* to be friendly and to have friends increase as we go up the scale. The low-dominance woman or man may not have a friend in the world, in spite of the fact of the passionate desire to be able to have friends and to behave as others do. Fantasies are often about having a true, loyal friend. The reasons for the inability to be friendly are many and must be obvious by now after the discussion above. Sensitivity, inferiority feelings, suspicion, the sense of isolation—all play their part.

### 21. Suggestibility, Hypnotizability

It would seem from our results that these characteristics are more complex than has usually been thought. It has already been indicated that with lower dominance-feeling, we get certain behaviors that can be considered as indicative of greater suggestibility. Certainly respect for prestige of any kind increases as we go down the scale of dominance. At the same time it has been the personal experience of the writer that the most hypnotizable subjects have been high in dominance-feeling. He has failed utterly in his few attempts to hypnotize low-dominance people deeply. Apparently the reasons for this were several. They could not relax as the high-dominance subjects could; they were afraid of the idea of hypnosis as the high-dominance women were not; and, finally, they became emotionally upset and excited by the close approach of the operator, becoming tense, breathing more rapidly, and with an accelerated pulse.

Thus we can say that social or prestige suggestibility has a fairly high negative correlation with dominance-feeling; that we seem to have a little evidence that hypnotizability is correlated with dominance-feeling; and, finally, that what little evidence we have indicates a lack of correlation of dominance-feeling with sheer ideo-motor suggestibility.

### 22. Likes and Dislikes, Aesthetic Tastes, Etc.

We can report only general and perhaps vague impressions on this subject, since no systematic investigation was made. Certain tentative hypotheses have been suggested by various incidental observations. It seems to us that with higher dominance there goes a certain robustness and heartiness of tastes. For instance, it seems that higher-dominance people enjoy eating and drinking more than lower-dominance people. They seem to like what might be called the hearty foods, strong cheese, red meat, strong drink, etc. They eat more and with more gusto. There is less genteel picking at a delicate salad and more "wading into" a meal.

A tentative exploration into aesthetic tastes indicates that research here promises to be fruitful. There are indications of deep-lying and characteristic differences in preferences for various kinds of music, poetry, painting, and writing. The low-dominance woman, if we are correct, would tend to like the delicate and lovely rather than the strong and crude in art, the precious rather than the forthright, the Mozart, let us say, rather than Beethoven, Raphael rather than Rubens, Keats rather than Chaucer. The tendency probably would be to dislike a sculptor like Gaston Lachaise, or painters like some of the modern American school, e.g., Burchfield, Marsh, Benton. Undoubtedly they would dislike Rabelais, D. H. Lawrence, or Dreiser.

These are intended only as suggestions for research rather than as definite findings. Certainly the Terman Masculinity-Femininity test (23), which probably correlates significantly with ego-level, indicates differences in tastes and likes with differences in personality position.

### 23. Leadership

It must be clear that the high-dominance woman would make the best leader. This we have found to be the case. The woman who is definitely below the middle of the dominance distribution is quite unfitted for leadership by the makeup of her personality. Furthermore, she does not want to be a leader except in her fantasies, for she is afraid of being in the forefront, she is afraid of responsibility, and she feels that she would be incompetent. In any case she is never chosen by the group.

The fact that the high-dominance women would make the best leaders does not guarantee that, in actual social life, they do in fact become the leaders. For one thing, many of them do not care for leadership in most instances, feeling the triviality of the work that is so often required. This is particularly true of the "secure" ones. The "insecure" ones, needing the reassurance of prestige more, are apt to accept or even seek for any leadership that will bring dominance status. Then, too, we must consider the fact that, when leaders are chosen by vote, other considerations besides competence enter. We found that the high-dominance woman is apt to be disliked by low-dominance women. The person who is apt to be chosen is the one who is of the mass or group but somewhat higher in dominance-feeling than the average of the group, probably someone at or near the 75th percentile of the group. The highest ones are apt to be impatient of triviality, gossip, small-talk, and the like, giving to the other women in the group the impression of being hard, cold, or snobbish. In any case we may say that the leaders in any field are practically certain to be in the upper half of the dominance distribution of the group.

### 24. Some Other Qualities

Filial love and responsibility is greater in those of low ego-level, all other things being held equal. That is, given a selfish, domineering, or hateful mother, a low-dominance woman is much more apt to be dutiful and give the appearance of love than a high-dominance woman.

Sheer general activity or energy seems to be completely unrelated to ego-level.

The love of adventure, new experience, novelty, and new ideas is seen more often in high- than in low-dominance people. For instance, the former are much more apt to try new foods, to like meeting new people, etc.

Pride is an extremely complex quality. It cannot be discussed in the simple terms we have used. Generally high-dominance people feel more "prideful" than low-dominance people, but this correlation does not often hold for prideful behavior, for the necessities of the situation and cultural pressures are also potent factors in the determination of such behavior.

Fear of ridicule, fear of disapproval, fear of not being liked, and fear of being hurt are all apt to be stronger in low-dominance people but are also related to ego-insecurity. For instance, all these qualities may be found in the compensator, who usually seems to be of about middle dominance-feeling. Sensitivity to rivalry is found most often in compensators.

### 25. Insecurity (Ego-Insecurity)

At present, this is little more than a deductive construct that has been forced upon us by the inadequacy, at certain points, of dominance-feeling to explain various kinds of behavior, particularly compensatory dominance behavior. Crudely conceived as it is, it is almost certainly independently variable, to a large extent, of dominance-feeling. We have found secure and insecure people at all parts of the dominance distribution. Secure people are at home in a friendly world, never think of suicide, are more apt to be deeply happy, are less apt to compensate, find it more easy to submit and be relaxed and soft when necessary or desirable, are more friendly, more calm, less emotional, less threatened by future emergencies, worry less, are less easily thrown out of their emotional balance, are less affected by the opinions or dislikes of other people, strive less for dominance status (recognition, glory, fame, etc.), are less apt to dominate others in their behavior if they are high in dominance-feeling, are less apt to think others are a challenge, are less "nervous," are less easily hurt. Insecure people will show opposite characteristics. They seem to feel generally that they live in a hostile, challenging world rather than a friendly, beneficent one. Some of these characteristics we have already related to dominance-feeling. This is not a contradiction. We are certain that dominance-feeling, important though it may be, is not the only important main variable in personality and social behavior. We feel that in the future some such variable as we have indicated roughly here as "ego-security" will also have to be invoked in order to give a fuller and more fundamental understanding of personality. Ruth Benedict (2) has recently given it a fuller cross-cultural reference, correlating it with the institutional stresses in various cultures.

### 26. Compensation

Of all the problems connected with this research, compensation still remains the most pressing as well as the most stubborn. We have little to add to the discussion in our previous paper (16), except that further investigation has confirmed the hypotheses there set forth, and also has indicated the greater stress that must be laid on the contributory factor of ego-security. We have continued to find highest percentages of compensation among Jewish women, next highest among women of Catholic background, and least among women of Protestant or non-religious background.

It is just the compensating case, for all the difficulty that it may be causing now, that promises to be the best point for study of a very vexing question, namely, the possible necessity of the invocation of "unconscious motivation" in our study.[4] While we feel sure that a technique such as ours, simple as it is, is nevertheless adequate for the study of relatively normal, well adjusted, secure personalities, we are just as sure that it is *not* in itself adequate to investigate the neurotic, insecure, anxious person. In such a person, we can learn a good deal by our form of questioning, but eventually we must feel baffled. We are presented with the choice of being quite empirical, and getting a fundamentally false picture of the personality (since our technique relies very largely on the subject's own awareness of his motivations), or else we embark on the sea of interpretation, which we explicitly set out to avoid. That is, we weigh, accept, reject, or modify what the subject says, rather than accept it at face value, as we can do with non-compensating cases.

Essentially the compensator is trying to convince himself as well as others, and sometimes he succeeds, at least unconsciously. As well

[4]The discussion that follows is due to an exchange of ideas with Dr. Erich Fromm.

as putting up psychological defenses in the realm of social behavior, he has put them up in his introspective world and is fooling himself as well as others.[5] It matters not that the experienced psychologist can often detect this "psychological front" very easily; we are now considering the validity of a technique that consists of using as ultimate data a person's own conscious self-estimate. On the basis of such statements in the interview, it has been necessary to rate as high in dominance-feeling some cases (compensators) who were surely not what they thought they were, and who would have been rated otherwise if we had permitted ourself access to the unconscious conflicts and motivations, and to interpretation. It might be said, then, that such people may have been consciously high and unconsciously low in dominance-feeling.

It must be understood that this is a theoretical, not a practical, question in the present investigation. Those cases in which unconscious motivations were felt to be primarily important were kept at a minimum, were dropped, or were avoided altogether. Our rough estimate is that such cases will be found to be no more than 10 to 15 per cent of the college population.

We may fairly say, then, that the general indications of our study are that the importance of unconscious motivations has been definitely overrated in the understanding of the personality of relatively "normal," well adjusted people. It has, however, turned out to be very important in the investigation of relatively "abnormal," poorly adjusted, insecure, or neurotic people. Even in such cases, however, simple interviewing can give us more insight than might have been expected. As an adjunct to customary psychoanalytic procedure, it might save much time.

## D. Discussion

### 1. The Problem of Definition

The reader will have noticed that an important theoretical difficulty was glossed over in the discussion of the data. We have spoken of the correlation of dominance-feeling with this or that, as if it were something separate and apart from all these behaviors. This is not the case. It is unfortunate that dominance-feeling, in itself, cannot be given very clear definition. The definition that we have used amounts to a list of the feelings it correlates with. But then the difficulty arises that a very important basis for the rating of dominance-feeling has been a list of just these feelings, involving the further problem of self-correlation.

[5]This may seem like interpretation rather than description, but it must be remembered that our definition of compensation was an objective one (16, p. 417).

The concept of the syndrome has been borrowed from the field of medicine, partially to meet these difficulties and partially because it seems to be an inevitable way of describing personality, which tends always to be a unified whole. The syndrome concept allows us to do what we usually must as scientists, namely, to analyze atomistically, at the same time that it forces us always to keep in mind the unitary character of large parts or the whole of personality. Definitions in terms of syndromes tend to be operational in nature and, therefore, probably, more valid and useful scientifically. We may then define dominance-feeling as a system of interrelated parts or units, and we present in this paper one aspect of this syndrome.

Other modes of definition are possible. Various grades or levels of dominance-feeling may be defined typologically in terms of the complex feelings of single actual or mythical people "typical" of each of the levels defined. Another possible definition is to speak of a factor "D" assumed to be at the bottom of all the interrelated parts of the syndrome. That is, all the parts may be assumed to be correlated because of common participation in a single course of energy or determination, perhaps similar to the Jungian *libido*. This latter type of definition would attempt to come to grips with the eventual necessity of advancing beyond mere descriptive definition. (The syndrome definition is an entirely descriptive one.) Since there is also some indication that endocrinological factors may be partially involved in the determination of ego-level, eventual definition may be psycho-physiological in part (6).

One positive statement can be made in this connection, namely, that definition in behavioral terms is definitely unsatisfactory. We have already discussed the lack of necessary relationship between dominance-feeling and dominance behavior. Because of this, one cannot be defined in terms of the other. While there is no doubt that behavioral study of personality must be made if we are to get a complete picture, there is equally little doubt that the naive behavioristic view of personality is quite unsound.

### 2. Patterning within the Syndrome[6]

We have so far discussed the parts of the syndrome as if they formed what Wertheimer calls an "and-sum," a mere additive summation of unrelated, equally valid items. It is necessary to point out that the case is quite otherwise, that there is patterning within the syndrome, that certain parts of it seem, in one sense or another, to be prior to other parts, that some seem to be sub-aspects of others, and that there is a

[6]I wish to thank Dr. Max Wertheimer for calling my attention to this point.

tendency for the various items to cluster together in spontaneous and "natural" groupings. For instance, conventionality, morality, modesty, and regard for rules seem to fall together very naturally, say, as contrasted with another group of clustering qualities, namely, high self-esteem, self-confidence, poise, lack of timidity and shyness, unembarrassability, and the like.

In spite of many attempts, no satisfactory system of groupings can be presented here, and we shall not discuss this question further. We do wish, however, to disclaim the apparent automism that seems latent in our presentation of the data.

### 3. Dominance-Feeling as Lack of Inhibition

Our data indicate that the higher people are in the scale of dominance-feeling, the more they are apt to lack tension, restraint, or inhibition, although this relationship is probably somewhat attenuated by a similar relationship of lack of inhibition with ego-security. This conclusion has been confirmed by Eisenberg (3) in his experiment with dominance-feeling and expressive movements. The high-dominance woman may be spoken of as psychologically free, easy, and relaxed. The low-dominance woman is strained, tense, and inhibited. It is difficult or impossible for her to drop her psychological guards or defenses. As a result, it is sometimes difficult for her to "submit" in a psychological sense, that is, to be friendly, to make herself vulnerable voluntarily, to expose herself psychologically, to let herself be seen.

In a sense, a high-dominance person is incompletely "socialized" in inner personality; the low-dominance person is "oversocialized." The former is apt to recognize, aside from expediency, few restraints beyond her own desires, or the rules that she herself has set up to guide her behavior. She is to some extent non-normal, as well as being individual and independent. Taboos, rules, conventions, laws mean less to her than they do to the average person. She has few guilt feelings and little conscience.

These considerations have suggested to the writer a hypothesis that offers a different view of dominance-feeling. That is, that the distribution of dominance, from high to low, may represent a steadily decreasing amount of psychological "freedom." As we go up the scale we find less and less inhibition (or what Freud calls super-ego). In other words, high dominance-feeling may be not so much a positive quality as a *lack* of something (restraint, inhibition, super-ego, etc.), which is acquired in a steadily increasing quantity as we go down the scale.

Such a way of envisaging the data would necessitate a complementary hypothesis: that the behaviors, attitudes, and feelings of the high-dominance woman are, so to speak, more "natural" than they are in the lower-dominance woman. What we have called low dominance-feeling or ego-level would then be thought of as a positive covering up of underlying, more deeply determined behaviors and feelings.

It will be seen that we have here many resemblances to the Freudian doctrine of structure of personality (4), with its stress on the ontogenetic primacy of the "id," from which develops the ego and all its sub-parts. The more primary impulses come from the *id*, and in a certain sense are "covered up," redirected, reshaped, or altogether denied. It is just this covering up, reshaping, or denying that we find so frequently in the low- and so infrequently in the high-dominance woman. Our analysis of sexuality and dominance (14) has shown that dominance-feeling and sexual attitude are very highly correlated. Sexual attitude was defined in terms of (at one extreme) complete acceptance of everything sexual, and (at the other end) complete sexual rejection. These amount to much the same as inhibition and lack of it, restraint and lack of it. The woman rated very high in sexual attitude accepts everything, promiscuity, homosexuality, masturbation, sadism, masochism, sodomy, coprophilia, cunnilingus, fellatio, and experimentation of every conceivable kind. It would seem as if every sexual impulse or desire that has ever been spoken of may emerge freely and without inhibition in these women. Exactly the opposite is true of the low-dominance woman. Here we have, then, a specific example of what is meant when we propose to think of the low-dominance woman as inhibited and restrained. If we are to take the psychoanalysts at their word, the presumption will be that sexual attitude has been "high" in all people in their early days, even in our low-dominance women. Presumably, also, some traces of this high sexual attitude are still present in the deeper layers of their personality, but these have been covered up or repressed. In the high-dominance women, on the other hand, where, according to our hypothesis, this repression has not taken place, this high attitude can be seen expressing itself openly.

This hypothesis is presented as an interesting possibility, rather than as one which we can prove at this time. It raises too many questions to be evaluated without further research.

### 4. The Role of Cultural Pressures & Social Norms

We have attempted to indicate throughout the tremendously important role of general and specific cultural influences on dominance-feeling. There is little doubt that any consideration of the etiology of dominance-feeling, its aims, techniques, and effects, must take primary recourse to the general cultural background, as well as the multitude of more local, specific, sub-cultural pressures and norms. We feel, for instance, that the easily observable fact of craving for dominance is culturally produced because of the presence of social norms that favor high rather than lower dominance-feeling, status, and behavior. Cultures are now known in which no such social norm exists, e.g., Arapesh, and in which the person who strives for dominance status is a deviant (17).

Whereas we have had to speak often of culture, it has not been necessary to speak of biological determination. It has been our opinion, and we are even more confirmed in it now, that the biological influences on personality have been exaggerated. In any textbook on the subject, one is apt to find far more space assigned to hormones than to social norms. We believe that this exaggeration will soon be found misleading and unproductive, and that social psychology will turn more and more to the study of man-in-a-culture rather than man-as-an-animal. We do not intend this as an all-or-none statement. Nor do we wish to exaggerate in the opposite direction. There is in psychology a definite place, even a need, for some concept of temperament, in the sense of deep-lying chemical, physical, innate determinants of the personality. Unfortunately, nothing can be said about this because so little constructive research on this point is available.

*5. The Character of Syndrome Change and Its Relation to Personality*

The syndromes, both of dominance-feeling and of dominance behavior, usually change as a whole and not piecemeal (see, for animals, 10, p. 270, and 13, p. 194). The separate parts of these syndromes are interchangeable and have similar or equivalent psychological meaning. This is true in humans as well as in animals, although not to the same extent (especially for behavior). The syndromes of feeling can be described with amazingly complex possibilities of alternative detailed expression.

The use of the syndrome concept has thrown an increasingly clear light on the useless and misleading character of the causality concept in dealing with personality. The eternal question has been "What *causes* this behavior?" and as a result psychologists have spent much time trying to discover whether shyness causes inferiority feelings or inferiority feelings cause shyness, whether social ease causes self-confidence or self-confidence causes social ease, and the like. The worst offenders in this regard have been the psychoanalysts. Because these characteristics or "symptoms" are part of an interrelated syndrome, they are always found to be correlated and present at the same time or in a certain sequence, and therefore, following an outmoded philosophy of causality, they are put down as cause and effect. From such a procedure, only confusion can follow, since, as may be clearly realized now, these "causes" are absolutely interchangeable.[7]

This principle has an even wider application, namely, to the relation of the syndrome as a whole to admittedly external influences, which have also been called "causes." We are convinced that, ordinarily, effective external influences, whether contemporary or historical, do not affect single parts of the syndrome, but *rather influence the syndrome as a whole.* Changes in behavior that appear, consequent upon these external stimulations, spring from or are related to changes in the general syndrome. They are not direct "effects" of the external influences.

Thus, for example, instead of saying that John underwent a traumatic experience that causes such and such behavior to appear and persist, we should rather say (in most cases) that such and such a series of shocks changed John's self-confidence (or self-esteem or dominance-feeling) *and all its correlates.* Since these syndromes of feelings and attitudes are to some extent automatically related to impulse-to-behavior, the behavior also changes, and we have John behaving as he now does.[8] That is, external circumstances change inner personality and also, consequently, change behavior to some extent.

It is easy to observe how this concept works in clinical practice when a patient is impelled, by some outstanding change in his behavior, to come for help. It is usually found, if this behavior has any relation to the dominance-feeling syndrome, that there has been a change in this syndrome, that it has changed as a whole, and also *that there have been widespread and interrelated changes in behavior at the same time.* The complaint may be, for instance, compulsive promiscuity, but thorough investigation, in perhaps four cases out of five, reveals many other behavior changes that are not so obvious, just as it reveals the ordinarily neglected fact that the dominance syndrome as a whole has also changed. Thus, to repeat, the formula would run: these experiences change the inner personality, and (since the personality is definitely related to tendency-to-behavior in such a way that changing the personality means automatically changing this tendency-to-behavior also), at the same time, they change the behavior (with culturally set bounds). External influences change or influence a whole human being, not merely a bit or a part of a human being.

[7]See Dr. Karen Horney's (5) concept of the "vicious circle," another attempt in this direction.

[8]We imply here a distinction between behavior and impulse-to-behavior. We do this advisedly. It is our conception that a wish, a feeling, or an attitude carries with it automatically a corresponding impulse-to-behavior. If it has not already been made obvious, it may be stated explicitly at this point that these impulses-to-behavior are part of the dominance-feeling syndrome. Of course these impulses-to-behavior often spill over into overt behavior, but, as we pointed out repeatedly, the overt behavior is far more subject to inhibition by cultural demands than is impulse-to-behavior.

## 6. Inner and Outer Personality

Much confusion in the study of personality could be avoided if sufficient account were taken of the important distinction between inner and outer personality (or inner personality and social behavior, or implicit and explicit personality) (21). We have demonstrated in previous papers that a certain behavior may be related to any one of several motivating or underlying states, and, conversely, that a certain inner state may be related to, or give rise to, any one of several behaviors. We have also demonstrated the uncertain correlation between dominance-feeling and dominance behavior, and have stressed the fact that one cannot predict accurately from one to the other. Furthermore, we have stressed what we consider to be a most significant fact, namely, that the inhibitory control by cultural pressures is far greater and more effective for dominance behavior than it is for dominance-feeling (or, to generalize, culture controls outer personality or behavior more than it does inner personality).

These facts, and the distinction (between inner and outer personality) that they support, are relevant to any discussion of that now-raging problem between specificity or generality of personality traits. In brief, our contention is that when inner personality is studied, generalized, persistent "traits"of personality may be found. When behavior, or "outer personality," is studied, then we are much more apt to find specificity of personality reactions. We feel, furthermore, that deduction from one kind of study to the other is risky, unless empirically supported.

To some extent, this would follow on a priori grounds from a consideration of the mode of cultural impacts on personality. The folkways that control behavior are often (not always) highly specific, and hold for definite situations and circumstances. For instance, in our culture, the circumstances under which we may appear in a swimming suit are very circumscribed and specific (22). The same is true for evening gowns, overalls, pajamas, etc. They are enjoined in one situation, forbidden in another. So with honesty behavior (aside from copy books and ethical treatises). Stealing pennies from a blind man's cup is absolutely forbidden; stealing pennies from large corporations is not (indeed, it is even encouraged in some quarters). The expression of hostility is highly socialized in the same sense. There are times when one *must*, other times when one just as surely must not. If this principle be granted, and it is also admitted that cultural control over social behavior is stringent, then we may begin to understand that specificity of social behavior is, at least partly, a function of the specific nature of the cultural control. This also explains in part the possibility of great changes in social behavior in an individual from year to year and from decade to decade.

It would be just as true that, where the folkways are patterned, this patterning would be reflected to some extent as patterning in the social behavior of individuals.

The situation is not the same for inner personality, which is also to a large extent a social product, but in a different sense. For it is when we deal with the interiorization of social norms that we encounter psychic inertia at its strongest. This interiorization takes place in the early life of the individual, and after that remains as a relatively stable portion of the personality. (It is this fact that makes us feel that we need not modify our conclusions even with the acceptance of a field of theory like Gardner Murphy's (19).)

Attitudes, feelings, affective sets, dominant motivations, and the like are, from all we know, formed and fixed at an early age. Some change undoubtedly occurs, which must surely be largely assignable to social influences. Such change, however, slow as it is, cannot be compared with the determination of the appearance of social behavior by the immediate social field. We need not be surprised, then, if inner personality is stable and enduring. (See also Adler's concept of "life-style.")

The implications of the foregoing distinctions are considerable. It must be obvious that a purely behavioral approach to personality takes the long way 'round, to say the least, and even, because of limitations of method, may possibly not even hope to learn all there is to learn about personality. This amounts to saying that what people feel, think, and wish is as important as what they do, if the aim is to understand personality. In this we agree with the psychoanalysts, who have long claimed that the academic psychologist scratched the surface and neglected the most important aspects of personality. At the same time, we do feel that it is quite possible to study inner personality in an acceptably scientific fashion.[9] Undoubtedly the most promising mode of approach available now is one that would simultaneously study both inner and outer aspects of important facets of personality.

### References

1. Adler, A. *Neurotic constitution.* New York: Moffat, Yard, 1917.
2. Benedict, Ruth. Anthropology and personality. Unpublished lecture, Cooper Union, November 14, 1937.
3. Eisenberg, P. Expressive movements related to feeling of dominance. *Arch. of Psychol.*, 1937, No. 211, p. 73.
4. Freud, S. *New introductory lectures in psychoanalysis.* New York: Norton, 1933.

[9]Such a study must deal necessarily with the problem of trust, faith, "transference," rapport, or whatever we may call it, that enables a subject to perceive the lack of a censorial attitude and consequently permits him to report freely and accurately his attitudes, wishes, feelings, etc. Without such a relationship between subject and investigator, inner personality cannot be studied directly.

5. Horney, K. *Neurotic personality of our time*. New York: Norton, 1937.
6. Levy, D. M. Aggressive-submissive behavior and the Frolich syndrome. *Arch. Neur. & Psychiat.*, 1936, **36**, 991–1020.
7. Linton, R. Unpublished lectures on culture and personality, 1937.
8. ———. *Study of man, an introduction*. New York: Appleton-Century-Crofts, 1936.
9. Maslow, A. H. The dominance drive as a determiner of social behavior in infra-human primates. (Abstract) *Psychol. Bull*, 1935, **29**, 117–118.
10. ———. The role of dominance in the social and sexual behavior of infra-human primates: I. Observations at Vilas Park Zoo. *J. Genet. Psychol.*, 1936, **48**, 261–277.
11. Maslow, A. J., and Flanzbaum, S. II. The experimental determination of the dominance behavior syndrome. *J. Genet. Psychol.*, 1936, **48**, 273–309.
12. ———. III. A theory of sexual behavior of infra-human primates. *J. Genet. Psychol.*, 1936, **48**, 310–338.
13. ———. IV. The determination of hierarchy in pairs and in a group. *J. Genet. Psychol.*, 1936, **49**, 161–198.
14. ———. Dominance-feeling and sexuality in women. *J. Soc. Psychol.*, 1942. **16**, 259–294.
15. ———. Personality and patterns of culture. In R. Stagner, *Psychology of Personality* (21). (pp. 408–428).
16. ———. Dominance-feeling, behavior, and status. *Psychol. Rev.*, 1937, **44**, 404–429.
17. Mead, Margaret. *Sex and temperament in three primitive societies*. New York: Morrow, 1935.
18. Murphy, G., Murphy, L., and Newcomb, T. *Experimental social psychology*. (2nd ed.) New York: Harper, 1937.
19. Murphy, G. Personality and social adjustments. *Soc. Forces*, 1937, **195**, 472–475.
20. Sears, R. R. Experimental studies of projection: II. Ideas of reference. *J. Soc. Psychol.*, 1937, **8**, 389–400.
21. Stagner, R. *Psychology of personality*. New York: McGraw-Hill, 1937.
22. Sumner, W. G. *Folkways*. Boston: Ginn, 1906.
23. Terman, L., and Miles, C. C. *Sex and personality*. New York: McGraw-Hill, 1936.

# 5

# Self-Esteem
# (Dominance-Feeling) and
# Sexuality in Women[1]

*A. H. Maslow*

## A. Introduction

This paper is one of a series presenting the results of a broadly comparative investigation of the dominance or self-esteem syndrome in animals and in humans, studied simultaneously from a biological and a cultural point of view. It was found, in the preliminary studies with monkeys and apes, that there was a remarkably close relationship between dominance and sexuality, so close indeed that we are now inclined to consider sexuality as a sub-pattern in the total dominance syndrome in these animals.

In view of the evidence presented in this paper, we can fairly say that the same conclusions hold true for the dominance syndrome in humans (within the restrictions set by our methods and by our type of subject).[2] The present paper tends to indicate that sexual attitudes and

From *Journal of Social Psychology*, 1942, **16,** 259–294. Reprinted by permission of The Journal Press.

[1]This research was supported in part by funds from the Carnegie Corporation, administered by E. L. Thorndike at the Institute of Educational Research, Teachers College, June, 1935, to February, 1937.

[2]It is well to express at once some of the theoretical qualms that the writer has about the data and conclusions presented in this paper. The whole field of human personality and sexuality is one in which direct experimental or observational data are practically impossible to obtain. All data presented in this paper have been gathered by questioning people and trusting their answers. Sometimes questioning takes more complex forms as in hypnosis, dream interpretation, free association, or as in the check questions asked of the subjects' husbands or relatives; sometimes the validity of the writer's trust in the answers of the subjects could be more firmly established by various ad hoc methods. But in the

behavior are as much or more truly and closely functions of personality and social and cultural relationships than of sheer biological endowment. This demonstration in no sense minimizes biological influence, for we have also demonstrated with our findings that sheer sexual drive has definite determinative value. But this paper is biological in an even more important sense, namely, it demonstrates that these same personality-sexuality relationships are themselves a biological fact since they hold across species lines; there is also some evidence that they hold across cultural lines. This is then both a biological and a cultural study.

For a discussion of the general concepts and other results of this investigation the reader is referred to other papers by the writer listed in the bibliography but especially to (13, 14). We shall here indicate only in brief outline what has been already presented in these papers.

## B. Definitions

*Dominance-feeling (or self-esteem),* is an evaluation of the self; operationally defined, it is what the subject says about herself in an intensive interview after a good rapport has been established. High dominance-feeling empirically involves good self-confidence, self-assurance, high evaluation of the self, feelings of general capability or superiority, and lack of shyness, timidity, self-consciousness, or embarrassment. Low dominance-feeling is seen as lack of self-confidence, self-assurance, and self-esteem; instead there are extensive feelings of general and specific inferiority, shyness, timidity, fearfulness, self-consciousness. Such people are easily embarrassed, blush frequently, are generally silent and tend to be incapable of normal, easy, outgoing social relationships or forward behavior.

*Dominance status* is a social relationship; it is an expression of social position with respect to another person, and is always relative to this other person. A person is in dominance status with respect to another when he feels stronger, more adequate, superior or dominates this other

last analysis we are still dealing with questions and answers, however complex they may be. This means that an element of faith in the truthfulness of the subjects is necessarily involved in the consideration of the data and conclusions.

The writer feels, therefore, that if the concept "scientific" be stringently interpreted, this is not a specific research, at least in the eyes of the purists. Even more strongly, it is his feeling that the problems set forth herein may actually be theoretically unsolvable with the methods we have available today if we are interested only in definitive solutions. Granted then that this may be an attempt to solve an unsolvable problem, the paper will be presented without too much cluttering up of the text with further apologies, questions, and cautions. The writer's own feeling is that it is quite scientific to use shaky data when it is not possible to obtain better data, one knows that the data are shaky, and the reader is warned that they are shaky.

person either overtly in behavior or implicitly in feeling. The dominated or less adequate person is said to be in subordinate status.

TABLE 1. Some Personality Variables that Make Up One Aspect of the Dominance-Feeling Syndrome

| High Dominance-Feeling | Low Dominance-Feeling |
|---|---|
| Self-confident | Timid |
| Socially poised | Shy |
| Relaxed | Embarrassable |
| Extroverted | Self-conscious |
| High self-esteem | More inhibited |
| Self assured | Modest |
| Feeling of general capability | Neat |
| Unconventional | Reliable |
| Less respect for rules | More honest |
| Tendency to "use" people | Prompt |
| Freer personality expression | Faithful |
| Somewhat more secure | Quiet |
| Autonomous code of ethics | Introverted |
| More independent | More inferiority feelings |
| Less religious | Low self estimate |
| More masculine | Somewhat less secure |
| Less polite | Retiring |
| Love of adventure, novelty, | More feminine |
| new experience | More conventional |
| | More conservative |

*Variables Relatively Uncorrelated with Dominance-Feeling*
Brooding, worrying, moodiness
Weeping
Nervousness and "nervous" habits
Jealousy
Anxiety
Happiness
Neurosis and maladjustment
Intelligence

*Dominance behavior* is sharply differentiated from dominance-feeling since there is rarely a one-to-one relationship between them. Dominance-feeling is only one of the determiners of dominance behavior. Other determiners are dominance status, compensatory efforts, specific training, the specific situation, and cultural pressures, both local and general. Diagnosis of dominance-feeling from dominance behavior alone is apt to be inexact. Examples of dominance behavior are bursts of temper, aggressive behavior, insistence on one's rights, free expression of resentment or hostility, openly overriding rules or conventions, arguing freely, etc.

## C. Method

The main method used for gathering of data was the intensive, semi-psychiatric interview. Since the term "interview" ordinarily means a procedure very different from the one used in this research, we must go into some detail to explain our procedure more fully.

In the first place, questioning was started only after a satisfactory rapport had been established between the interviewer and the subject. This means mostly a frank, friendly, trusting relationship of an equalitarian rather than dominance-subordination type.

In the second place, the investigator subordinated objectivity and routinized procedure to the necessities of the separate situations presented by each different subject. Each one was treated as a unique individuality to be understood and interacted with in a different way. The investigator attempted always to be sensitive and adaptable to these widely varying situations. He conceived his first business to be to understand the person before him *as an individual,* and only then to try to follow through the more specific demands of the research. Our method is, then, a fusion of the clinical and experimental approaches.

Another difference was the extreme flexibility of the interview itself. In the beginning stages of the research, all questioning was purely exploratory. The only cues available were those obtained from the previous work with infra-human primates, from general clinical experience and from study of the writings of Adler, Freud and others. With each subject more was learned and lists of questions could be made. These lists expanded as time went on, even though questions found useless were dropped from time to time. These questions were, in any case, no more than a list of cues. For instance, the word "self-conscious" served as a reminder to find out all that was possible about this topic. The particular questions were determined by the particular situation and subject, her general level of self-esteem, her security or insecurity, her loquacity, her cooperation, etc.

As a result, our data are not quite comparable for all our subjects, not in the sense that they do not mean the same thing when we do have data, but rather that we do not have complete data for all subjects.

In addition, some of our knowledge of people with low self-esteem was obtained in a rather incomplete form. That is, one person would be willing to talk about her personality but not about her family; another might be willing to speak about certain aspects of her sexual history but not about others. Such people have been only partially useful for our statistical tables but have nevertheless been valuable in furnishing us with a more adequate appreciation of the personality and sexual outlook of such women. General clinical experience also contributed to this backlog of general information about women with low self-esteem.

### 1. Variables Studied; Rating Scales

The list of variables which were correlated is:
1. Rating for dominance-feeling (or self-esteem).
2. Rating for sex drive.

3. Rating for sex attitude.

4. Presence or absence of technical virginity (if married, whether or not virgin at time of marriage).

5. Promiscuity (number of men with whom sex relations were had).

6. Presence or absence of any history of masturbation since puberty, no matter how infrequent.

7. Score in the Maslow "Social Personality Inventory," a paper and pencil test of dominance-feeling (self-esteem).

We used for our guidance roughly constructed 9-point scales of sexual drive and sexual attitude. These are not reproduced here for fear that they would give a spurious impression of exactness and objectivity. In actuality these variables were rated not only by objective scales but also by a careful judgment about what they would be theoretically if there were no other factors in the picture. That is, the attempt was made to discount the influence of other determiners of sexuality, *e.g.*, whether husband was loved or not, opportunity, fatigue, compensatory efforts, etc. Such ratings are objective only in a very broad sense, i.e., another judge would probably assign the same rating only if he knew *all* the relevant information, rather than just the reports of sexual behavior and feelings in isolation.

In making the rating of sex drive we proceeded from no fixed principle or single definition of sex drive. Our rating is a compound of many elements reported by the subject in response to direct questions after rapport had been established.

1. Frequency and intensity of local genital reactions, and of conscious sexual relations or masturbation, actual or desired.

2. Percentage frequency of climax in heterosexual acts, the ease or difficulty of achieving the climax, the kinds and amount of stimulation needed to come to it, and its intensity (in terms of overt loss of control, sounds, etc., and in terms of introspective description).

3. Subject's estimate of ease of excitability.

4. Number and extent of erotogenic zones of the body reported by subject.

5. Number of everyday stimuli consciously regarded as sexual stimuli.

It is possible to quarrel about any single one of the questions asked to elicit this information, and one must admit that any sexual response whatsoever is of course a resultant of many factors aside from sex drive itself. For instance, the frequency of conscious sex desire probably is as much a function of inhibition or repression as of sex drive. It was in making this rating that the weakness of the question-answer method revealed itself clearly.

Taking the list as a whole, however, with its close emphasis on physiological reaction, we must say, that in spite of our many theoretical qualms, we have found it useful. It is especially so when we are comparing people at the same level of dominance-feeling and sexual experience. At such times, the fact is brought forcefully home that people vary in their physiological endowment.

Generally it must be remembered that such mistakes as were made in this sex drive rating would in any case tend to make it correlate too highly with self-esteem, sex attitude, and sex behavior.

### 2. Unconscious vs. Conscious

The possibility of unconscious falsification or repression has been neglected, advisedly (in the writing of this paper, *not* in the investigation itself). There are many reasons for this: (*a*) any other procedure would have created tremendous experimental difficulties; (*b*) on general grounds of scientific parsimony, it was thought wisest to see what could be done with the simplest concepts available; (*c*) our subjects were relatively "normal" (as distinguished from "neurotic") and a good many experimental psychologists feel that extensive and important unconscious influences and sexual repressions are less frequent or less crucial in normal people than in neurotic individuals; (*d*) our search was for heuristic concepts that would be useful in further researches.

In general, the feeling of the writer is that this non-use of the concept of unconscious repression and falsification has been justified by the results. It should be mentioned here that we feel our data on personality and sex to be quite compatible with those obtained by the group of sociologically oriented psychoanalysts—Horney, Fromm, Kardiner, etc. The concepts of character structure elaborated by them are different from those indicated by our data, but it is the writer's feeling that they lead in the same direction of considering conscious self-confidence or self-esteem or a similar concept to be a fundamental and important determining force in a descriptive dynamic analysis of the normal adult personality, and particularly in the sexual life.

The writer must admit, however, that for more complex cases, e.g., neurotics, his simple methods are quite inadequate to reveal the unconscious motivations which undoubtedly exist and are an important factor in the personality. All the questioning in the world will then be useless (unless interpretations are also made) since the subject herself does not know the whys and wherefores of her feelings and behavior. In such people, a rating of dominance-feeling is often (not always) meaningless. Accordingly such people have not been used as subjects in our criterion group.

### 3. Sampling Errors

When this research was about half completed, certain very important facts became apparent, that seemed to limit not only the usefulness of the research, but also to cast a definite shadow of doubt on previous sexological studies.

At this point about 90 per cent of our subjects were in the middle and high dominance groups and only about 10 per cent were low dominance women. It is necessary to examine carefully the method of getting subjects for our research to understand this fact. A good many of these people were volunteers, people who had heard of the research and were interested in helping it. Thus a large percentage were graduate students. These tried to get their friends to submit to interviewing also. Many other people were approached with a request to be subjects but the writer never insisted or urged his case. People who showed any signs of distaste or withdrawal or hesitancy were not bothered further. At this point the only low dominance subjects we had were graduate students in psychology who felt it to be their scientific duty to submit to interviewing.

A survey of the data at this point revealed the startling fact that *all* our low dominance subjects were virgin, were non-masturbators, were low in sexual attitude, etc., so that in spite of the fact that at this point in the research only about 30 per cent of the total group of subjects were virgin, 100 per cent of the low dominance group were virgin.

At this point special efforts were made to inveigle low dominance women into the research. The writer devoted himself to the hasty construction of a crude paper and pencil test for dominance-feeling with which large populations could be tested and subjects selected. [The unexpected success of this test led to the final construction of the *Social Personality Inventory* (16).] From the large groups of people tested in various college classes, the writer selected out enough low dominance subjects to make the distribution more balanced, always also selecting out an almost equal number of high dominance subjects to control out the various special factors bound up with attendance at a particular school, etc. These people were actively approached, the whole research was carefully explained, the difficulties presented and a personal plea for coöperation was then made. Of all these people, the writer remembers only one or two that refused. The others, in spite of their obvious reluctance, usually decided to submit to interview. The interviews with these subjects were particularly long, careful, and thorough.

As we continued working with these subjects, our percentage of virginity went higher and higher, while the percentages of masturbation and promiscuity went lower and lower.

This history becomes very important when we examine the various sexological researches in the literature, and realize that most of the data obtained, e.g., by Hamilton (5), are probably from high-dominance men and women and that therefore they must be considered to some extent unrepresentative and a product of bad sampling. Any study in which data are obtained from volunteers will always have a preponderance of high dominance people and therefore will show a falsely high percentage of non-virginity, masturbation, promiscuity, homosexuality, etc., in the population. This criticism must be directed to some extent against even such figures as Dickinson's (2, 3) for we know that the low dominance woman shuns pelvic examination whenever possible, and will not volunteer comments about her sexual history. Any study, also, which relies for its data on anonymous questionnaires must meet the same criticism, especially if partial mail returns are obtained, for it is probable that a far higher percentage of low dominance individuals will not return their questionnaires, e.g., Davis' studies (1).

Our device for controlling this factor of selection is, in addition to the deliberate selection of low dominance cases, the use of a statistic which obtains its final figures by averaging the sum of the averages for each of the deciles of dominance-feeling. Thus the raw percentage of virginity in our total number of subjects is 59 per cent, but by the aforementioned technique the figure is 71 per cent. For our criterion group the raw percentage of virgin subjects is 52 per cent but by controlling the factor of dominance-feeling, the percentage obtained is 66.5 per cent. These differences exist even after we have succeeded to some extent in obtaining a more equable distribution of cases with low and high dominance-feeling. These "prediction tables" are presented in Tables 3 and 4.

### 4. Some Theoretical Difficulties

There are numerous theoretical difficulties to be met with in this type of research.

The most difficult to handle has been a methodological one, namely, the study of parts of an inter-related whole with analytic or atomistic techniques. For instance, every effort has been made to treat sex drive as a variable separate from and independent of self-esteem or sexual attitude, when it is obvious that it is *not* separate or independent. In a certain sense, then, we have isolated artificially, unisolable variables in the effort to prove in the end that they are all related to each other. Sex drive, let it be said then, is an artificial heuristic concept and not an empirical, directly observable fact. In part this difficulty has been surmounted by what the writer considers a valid synthetic-analytic technique. This, briefly, consists of studying a particular aspect of personality against the background of a previously acquired knowledge of the total personality. This means a certain loss of objectivity in the conventional sense, but a tremendous increase of validity.

Another difficulty is obvious. What relation do these data bear to the Freudian and Adlerian theories? In a certain sense our data have no bearing whatsoever upon these theories, for we have worked only with conscious, reportable data in the writing of this paper (although as might be expected, other data have also been obtained). And still we feel constrained to record our opinion that these data do have a wider validity and do to some extent bear on the depth theories, particularly on the libido theory as presented, let us say, by such writers as Abraham. The writer himself cannot claim ever to have been able to understand just what *the* libido theory was. For that matter it is very doubtful whether there ever was any single "libido theory" that could either be accepted or rejected. Today even many orthodox Freudians have watered it down to a mere insistence on the potency of drives or to a stress on somatic causation, which the writer is of course completely willing to accept (as who is not?). It is interesting that some analysts who have seen our data feel that they do not contradict "the" libido theory; others just as firmly feel that they do. Obviously they have different theories in mind.

Another theoretical difficulty which by now is certainly apparent is that of drawing a line between the "normal" and the "neurotic" individual. Our so-called criterion group of 70 individuals, it was stated, were relatively normal people. What this means to the writer has been fully presented elsewhere (17) and we need do no more than express the beliefs underlying this research. These are (*a*) that a differentiation between normal and neurotic must be made if the words are to mean anything. These are relative words of course but it is a disservice both to semantic principles and to psychology to say therefore that everybody is neurotic; (*b*) this line, though it must be drawn is certainly not a clear one. Normality is a matter of degree. (*c*) A concept of neurosis very largely acceptable to the writer is that presented in Horney's writings. (*d*) We feel that there are remarkable qualitative as well as quantitative differences between normal and neurotic people, and it seems certain that these are not merely operational, methodological differences.

### 5. Security and Self-Esteem

In general our results hold for average, normal members of our society. Since our society tends to general insecurity, the average citizen may be expected to be fairly insecure. Wertheimer has pointed out that any discussion of dominance must be a discussion of insecure people, that is, of slightly sick people. Our data show this to be true. Study of carefully selected psychologically secure individuals indicates clearly that their sexual lives are little determined by dominance-feeling. In fact, in such people, the phrase, dominance-feeling, is a misnomer. High self-esteem in secure individuals results in strength rather than power-seeking, in coöperation rather than competition. High self-esteem in insecure individuals eventuates in domination, urge for power over other people and self-seeking. Since these researches were started with the use of the concept of dominance-feeling, we have retained it, using it, however, interchangeably with the term self-esteem throughout this paper.

## D. Quantitative Results

The specific results are presented in Tables 2 to 6. The results are presented in two forms always, one for the total group of subjects, and one for the criterion group. The criterion group was selected by excluding people over 28 years of age, Catholic and Jewish women, married women, and severely maladjusted women. The exceptions to these rules were a few women who had been married only a year or two and also a few women of Catholic background who were not now practicing Catholicism. The total group numbered 139, the criterion group about 70. As has already been explained, we do not have complete data for all subjects. The number of subjects involved in each correlation therefore will vary.

Generally it will be noticed that correlations for the criterion group are higher than for the total group in spite of the fact that the number

TABLE 2. Intercorrelations of Various Scores and Ratings

|  | Dominance Test Score | Sex Drive | Sex Attitude | Virginity | Masturbation |
|---|---|---|---|---|---|
|  | | *Criterion group* | | | |
| Dominance rating from interviews | .90 | .20 | .85 | −.81 | .53 |
| Dominance test score | | .17 | .71 | −.66 | .41 |
| Sex drive | | | .43 | −.36 | .51 |
| Sex attitude | | | | −.89 | .68 |
|  | | *Total group* | | | |
| Dominance rating from interviews | .89 | .14 | .83 | −.73 | .42 |
| Dominance test score | | .10 | .72 | −.60 | .30 |
| Sex drive | | | .34 | −.24 | .25 |
| Sex attitude | | | | −.82 | .55 |

TABLE 3. Percentage of Masturbators in Each Decile of Dominance-Feeling as Measured by the Social Personality Inventory with a Corrected Prediction of Masturbators in the Theoretical Population at Large (See text for explanation of this corrected prediction.)

| Dominance Scores Arranged in Deciles (highest scores at top) | | Percentage of Masturbators | | | |
|---|---|---|---|---|---|
| | | Criterion Group | | Total Group | |
| | | % | N | % | N |
| 61 - | 182 | 64% | 25 | 70% | 44 |
| 32 - | 60 | 50% | 6 | 54% | 13 |
| 16 - | 31 | 75% | 4 | 71% | 7 |
| 1 - | 15 | 33% | 6 | 50% | 8 |
| 0 - | −12 | 25% | 4 | 57% | 7 |
| −13 - | −28 | 40% | 5 | 62% | 8 |
| −29 - | −40 | 33% | 3 | 20% | 5 |
| −41 - | −58 | 50% | 2 | 20% | 5 |
| −59 - | −81 | 0% | 3 | 29% | 7 |
| −82 - | −145 | 17% | 6 | 30% | 10 |
| Predicted estimate of percentage of masturbators in a general population comparable to ours (obtained by averaging the percentages for all the deciles). | | 38.7% | | 46.3% | |

of cases is considerably smaller. This supports our contention that in this type of investigation homogeneous groups are necessary for the best results. Our experience has shown us that differences in religion, cultural background, socio-economic status, marital condition, and geographic differences all have attenuating effects on correlations between self-esteem and sex behavior. We shall, then, henceforth discuss only the correlations obtained in the criterion group in spite of the fact that because of smaller number of cases they are less reliable statistically than those obtained with the total group.

We may say here at once that we have little faith in the absolute value of these correlations as true expressions of the quantitative relationships involved. We shall place much more emphasis on the generalized qualitative relationships as they impressed the experimenter, that is, on clinical rather than statistical correlations. We have used these statistical correlations almost solely for the sake of comparisons between dominance-feeling and sex drive, as they relate to sexual behavior and attitude.

An inspection of Tables 2-6 shows that closer correlations exist between promiscuity, masturbation, sexual attitude, and dominance-feeling (measured both by rating and by test score) than between these sexual variables and sex drive. Masturbation correlates about equally with sex drive and with dominance-feeling, but we must not neglect the fact of self-correlation, that is, the rating for sex drive depended to some extent on the presence or absence of masturbation. This factor of self-correlation

TABLE 4. Average Promiscuity Index and Percentage of Virginity in Each Decile of Dominance-Feeling, as Measured by the Social Personality Inventory, with a Corrected Prediction of Virginity in the Theoretical Population at Large

| Dominance Scores Arranged in Deciles (highest scores at top) | | Criterion Group | | | Total Group | | |
|---|---|---|---|---|---|---|---|
| | | % of virgins | Promiscuity | N | % of virgins | Average promiscuity | N |
| 61 - | 182 | 35% | 6.5 | 26 | 41% | 4.4 | 51 |
| 32 - | 60 | 29% | 2.6 | 7 | 33% | 3.5 | 15 |
| 16 - | 31 | 25% | 3.5 | 4 | 50% | 1.9 | 8 |
| 1 - | 15 | 33% | 2.0 | 6 | 40% | 1.8 | 11 |
| 0 - | −12 | 80% | 2.4 | 5 | 75% | 1.6 | 8 |
| −13 - | −28 | 80% | 1.4 | 5 | 80% | 1.0 | 10 |
| −29 - | −40 | 100% | 0.0 | 3 | 100% | 0.0 | 6 |
| −41 - | −58 | 100% | 0.0 | 4 | 100% | 0.0 | 9 |
| −59 - | −81 | 100% | 0.0 | 4 | 100% | 0.0 | 8 |
| −82 - | −145 | 83% | 0.2 | 6 | 85% | 0.2 | 13 |
| Predicted estimate of percentage of virgins in a general population comparable to ours (obtained by averaging the percentages for all the deciles). | | 66.5% | | | 70.4% | | |

TABLE 5. Relation of Promiscuity to Presence or Absence of Masturbation; Promiscuity Index Equals Number of Men with Whom Sexual Relations Have Been Had

| | | |
|---|---|---|
| Criterion group (N = 71) | | |
| Average promiscuity index of masturbators | 7.8 | (N = 37) |
| Average promiscuity index of non-masturbators | 0.3 | (N = 34) |
| Total group (N = 124) | | |
| Average promiscuity index of masturbators | 5.3 | (N = 73) |
| Average promiscuity index of non-masturbators | 0.5 | (N = 51) |

TABLE 6. Relation of Virginity to Presence or Absence of Masturbation

| | Masturbation | Non-Masturbation | |
|---|---|---|---|
| Criterion group (N = 71) | | | |
| Virgin | 24% | 76% | N = 37 |
| Non-virgin | 82% | 18% | N = 34 |
| Total group (N = 127) | | | |
| Virgin | 42% | 58% | N = 69 |
| Non-virgin | 78% | 22% | N = 58 |

also shows its influence in the slight discrepancies between the correlations with dominance-feeling score. It must be remembered that the rating was made after an exploration of the whole personality *including sexual attitudes and behavior.* This is not true for test score, which is based entirely upon non-sexual questions. Incidentally, the writer feels that the remarkably close correspondence (in spite of the above factor of self-correlation) between the correlations obtained with test score and with rating is a convincing proof of the validity and objectivity of the interview procedure and of the data obtained in these interviews.

The highest correlations obtained, as might be expected, are between sexual attitude and sexual behavior. The correlations between sex drive and sex behavior and attitude are probably too high, first because of self-correlation, and second because it was very difficult to get this rating disentangled from personality and cultural factors. The writer feels that if ever some perfectly physiological basis for sex drive is found that is measurable, say, by sheer blood level of the oestrin hormone, that the correlations with sexual behavior would be lower than those we have obtained.

We are not stressing in this paper the relations between sexual behavior and attitude and ego-security. These will probably be presented in future papers. We may, for the moment, however, point to the differences in correlations between sex drive and masturbation in the Criterion Group and in the Total Group. In the latter group, the factor of ego-security was not as well controlled as in the Criterion Group. We attribute this drop in correlation from .51 to .25 to the intrusion into this picture of the factor of ego-insecurity. It will be observed that no other correlation is as much affected as this one.

Table 6 shows that masturbation and non-virginity go together more than do masturbation and virginity. This indicates that masturbation in normal people need not be thought of only as a method of compensating for lack of love or heterosexual experience, nor that it is solely a product of fear of heterosexuality.

It will be noticed that the correlations between sex drive and dominance-feeling are low ($r = .10 - .20$). Clinically we found almost no predictability at all.

### 1. Validity and Reliability of the Statistical Results

It is necessary to indicate here what we believe to be the shortcomings of our statistical data.

1. The subjects that we had available are not evenly distributed, nor are there enough cases at some levels of self-esteem.

2. The bi-serial correlations may not be used as absolute quantitative measures since they are valid only when used for normal distributions and for greater number of cases than we had available.

3. Our quantitative ratings are in any case subject to a large number of criticisms which have already been discussed; the most important being that they are too subjective.

4. The question of truthfulness of certain answers in the interview must be considered as a possible attenuating factor. The writer believes

that he was able to get frank, truthful answers, but it is difficult to prove this.

5. Self-correlation is present to some extent in correlation between ratings, e.g., the rating for dominance-feeling was made partially on the basis of sexual data. This factor turned out to be quite negligible, for correlations with dominance test scores are just about the same as with dominance rating.

### E. Qualitative Results

*1. Cultural, Religious, Background Differences*

Sexual behavior, and to a lesser degree, sexual attitude, is a very sensitive resultant of many diverse influences, of which self-esteem and sex drive are only two. For instance, Jewish women, who have been found in general to be higher in dominance-feeling, and even more so in dominance behavior, than either Catholics or Protestants, nevertheless show higher percentages of virginity than either of the other groups. This has nothing to do with religion as such because very few of our Jewish subjects had ever been religious. When subjects *were* religious, whether Jewish, Catholic, or Protestant, they were much more apt to be virgin, not to masturbate, and to have lower ratings for sex attitude.

The Jewish women as a group were found to be markedly ambivalent toward sex, being attracted and frightened by it simultaneously. We have elsewhere (13) propounded the tentative hypothesis that their compensatory dominance behavior is partly a function of cultural insecurity; i.e., belonging to a cultural sub-group that is somewhat rejected and segregated by the larger group. The sexual findings for these women may also be a function or result of this same cultural position.

We have too few Catholic subjects for any final conclusions.

Certainly our data seem to indicate differences as a result of different religious or sub-cultural backgrounds. In dealing with individuals (rather than groups), this is even more apparent. So also are differences in educational background, differences in kind of parents, etc.

Geographical or sectional differences also seem to be possibly important. Subjects originally from the South carried with them a tradition or emphasis on purity, virginity, etc. "Being a lady" and "being common" were two sharply distinct things for them.

Certain kinds of progressive education or the influence of sophisticated parents seem also to instill a freer attitude toward sex, although it does not seem to affect actual sex behavior very much. On the other hand, being brought up by grandparents gave two subjects, both high in dominance, a more Puritan, antagonistic attitude toward sex.

### 2. Homosexual Behavior

Five of our subjects had had active homosexual experiences. Only one of these could be called "really" homosexual, preferring it to contact with men. Three of these were rated 9 in dominance-feeling (highest possible rating in our nine-point scale), one 8, and the "real" homosexual, 7. Of our total group of subjects six were rated 9 in dominance-feeling. In this group of six, of the three who had *not* had homosexual experiences, two consciously desired it and the last was not averse to it. The only other two subjects who admitted homosexual desires were rated 8.

Two of our subjects had had passive homosexual experience. One was rated 5.5 in dominance-feeling, the other 4.5 (5 is the median rating).

The implications are obvious even if our numbers are not great. In women with *very* high dominance-feeling, the probability is much higher than it is in the general population, that investigation will find either active homosexual episodes in the history or else conscious tendencies, desires, or curiosity.

In only one of these people was the homosexuality preferred or long continued. It came usually either from intense curiosity or from the inability to find a man suitably high in dominance-feeling as a mate. In these cases when a suitable man came along, the homosexuality was dropped at once.

In our two cases with passive homosexual episodes in the history, both were well-sexed, and at the time somewhat afraid of men and sex in general. Both were virgins. Conscious guilt feelings were present in both of these, but in *none* of the high dominance women. Both eventually turned to heterosexual interests.

Our one homosexual by preference (of course not included in our criterion group of "normal" women) did not look masculine but behaved so in many ways, preferring men's clothes, occupations, sports, etc. Sexual relations with men were reported but with no pleasure. They were indulged in "only to keep up a front" (the girl was terribly afraid of discovery).

Her history consists of the seduction of one girl after another in a very systematic fashion, always selecting women who "challenge" her. They are always taller than she is, always beautiful and feminine, and she is initially attracted because they dislike her, are antagonized by her, or are aloof and stand-offish. She is not attracted to those who obviously like her. She systematically, over a long period of time, gets them to tolerate holding hands, embracing, kissing, etc. The climax comes at the moment when she first induces orgasm in her partner: "At such times I get a feeling of smug power, and of great satisfaction." Her own orgasms come much later in the history of the relationship and are definitely not the primary goal in the seduction.

It is obvious that these findings (in the normal women) suggest an interpretation of homosexual behavior in terms of dominance which appears to be far more valid and useful than a purely physiological interpretation. The reader should compare these data and interpretations with our data on infra-human primates (12). An identical conclusion was reached therein.[3]

### 3. The Influence of Sexual Position

The facts upon which any theorizing must be based are as follows: Many of the women very high in dominance-feeling get a tremendous thrill out of occasionally assuming the above position in the sexual act; such behavior is unthinkable for women low in dominance-feeling; in those couples in which the wife has dominance-status over the husband, these women to some extent, regardless of level of dominance-feeling, are impelled to assume this position as the only or the best means of obtaining erotic pleasure. It will be remembered that certain relevant data are available in monkeys also, with respect to the dominance meaning of "above-ness" and "below-ness" in sexual behavior. In these animals we came to the conclusion that the face-to-face sexual position also had dominance meaning. This position was observed only in pairs in which the animal in subordinate status had, at the same time, high dominance-feeling. Our interpretation was that such a position signified greater equality than the ordinary dorso-ventral sexual position. This conclusion was further supported by the observation of the frequency of this face-to-face position in chimpanzees, in which dominance-subordination is of the friendly, more equal type. It is also found frequently in marriages of secure people for whom dominance-subordination usually is not a factor (in which status is equal).

These data clearly indicate the possible psychological and even biological importance and meaning of sexual position. The above position often has a deep connection with dominance, both feeling and status, and the below position seems often to be connected with subordinate status and feeling, although this latter connection is more influenced by other variables than is the former. For instance, we are forced to the conclusion that, in certain women whose high self-esteem is of the "ego-secure" type, the below position seems to carry with it no implication of submissiveness nor the above position any implication of dominance (the sexual act is not for them a "dominance act"). Also religious dogma has standardized the below position as "normal" for women. It is interesting to notice in this connection that in our couples in which the women

[3]These comments of course do not purport to be a general theory of human homosexuality.

assumed dominant status and the above position, they all reported feeling "forced to do it," and that they felt that somehow they were not "normal." We have also two subjects who felt dominant to their husbands but nevertheless submitted to sexual relationships. Both were psychologically frigid with their husbands and both preferred the position in which, lying side by side, the man made entrance from behind. The statements of both women indicated that any other position would have indicated participation and neither felt that she was participating. This was a way then of saying, "I am outside of this affair."

The almost universal prevalence of the ventro-ventral position in most of the cultures of the world indicates closer, more friendly, more equal relationships between the sexes with mutual participation than is the case in animals. It is the writer's impression, although he is not at all certain of this, that in those cultures in which the dorso-ventral position is the more common one the men are completely dominant over the women and do not value them as individuals. The converse seems not to be true, however, for there are cultures of this latter type in which the ventro-ventral sexual position is the rule.

Possibly, more data on the sexual behavior of the primitives would yield us easy answers to many of our questions. For instance, such behavior as the following seems to the writer to be of great value in any general consideration of relationships between dominance and sexual behavior. In the Trobriand Island (11) a commoner man married to a noble woman is not allowed to be physically above her in the sexual act. Among the Arunta of Australia (18) some women, known as "Alkner-intja," refuse to submit to men. Men are afraid of them and at the same time very much attracted to them. To have had sexual relations with such a woman is a matter for boasting. An interesting folk-belief is that if a man dreams of an "Alknerintja" woman he must get up at once and run away or else she will put him on his back, sit on his erect penis and force him to the female role. In the few reports the writer remembers of groups in which women raped men, the procedure is to place him on his back and sit on the erect penis, thus assuming the above position.

*4. Dominance in Sex and Marriage*

In general our main conclusions are as follows. The best marriages in our society (unless both husband and wife are definitely secure individuals) seem to be those in which the husband and wife are at about the same level of dominance-feeling or in which the husband is *somewhat* higher in dominance-feeling than the wife. In terms of status this means that marriages with equality status or "split-dominance" status, or the husband in dominant status (but not markedly so) are most conducive to happiness and good adjustment for both husband and wife. In those marriages in which the wife is definitely dominant over her husband, trouble is very likely to ensue in the form of both social and sexual maladjustment unless they are both very secure individuals. This seems to be true also, but to a lesser extent, in those marriages in which the husband is *very* markedly dominant over his wife.

It follows from these statements that we should expect a greater incidence of divorce among such couples. A group of about 20 divorced women given our test for dominance-feeling scored significantly higher, on the average, than a comparable group of married women. It is interesting to notice that all of these cases but one fell at the middle of the range for dominance-feeling or above. The one exception was just as definitely below the median. No information could be elicited from her about the situation leading up to the divorce. However, the study of several marriages in which the husband was very much more dominant than the wife indicated that the marriages were in all cases not as happy as the equal ones. The husband was apt to feel conscious or unconscious contempt for the wife, to look down upon her and to lack respect for her. She was apt to become very insecure, to develop anxiety and jealousy and to be generally unhappy.

A confirmation of our finding about divorced women is found in an article by Johnson and Terman (9). The picture that they have derived of divorced women with personality tests is almost exactly like the one we have drawn of the high-dominance woman. For instance, to select only a few of the items, they found divorced women to be, on the average, high in volitional strength, tolerance, self-assertiveness, initiative, decisiveness, self-reliance, independence, ambition. They were more accustomed to take the lead in activities, more willing to be different or unconventional, and more able and willing to take jeers and criticism when they knew they were right. They were less docile and compliant, preferred working for themselves to taking orders. They blushed rarely. In general they lacked the element of sweet femininity but commanded respect for rugged strength, self-sufficiency, and detached tolerance.

Another very interesting finding in our investigation throws some light on an essential mechanism underlying promiscuity, one that we have seen often mentioned in the literature. Married men and women who were also promiscuous, very frequently were quite sure that sheer sexual pleasure and satisfaction was for them confined to the relations with the spouse. Other emotional needs were satisfied in their extramarital affairs, namely, the desire to be sure they were still attractive, the thrill of novelty, unconscious hostility for the spouse, and often, frankly and consciously, the desire to conquer, to "collect scalps." Most subjects of all kinds admitted that a long-continued permanent relationship seemed to be necessary for the fullest sexual (physiological) pleasure and happiness. In promiscuity this was most often not the aim, nor could it be attained easily even when it was the aim, since it was displaced by the desire to impress, the desire to shine by comparison with other sexual partners, the wish to break down aloofness, coldness, snobbishness, etc. In a word, such hasty copulations are most often best viewed, not as sexual affairs, but as what might be called "dominance affairs" or "insecurity affairs."

The Don Juan (and the Dona Juana) has often been described in the literature as a person who bolsters up an insecure ego by convincing himself and others that he is a strong, conquering and desirable man (or woman). Our data supports such interpretation in a good many cases.[4] From such individuals we get reports that the greatest thrill comes not at the moment of the subject's climax, but at the moment of the partner's climax, for such seems to be the moment of conquering.

In such men, it is interesting to see the continued recurrence, in conversation about a snobbish or aloof woman, of the phrase, "She ought to be raped" as if this were the ultimate humiliation that would bring her to her (psychological) knees and allow the man to feel superior. Such aloof men and women are continual challenges and seem highly attractive sexually to the high-dominance person who is also somewhat insecure. So long as they hold off and fail to make love, they remain attractive, challenging, and superior. As soon as they succumb they have lost their value and are cast aside once the first thrill of conquest is gone. These findings are not true of the secure person and they become untrue for insecure high-dominance people who eventually attain psychological security.

We can say that monogamy, in our culture, if the pair are well matched psychologically (and, consequently, sexually) seems to be far preferable to promiscuity as a channel for sheer sexual satisfaction but does not satisfy the emotional needs of people with ego-insecurity of some sort.

### 5. The Meaning of the Sexual Climax

Attention was called to the possible psychological meaning of orgasm when our most highly sexed subject, a nymphomaniac (also in the highest dominance bracket)[5] reported that she had not had orgasm

---

[4]Not in all, however. This is too easy an explanation of promiscuity. Other factors are also part of this picture; e.g., a strong sex drive, high sex attitude, high dominance-feeling with its lack of inhibition, etc.

[5]A nymphomaniac is ordinarily defined as one who cannot control her sex urge, and who is insatiable. Usually, however, it is reported that such women do not have orgasm. This was not true in this case even though she conformed to the requirements of the usual definition. See Hamilton (p. 223) who says, "Compulsive promiscuity, including those extreme cases ... labelled 'nymphomania,' is probably never found among women who can have the climax." Most of our subjects who could be called "compulsively promiscuous" were capable of having the climax. Hamilton's statement may or may not be true of neurotic women; it certainly is not true of "normal" women (6).

with two particular men. This was quite unexpected in view of the fact that she could have orgasm merely by looking at a man. Her statement was, "I just couldn't give in to them. They were too weak." She had felt completely dominant over these men.

Another of our insecure subjects in the highest dominance group who had a strong sex drive and who felt dominant to most of the many men with whom she had sexual relations, reported lack of orgasm with most of them and went to extreme lengths to "show them I didn't give a hoot," such as chewing gum and smoking cigarettes during the sexual act.

Another subject, divorced from her husband, reported that she had tried desperately not to have orgasm with him because she hated and scorned him so. When she could not help herself, because of her high sexuality, she inhibited completely any overt indication of what was happening to her. "I wouldn't give him the satisfaction." She despised herself for not being able to prevent the climax.

In cases of middle dominance-feeling and average sexuality, the presence of the orgasm is a fairly good sign of a feeling of love of the husband. If she does not feel loved or secure, the orgasm will be inhibited unless she is strongly sexed. This will also be true very frequently when a wife is dominant over her husband. In two of the subjects whose husbands were instructed concerning suitable dominance behavior, the orgasm was eventually induced.

In the homosexual subject reported above, it will be remembered that inducing the climax in her partner was the high spot and the goal toward which all her activity was pointed. In the men that we have interviewed this also seemed often to be the case, at least in those with higher dominance-feeling. One (rather insecure) man reported that he always had a feeling of exultation at such a moment. Also it appears fairly frequently that such men will not be satisfied with wives who do not have orgasm, and to the researcher, there seemed to be some undermining of their dominance-feeling when they "failed," as they so often put it. One wife reported faking the orgasm when it did not come spontaneously "in order not to make him feel that he isn't good enough."

It would seem then that the orgasm has psychological values for the woman. With it she may "give in," make herself vulnerable, and to a certain extent, put herself into subordinate status. For a man to induce the orgasm in a woman supports his dominance-feeling and also, for the moment at least, gives him dominance status, especially if the sexual position is psychologically suitable. We may make the finer distinction between what we may call dominant and subordinate orgasms. Women may achieve the first by assuming the above position, by being active homosexuals, or by being in charge of the whole sexual situation, as with a much younger man. The first type carries with it feelings of triumph, of exultation and of bigness, strength and masculinity.

Such feelings and distinctions are strikingly absent in the "equal" or "secure" marriage, in which also the various sexual positions seem to lose some or all of their dominance meaning. In this type of marriage, we may say in general that the concept of dominance is of little direct use. (This is generally true for secure people.)

### 6. Personality and Lovemaking

Practically all the books on sexual and love technique make the stupid mistake of assuming that all women are alike in their love demands. And so we find that general instructions are given to apply to all lovemaking as if one woman were equal to any other woman. That this is completely absurd must already be self-evident from our previous discussions. They are even more absurd when they speak as if the sexual act were merely a problem in mechanics, a purely physical act rather than an emotional, psychological act.

Our data are best presented if we make three general groupings: low, middle, and high dominance. For these groups the concept of the ideal man, of the ideal love act, and of lovemaking in general vary widely.

*a. The Ideal Man.*   For the woman who is high in dominance-feeling, only a high-dominance man will be attractive. He must be highly masculine (psychologically at least), he must be self-confident, fairly aggressive, and even "cocky," sure of what he wants and able to get it, generally superior in most things. Strength and forcefulness of personality are stressed. As we go down in the dominance scale, we find our subjects beginning to stress more and more such qualities as kindness, amiability, love for children, sympathy, gentleness, consideration, romanticism, sentimentality, faithfulness, and honesty. Our middle subjects were somewhat repelled by and afraid of the kind of man attractive to the high-dominance woman. Such men, they feel, are not soft enough, are "too highly sexed," and apt to be too brutal and animal. Generally we might say that the tendency in high-dominance women is to seek a good lover, while middle-dominance and low-dominance women tend rather to seek a good husband and father, an adequate man rather than an outstanding man, a comfortable and "homey" man rather than a man who might inspire slight fear and feelings of inferiority.

We know much less about the ideal man for the low-dominance woman. At times it appears as if there weren't any, at least for those who are also insecure; they are afraid of all men and distrust them. However, children are usually desired and therefore men and sex are unfortunate, even disgusting, necessities. Here too we find that the principle of homogamy holds, of like marrying like. It is the low-dominance man who is acceptable, the gentle, timid, shy man who will adore at a distance for years before daring to speak, who also is afraid of sex as such. It is the writer's impression (with inadequate data) that certainly the low-, and often middle-dominance woman chooses a man to whom she can feel maternal at times.

Looked at from another angle, we see amazingly good adaptations in this sphere. For instance, there are roughly about equal percentages of high-dominance men and women, and so on down the scale of dominance-feeling. It seems possible to say, psychologically, that with respect to the one characteristic we have studied, there is a man for every woman. Also we find in men and women at various levels of dominance-feeling almost perfectly complemental characteristics. The high-dominance woman demands only a high-dominance man, but also the high-dominance man prefers the high-dominance woman. The low-dominance woman dislikes or is afraid of sex; so also is the low-dominance man. The middle- and low-dominance woman wishes romance, flowers, dim lights, illusions, sentimental gestures and poetry. These are just what the middle- and low-dominance man is inclined to give.

*b. Ideal Lovemaking.* The average high-dominance woman in our insecure society prefers straightforward, unsentimental, rather violent, animal, pagan, passionate, even sometimes brutal lovemaking. It must come quickly, rather than after a long period of wooing. She wishes to be suddenly swept off her feet, not courted. She wishes her favors to be taken rather than asked for. In other words she must be dominated, must be forced into subordinate status.

For the middle-dominance woman gentler, long-prolonged wooing is considered ideal. In lovemaking, sex as such must be hidden, swathed about with veils of love words, gently and carefully led up to. It must be preceded by a general atmosphere of the type supplied by soft music, flowers, and love-letters. There must usually be a process of habituation and adaptation to the man and to the situation.

So marked are these differences that we may say, with some inaccuracy but with illumination, that the high-dominance woman unconsciously wishes to be raped; the middle-dominance woman to be seduced.

As for the low-dominance woman, it is difficult to know what she wishes. Perhaps it may be fair to say that any commerce with sex will be for the purpose of reproduction or to "satisfy her husband" (except when there is a very high sex-drive). In one subject (dominance rating, 4; sex-drive rating, 9) divorce came after she had a child. In another (dominance rating, 2; sex-drive rating, 5) where there is no possibility of a child, sexual relations are entirely refused to the husband. In the first of these two subjects the high sex drive has led to some promiscuity, attended by terrific guilt feelings. In some others, regardless of their fears before marriage, some degree of reconciliation and sometimes even liking for it is achieved after marriage if they are not too insecure.

*c. Concept of Marriage.* As might be expected, the different types of women have different philosophies of marriage. A good deal of what might be said here can be directly deduced from the observations reported above. In addition, however, we can point out here that there is also variation in monogamous ideal. Most women insist on monogamy for themselves and their husbands. As we go higher in the scale of dominance, we are told that some promiscuity is expected in the husband and that there is nothing to do about it but adjust to it. Still higher in the scale, overt wishes are expressed by the subjects with relation to extra-marital activity. And, finally, in our highest dominance brackets, we find that the double standard has disappeared; that if the husband is to have extra-marital relations, so also will the wife. Of these subjects, those that are more highly sexed frequently do have extra-marital relations. The monogamous ideal and the acceptance of the double standard are thus seen also to vary with personality position in the dominance scale.

### 7. Sexual Attitudes, Tastes, and Behavior

The concept of sexual attitude as we have used it is not too well defined. What does it mean in terms of specific behavior and tastes?

Ratings were made on a nine-point scale. One extreme is a highly pagan, positive, uninhibited acceptance of anything sexual. The other extreme is a highly "Puritan," inhibited, negative and rejecting attitude toward sex. People who rate high can be said to love sex as such and for its own sake, to regard it as one of the world's best "goods," to approve of all aspects of it, and to regard everything connected with it as good. People who rate low are afraid of it, disgusted and revolted, and feel it must be controlled or justified by babies. For them it is justifiable only as a necessary preliminary to having children, or a necessary concession to the husband. These are the people who cry out and complain that God or nature could have done things in a better way. "Why is it necessary to be an animal before I can have a baby?" If a low sex attitude goes with an average or high sex drive then there is trouble indeed. Horrible guilt feelings, continual self-castigation, disgust and horror, repression and conflicts of all kinds are the lot of such a person. The following is a characteristic statement by a low-dominance woman (dominance rating, 3; sex attitude, 3).

> When I think about sex, I feel Nature could have fixed up a better method—it's rather stupid. It seems so similar to animals, it reminds us

we haven't evolved very far. In looking forward to sex, I think I'd be ashamed. I can never understand how people can do it. The sexual organs are the ugliest part of the body.

This subject with a low sex drive is fairly well adjusted and has no trouble in maintaining her attitude. In another and similar subject, who, however, had a strong sex drive and had been driven into some promiscuity, there were violent reactions against herself—weeping, self-punishment, and some suicidal thoughts. Such people, when they marry, live highly restricted sex lives.

At the other extreme, however, we find a tremendous flowering out of all kinds of sex behavior—cunnilingus, fellatio, unusual sexual positions, much experimentation, even homosexuality or group sexual activities in a few instances.

For instance, cunnilingus is liked very much and indulged in as frequently as possible by a large proportion of the subjects who rate in sex attitude from seven and up, and by practically none who rate five and below. (Because of the very high correlation—$r = .85$—between dominance rating and sex attitude, these remarks hold true for either dominance or sex attitude.) To a somewhat lesser extent the same is true for fellatio. Generally the higher the dominance (with ego-security held constant), the greater attractiveness the penis has for handling, looking at, and thinking about. High-dominance women ordinarily think it to be a very beautiful object in a truly aesthetic sense. Through most of the rest of the population it is considered to be either ugly or neutral in appearance. Incidentally, it is beginning to appear as if exactly the same were true in male attitudes toward the vagina and external pudenda.

This is only a sample of the general attitude of high-dominance people toward sex and sensuality in any of its aspects. Every aspect of it is eagerly, enthusiastically accepted and warmly thought of (where ego-insecurity is not too great), experiments of all kinds are made, all sexual acts are thought of as "fun," rather than as a serious business. Very frequently, in a marriage between high-dominance people, it is found that there has been experience, if only a single experiment, with practically every form of sexual behavior known to the psychopathologist as well as the sexologist, many involved and curious positions or combinations of positions in this sexual act, sodomy, homosexuality, cunnilingus, fellatio, sadism-masochism, exhibitionism, and even coprophilia, sexuality in a larger group, etc. These acts have no pathological tinge nor are they pathogenic in any way. It would appear that no single sexual act can per se be called abnormal or perverted. It is only abnormal or perverted individuals who can commit abnormal or perverted acts. That is, the dynamic meaning of the act is far more important than the act itself.

The strong tendencies to promiscuity found in higher-dominance people also illustrate the point, as does the widespread incidence of masturbation in these people, both before and after marriage (after marriage only when there is deprivation of opportunity for the sexual act). In such people, masturbation is often (not always) found to be a highly sensual affair, protracted and making use of all sorts of titillating and stimulating thoughts, objects and acts. In both masturbation and sexual intercourse the whole body rather than just the restricted genital area, is apt to be involved. Every spot or area that is erotically stimulable is apt to be enlisted in the game that the act has become, and in building up to a tremendous orgiastic climax.

The dreams and fantasies of high-dominance women are of great interest in this connection. In the first place, open dreams of the sexual act are practically restricted to the upper half of the distribution of dominance-feeling in the population. In the lower half of the distribution the "sexual" dreams are always, except in highly sexed women, of the romantic sort, or else are anxious, distorted, symbolized, and concealed. The sex dreams of the high-dominance woman are open, promiscuous, and reflect the same sensuality and desire for wide sexual experience found in the daily life. Thus they dream of intercourse with practically any attractive man met recently, or less often, of a "man" with no particular identity, often with a tremendously enlarged penis. Rape dreams or prostitution dreams are fairly often reported in which the dreamer is forced to submit sexually to a large number of brutal men. These dreams are highly excitable and enjoyable to the high-dominance woman, and of course to the low-dominance woman completely horrifying. Dreams and fantasies of sexual relations with negro men, large, husky, and beautifully built are reported by women in the highest brackets of dominance (except women from the south). A few reports of sexual dreams about animals, chiefly horses and dogs, have been made by women in the highest bracket who were also highly sexed. It must be emphasized that all these dreams reflect desires consciously felt in the waking life also. The same subjects are reported in the masturbation fantasies of high-dominance women.

We have previously pointed out (14) that there is a high correlation between dominance-feeling and liking for nudity. This correlation is just as high of course between sexual attitude and nudism. High-dominance people (if not too insecure) have little or no fear of the body or of any of its functions. Thus the sexual organs are not feared, are even especially attractive. This holds true even in like sex groups. Low-dominance men or women hide their sexual organs even in those situations, e.g., gymnasium, swimming pool, etc., where it is more inconvenient to hide than to reveal. In high-dominance marriages urination and sometimes even defecation is not considered a private matter particularly. Nor in such marriages is menstruation hidden from the husband.

Another characteristic of high sexual attitude and high dominance-feeling is the free use of words and phrases ordinarily considered to be obscene or "dirty," words that are apparently completely tabooed by low-dominance men and women.

Generally the sexual act is apt to be taken not as a serious rite, with fearful aspects, and differing in fundamental quality from all other acts, but as a game, as fun, as a highly pleasurable animal act. Such couples speak about it freely to each other, smacking their lips over anticipated or remembered pleasures, and becoming excited all over again in the process.

All these characteristics of high-dominance people (high self-esteem) must inevitably remind us of our previous interpretation of the dominance-feeling as a degree of repression or inhibition. Thus we may characterize high-dominance people as uninhibited or unrepressed, as people whose fundamental impulses, animal or otherwise, are more apt to come out freely into behavior, within limits set by the society. Low-dominance people (low self-esteem) are far more strongly socialized or inhibited.

### 8. Sadism-Masochism

Our data on this subject are somewhat confusing, probably because of our inability to disentangle clearly direct cultural effects from effects of sex drive and dominance-feeling. Generally our data must be discussed against the background of the standardized cultural formulation that women in love and sex relations are supposed to be yielding, submissive, and even to some extent masochistic. Such tendencies, sometimes stronger, sometimes weaker, can be seen in practically all our subjects. Peculiarly enough, it is just those few women who show no signs of this culturally expected attitude of deference to men in whom we find what seems to be a much more truly masochistic attitude (in a psychological rather than a cultural-conventional sense).

What we may call cultural-conventional submissiveness or masochism is the sort of attitude that expresses itself in preferring to be hugged tightly rather than gently and to be slightly hurt in love-making, that delights in the superior physical strength, height, hardness, and initiative of the male, and that generally regards men as superior to women.

On the other hand, in the high-dominance woman *who is also definitely insecure*, we find often the more classical sexual-pathological picture of close relationship between pain and sexual pleasure. For instance, in one case, a rather promiscuous negress had finally fixed on one man, had lived with him for several years with only one or two lapses from faithfulness. She clung to this man because of his tremendously large penis. She reported dreadful pain in the sexual act, but it seemed that just when the pain was greatest so also was the pleasure greatest. The highest-dominance women reported rather regularly in their fantasies and in their consciously drawn picture of the ideal sexual partner, men with enormously large sexual organs, large enough to cause pain. It will be remembered that these women reported that the idea of being raped, if not actually attractive, at least was sexually exciting. They definitely prefer rough to gentle love making (except when the sex drive is low).

It was to be expected from the findings of various of the psychoanalytic psychiatrists that we should find in just these "masochistic" women, an equal amount of sadism. Wherever one was found, so was the other and usually in just about equal proportions.

Perhaps the best way to describe the situation is to say that in these few women, they strive incessantly to dominate all with whom they come in contact and tend to be sadistic in their dominance in so far as they are allowed to by cultural formulations. They do seem to get a sexual thrill of a certain kind from this behavior. But when a man comes along who cannot be dominated, who proves himself stronger, then these women tend to become definitely masochistic, and to glory in being dominated. Apparently the sexual pleasure so derived is strongly preferred over the other kind of thrill derived from dominating.

One such subject described her sexual life as a continual hunt for a man who was stronger than she was. After a long career of promiscuity, she found such a man and married him (and is still as much in love with him as when she married him some years ago). However, she describes her married life in the same way, as a continual testing of his strength. She actually picks fights in which he becomes violent and which usually end in virtual rape. These incidents provide her with her most exciting sexual experiences.

While this case is the most extreme and the most neurotic recorded in our case histories, the same thing seems to be true in other high-dominance women, if in a more diluted form. The insecure high-dominance woman in our society is usually looking for a man who can dominate her. In order to do this, he must of course have extremely high self-esteem.

We can probably extend this rule to almost all insecure women in our society, however high or low their self-esteem may be. As they describe their ideal men they describe men who are somewhat more dominant than they, men who are superior and stronger. Some even describe men who are *much* more dominant than they. However, in reality the good matches that are made are of the type in which the man is *somewhat* more dominant. For one thing, the man who is much more dominant than a particular woman is usually not interested in her or attracted to her. For another thing, she, when she meets him, realizes that she is somewhat afraid of him, disapproves of him and his way of life, and even is apt to dislike him.

We do not wish to give the impression that this power philosophy of sex is universal. The extreme picture that we have given is characteristic of only a small per cent of the population, those that are very high in dominance-feeling and are also very definitely insecure. People who are secure show no sadism-masochism at all, nor do they seek to dominate or be dominated, no matter at what level their self-esteem may be. Here again we have a beautiful example of the sexual selection mechanism that draws to each other just those who are similar and can therefore satisfy each other's needs. Such a woman as we have described above usually finds and selects just that man who can give her what she wants, and who will find in her just what he desires in a wife. As a matter of fact the man that she married was also extremely high in dominance, high in dominance-feeling and definitely insecure. From a man who was just as high in dominance but was secure, she could not have received the domination, vigor, and aggressive strength that she needed. Such a man is more apt to be kind and cooperative, desiring a wife who is his equal, not one whom he has to beat into line. It is our very strong impression that the principle of homogamy holds strongly in the sphere of self-esteem.

We may now draw the general rule from the data we have presented above. This is, that for relatively insecure people sex is a power weapon, that it is in myriad ways related to dominance-feeling and dominance-status, and indeed may be considered itself simply as a kind of dominance or subordination behavior or at least as a channel through which dominance-subordination may be expressed. In general it has far more intimate relationships with dominance-feeling than it has with physiological drive. This may be interpreted as a definite corroboration of the Adlerian theory of sexuality, at least in its most fundamental emphases, in so far as it applies to our society taken in general as a relatively insecure society. The Adlerian theory definitely does not hold for people and societies that are secure, but Adler, in his later writings, seemed to realize this also.

This does not mean that our data contradict the Freudian sexual theories in toto. Freud has said, at one place or another, practically everything that may be said about the sexual life, even if this has often seemed to place him on both sides of the fence at the same time. Thus we can contradict specific statements that he has made only to find that he himself has contradicted them elsewhere. We do not mean this to be a carping criticism, for it seems to mean only that Freud saw clearly *all* the clinical facts and would not omit mention of them, even if they did not quite fit into his theoretical constructions. Neither do we mean to imply that we must accept *either* the Adlerian *or* the Freudian approach to sexuality. Freud himself has incorporated much of the Adlerian insight into psychoanalysis by the simple method of translation, and Adler has paid Freud the same compliment.

### 9. Comparison with Animal Data. See (12)

If we compare the two sets of data we find a series of startling parallels and similarities. In general it is fair to say that human sexuality is almost exactly like primate sexuality with the exception that cultural pressures added to the picture, drive a good deal of sexual behavior underground into fantasies, dreams, and unexpressed wishes. What we have to dig for in the human being we can see overtly in the infra-human primate. It should be noted that the picture of human sexuality that we have drawn has been mostly of the somewhat insecure type. The closest analogy is with the sexual behavior of the baboon and the macacus rhesus. The sexual life of the secure person is more closely paralleled by that of the chimpanzee, which has a different quality of dominance from that of the baboon and macacus rhesus (15).

The most important common conclusion for the two groups, human and infra-human, is that dominance is a more potent determiner of, or is more closely related to, sexual behavior than is sexual drive. In both groups, sexuality may be used as a power weapon in the Adlerian sense. One form of human homosexuality may be explained in the same way as in the monkey. This is also true for one aspect of sadism-masochism, which were found to go together in the human being as they did in the macacus. In human beings, as also in monkeys and apes, sexual position was found to have definite psychological significance. In both groups, it was found necessary to treat as separate, sexuality and reproduction. Both groups are relatively free from sexual cyclicity, the human group even more than the infra-human. This relative freedom from cyclicity in the human being is certainly more complex than in the infra-human, for cultural factors are certainly involved as well as biological differences.

The chief difference we wish to point out between the sexuality and dominance of animals and humans is that dominance, and consequently sexual behavior, is determined in the monkey almost wholly by social position. While it was found to be true that there were individual differences in what may be called by analogy dominance-feeling, still this was a minor factor as compared with dominance-status. What this means essentially is that practically all determination and inhibition of behavior in the monkey is due to external, immediately-present social forces (the presence of other animals). In the human being, we have a tremendous expansion of the importance of *internalization* of these social forces, so dominance-feeling becomes far more important and dominance-status far less important in determining attitudes and behaviors in the sexual sphere. We can rate most human beings in our society as generally bold or timid, but for the monkey, we are forced in almost all cases to specify the particular social situation in which he is at the moment. There are human beings who are inhibited in the presence of practically all of their peers, but there exist few such monkeys and these are the products of exceptional circumstances.

Other possible phrasings are in terms of super-ego or conscience or socialization which are far more highly developed in the human being than in the monkey. Inhibitions for the monkey are practically always external; for the human being they are much more often internal.

### F. Summary and Conclusion

Using a clinical-experimental methodology, combined with certain quantitative ratings, the general conclusion was reached from both quantitative and qualitative data that sexual behavior and attitudes were much more closely related to dominance-feeling than to sheer sexual drive in our subjects. This same conclusion had been drawn for infra-human primates in previous investigations. Other similarities in findings for these two groups were also pointed out. The most important difference pointed out between monkeys and humans was that in the extent of internalization of social inhibitions.

### References

1. Davis, K. B. Factors in the Sex Life of Twenty-Two Hundred Women. New York: Harper, 1929.
2. Dickinson, R. L., & Beam, L. One Thousand Marriages. Baltimore: Williams & Wilkins, 1932.
3. ———. The Single Woman. Baltimore: Williams & Wilkins, 1932.
4. Freud, S. Three Contributions to the Theory of Sex (4th ed). Washington: Nerv. & Ment. Dis. Pub., 1930.
5. Hamilton, G. V. A Research in Marriage. New York: Boni, 1929.
6. ———. The emotional life of modern women. In Woman's Coming of Age (ed. by Schmalhausen, S., & Calverton, V.). New York: Liveright, 1931. (p. 207–229.)
7. Horney, K. The Neurotic Personality of Our Time. New York: Norton, 1937.
8. ———. What is a neurosis? *Amer. J. Sociol.*, 1939, **45,** 426–432.

9. Johnson, W., & Terman, L. Personality characteristics of happily married, unhappily married, and divorced persons. *Charac. & Personal.*, 1935, **3,** 290–311.

10. Landis, C., *et al.* Sex in Development. New York: Hoeber, 1940.

11. Malinowski, B. The Sexual Life of Savages. London: Routledge, 1929.

12. Maslow, A. H. The role of dominance in the social and sexual behavior of infra-human primates: III. A theory of sexual behavior of infra-human primates. *J. Genet. Psychol.*, 1936, **48,** 310–338.

13. ———. Dominance-feeling, behavior, and status. *Psychol. Rev.*, 1937, **44,** 404–429.

14. ———. Dominance-feeling, personality, and social behavior in women. *J. Soc. Psychol.*, 1939, **10,** 3–39.

15. ———. Dominance-quality and social behavior in infra-human primates. *J. Soc. Psychol.*, 1940, **11,** 313–324.

16. ———. A test for dominance-feeling (self-esteem) in college women. *J. Soc. Psychol.*, 1940, **12,** 255–270.

17. Maslow, A. H., & Mittelmann, B. Principles of Abnormal Psychology. New York: Harper, 1941.

18. Roheim, G. Psycho-analysis of primitive cultural types. *Int. J. Psycho-anal.*, 1932, **13,** 2–223.

19. Terman, L. Psychological Factors in Marital Happiness. New York: McGraw-Hill, 1938.

20. Wexberg, I. The Psychology of Sex: An Introduction. New York: Farrar & Rinehart, 1931.

## Editor's Introduction
## to Paper 6

The next paper, published in the *Journal of Social Psychology* in 1943, in the depths of World War II, focuses again on the question of genuine "dominance" versus mere "domineeringness." And this time the question is taken up with an eye toward the issue of psychological health. Why is the authoritarian person the way he is? Because he is insecure. And why is he insecure? Because his "basic needs" have not been satisfied. In the paper that follows this one, we shall see this matter of "basic needs" discussed in full measure.

# 6

# The Authoritarian Character Structure*

## A. H. Maslow

In this war it is difficult to differentiate our friends from our enemies. The usual criteria that have been used in the past fail us now. But even so, our press and our leaders come back to them again for lack of something better. A fascist cannot be defined by his geographical location, his nominal national citizenship, the language he speaks, his religion, his skin color or other racial characteristics, his economic class, or even social caste. Any of these determiners may be involved in any individual case, but none of them will serve for all cases. To make the situation worse, we cannot even trust what people say or do, for personal expediency as well as covert loyalties may cause the most astounding shifts in policy or in behavior. It may be pointed out finally that in the last analysis even the conscious belief of the subject about himself is not altogether trustworthy, for there are many who tend unconsciously in the authoritarian direction.

The psychologist now has available data and principles that can certainly help in clearing up these confusions, so that by making basic

From *Journal of Social Psychology*, 1943, **18**, 401–411. Reprinted by permission of The Journal Press.

*This paper is the result of five years of off-and-on clinical study of authoritarian individuals in our society. This study was stimulated primarily by a series of lectures on the subject by Dr. Erich Fromm, then of the International Institute of Social Research. Fromm's recent book, "Escape from Freedom," presents some of his conclusions on authoritarianism. Since I have found myself in disagreement with him at certain basic theoretical points (even though in agreement on most else) and since the subject is of such obvious importance today, it seemed justifiable to present this differently centered point of view of the same subject matter, even though he has discussed it so well. A summer's field work with the Northern Blackfoot Indians, made possible by a grant-in-aid from the Social Science Research Council, has also influenced this paper.

issues more clear, he can help in the task of separating our friends from our enemies in our own country as well as others. These criteria are not offered as sufficient in themselves. That would be over-psychologizing of the worst sort. But, taken together with other characteristics of the individuals under consideration it should be possible with them to make diagnosis and understanding easier and more certain.

Any discussion of the concept of character structure must make its peace with field theory before it starts. It is common for any discussion of character structure to be attacked immediately on the grounds that it over-psychologizes what is essentially a person-world interrelationship. I do not think this is true. It is certainly both useful and possible to focus our attention on one or the other member of this relationship. This paper proceeds from the conviction that the almost exclusive attention to economic, political, social, and other cultural forces to the neglect of the psychological factors involved, has been a dis-service to the true understanding of the inter-relationship between the individual and the world in which he lives.

The concept of character structure has, in any case, to be understood as a final crystallization of many determining forces. Of all these forces, it is conceded that the most important is probably all the situations or fields through which the organism has passed in its life history. That is, the character structure may be considered to be largely (though not altogether) the reflection in the individual of all the environmental forces that have ever impinged upon him. This is even more specifically true of the concept of the "world view" to be discussed below. I, therefore, conceive the concept of character structure, as well as world view, to be an intersection of psychological and sociological concepts.


### The World View (Weltanschauung)


Many characteristics of the authoritarian person are already well known. Some of them are listed below. But these characteristics have not been tied together under a unifying principle which could succeed in giving them a hanging-togetherness and make possible a unified understanding of the total personality. This has encouraged many to consider an authoritarian as simply an eccentric or "crazy person" who is ultimately impossible to understand. But this is not so. Such people have a logic of their own which integrates all life for them in such a way as to make their actions not only understandable, but from their own point of view, quite justifiable and correct. This diversity of single characteristics can be understood only, I believe, by understanding the basic philosophy of the authoritarian person. This basic philosophy I shall call the "world-view."

Like other psychologically insecure people, the authoritarian person lives in a world which may be conceived to be pictured by him as a sort of jungle in which man's hand is necessarily against every other man's, in which the whole world is conceived of as dangerous, threatening, or at least challenging, and in which human beings are conceived of as primarily selfish or evil or stupid. To carry the analogy further, this jungle is peopled with animals who either eat or are eaten, who are either to be feared or despised. One's safety lies in one's own strength and this strength consists primarily in the power to dominate. If one is not strong enough the only alternative is to find a strong protector. If this protector is strong enough and can be relied upon, then peace of a certain sort is possible to the individual.

So we may say in more psychological terms that the authoritarian never loves nor respects other human beings any more than the animals in the jungle can be said to love or respect each other. In the last analysis, the alternatives are to fear or be feared.

Once granted this world-view, everything that the authoritarian person does is logical and sensible. We can easily see this for ourselves, if we can only imagine ourselves to be in an *actual* jungle peopled with *actual* wild animals. Then it is obvious that we must have many or all of the authoritarian characteristics if we are to survive. To speak of love, kindness, coöperation or the like in such a situation would be sentimental and unrealistic, like saying, "Let the lion and the lamb love each other" or, "Let us not be suspicious of the lion, for if we are good to him we shall see that he loves us," or, "It is just because we defend ourselves that the tiger attacks us."

If the world is actually jungle-like for an individual, and if human beings have behaved to him as wild animals behave, then the authoritarian is perfectly justified in all his suspicions, hostilities, and anxieties. If the world is not a jungle, if people are not completely cruel, selfish, and egocentric, then, and only then is the authoritarian wrong.

### The Tendency to Hierarchy

This is the tendency to regard most or all other human beings as challenging rivals who are either superior (and therefore to be feared, resented, bootlicked, and admired); or inferior (and therefore to be scorned, humiliated, and dominated). People are ranked on a vertical scale as if they were on a ladder, and they are divided into those above and those below the subject on this ladder.

The democratic person in contrast tends (in the pure case) to respect other human beings in a very basic fashion as *different* from each other, rather than better or worse. He is more willing to allow for their own tastes, goals, and personal autonomy so long as no one else is hurt thereby. Furthermore, he tends to like them rather than dislike them and to assume that probably they are, if given the chance, essentially good rather than bad individuals. We shall give the name "perception and appreciation of difference" to the democratic way of viewing individual differences (in contrast with the authoritarian tendency to hierarchy). Here the stress is first of all on the fact that people are human beings and therefore unique and respectworthy, and only secondarily upon the fact that they may then be ranked for superiority and inferiority. It is as if they were to say "All people are human beings, but they vary in their gifts." Let it be understood that it is possible with relation to this appreciation of difference to speak of inferiority and superiority, but we must define these terms in different ways. Of course, the authoritarian also perceives differences. But for him, as Fromm points out, "differences are necessarily signs of superiority and inferiority. A difference which does not have this connotation is unthinkable to him."

## The Generalization of "Superiority-Inferiority"

The authoritarian tendency to classify all other human beings into two groups determined by the relation of superiority or inferiority to the subject is furthermore marked by a tremendous over-generalization, namely, to regard the "superior" or stronger person as superior in everything, as generally superior, and to regard the "inferior" person as inferior in everything (since, in a jungle, strength is the only quality that ultimately matters).

For the democratic individual a judgment of superiority and inferiority tends rather to be specific, realistic, and functional. He refers to a particular quality or capacity rather than to the whole person, i.e., "He is superior because he can do this particular thing well." Furthermore, the measuring stick against which this democratic superiority is measured is sometimes not so much the subject's ability but rather the goals, motivations, and tasks of the individual who is being judged. In democratic superiority or inferiority, let us repeat, the basis for comparison is in relation to tasks and problems to be solved; in authoritarian superiority the comparison is made not in terms of tasks or efficiency, but in over-generalized terms which are related to the subject who does the comparing.

## Drive for Power

The authoritarian person tends to have a strong drive for power, status, external prestige (since in the jungle, power is so necessary). In extreme cases it can be said that he has a psychological *need* for power which may actually be overtly observed, especially in the person tending toward neurosis (see writings of Adler, Horney, Fromm). Furthermore, this power is defined characteristically in terms of power over people. The person with democratic character structure tends first of all to be less concerned with power, status, and prestige and secondly, to define it characteristically in relation to power over problems and tasks rather than over people. It is, furthermore, characteristic of the authoritarian individual that if he does have power, he tends to use it primarily to assuage his own psychological needs, that is, in a selfish way, and secondly he tends, especially when challenged, to use it in a hard, cruel, or even sadistic fashion. Conversely it is characteristic of the person with democratic character structure that if he does have power he tends to use it, less for personal needs and more in terms of the needs of the group over which he has power.

The reader may find it useful, as I have, to say arbitrarily that it is the authoritarian who seeks for "power," the democratic person who seeks rather for "strength." Power, used in this way, is the symptomatic expression of thwarting of the person's basic needs for safety, belongingness, or love. The true (unconscious) aim of power seeking is then not power per se, but other unconscious psychological satisfactions which the subject fallaciously hopes power will bring. "Strength" in contrast is used to imply capacity to solve problems external to the subject's psyche, that is, social problems, intellectual problems, problems of the real world.

## Hostility, Hatred, Prejudice

This is one of the best-known characteristics of the authoritarian person and need not be discussed at length. It is necessary to point out only that its object is, psychologically, an accidental or fortuitous choice. For instance, anti-Semitism or anti-Catholicism, or anti-negroism are none of them theoretically necessary attributes of authoritarianism. What *is* necessary is hatred and hostility against *some* group or other, whichever happens to be most convenient. Theoretically it might just as easily be people with long ears, or blue eyed people, or poets, or butchers, or bald men. Only hatred for a scapegoat is constant here, not the choice of the scapegoat.

## Judging by Externals and Judging by Internals

Another distinguishing characteristic of the authoritarian is that external signs of strength, prestige or dominant status, e.g., titles, money, power over other people, family name, noble birth, etc., are very important in determining who is superior and who is inferior. In part this judgment of respect comes because of the fact that the ones with prestige have the power of hurt over him. But this is not all there is to it. There seems to be a spontaneous flow of respect and even abasement because of the sheer fact that they are rated as "superior," no matter for what reason. For the democratic person these external signs and marks and symbols are less important than the essential character or personality or capabilities of the person being judged. He is apt to judge by internals rather than externals. (Although of course externals may have some influence also). It is not enough for him that the person being judged has titles or honors or is a celebrity. He must also be a good human being. Or we may say it another way. He customarily gives his permanent respect only to people who are worthy of respect for functional reasons. He does not give his respect automatically simply because he is supposed to, or because everybody else respects this person.

## Single or Multiple Scales of Value

In the authoritarian, as we have seen, there is the tendency to have but one scale of values by which to measure all people and all achievements, which is in terms of the personal and social over-generalized superiority or inferiority we have spoken of. In western civilization this inferiority or superiority most often comes on some such single basis as wealth, noble birth, family name or the like (anything that will give power over people). The authoritarian will automatically have the tendency to defer to these superior people no matter what the field may be, no matter what the question at issue, simply because they rank high on the dominating scale of value. The democratic person, on the other hand, will tend to recognize many scales of values and is much more ready to consider scales of value which are different from his own. Furthermore these scales of value tend to be specific and functional. He will respect the man who is a better historian if the discussion is about history, but will not necessarily therefore respect him in other fields in which he is inferior. Furthermore he is more ready to admire John Doe because John Doe has achieved out of life what he, John Doe, wanted to achieve, e.g., he has become the best chemist or the best baseball player, or the best novelist or whatever, even if no one of these achievements is important for the judger himself.

In addition for the authoritarian every person with a different scale of values tends to be, to some slight extent at least, a threat. For the democratic person this is most often not so. If someone else has different values, he is not threatened thereby.

### The Identification of Kindness with Weakness

Consciously or unconsciously the authoritarian will tend to identify kindness, sympathy, generosity with weakness (inferiority) and to identify cruelty, brutality, selfishness, or hardness with strength (superiority). The democratic person has, because of his character structure, no such tendency, or even a tendency in the opposite direction. Courtesy, honesty, and a good many other qualities which we consider to be good, an authoritarian will consider simply to be weak or foolish, or degenerate. This is not as arbitrary and senseless as it appears to be. If we go back to our original analogy and understand that our authoritarian is actually living in a psychological jungle, then the lamb who trusts the lion, who believes what he says, who is kind to him, is in actuality an idiot, and such behavior is in actuality dangerous. If we were to grant the authoritarian's postulate that everyone is out for himself, that everyone is selfish and the like, then a man who does trust anyone in the world of thieves is actually someone to be despised as unrealistic.

### The Tendency to Use People

It is easy to see from all the characteristics we have discussed so far that the authoritarian will be very apt to regard other human beings only as tools, as means to his end, as pawns on his chessboard, as objects to be exploited. In the extreme we may even detect the tendency to regard inferior people as not quite human so that it doesn't matter so much if they are pained or deprived or exploited or even killed. This too is logical granted the authoritarian's fundamental outlook on the world that one must kill or be killed. Furthermore, the very act of killing or hurting or exploiting, is in itself, a kind of validation or proof of his superiority and strength.

The democratic person, living in a different psychological world, tends, much less often, to "use" other human beings, since he regards them as brothers rather than as rivals, as unthreatening rather than as threatening. This reaction is just as logical as the authoritarian's reaction to his world.

## The Sadistic-Masochistic Tendency

It is for most of us in our society, fairly easy to understand that a person should want power. We can with little difficulty understand Mussolini's desire for power (even though our unconscious motivations to power may be different) but it is less easy to understand motivation of the one who gives up his life for Mussolini. How about the authoritarian who is in the subordinate position? We must understand clearly that the tendencies of which we have spoken, have two sides both of which exist in the same person. Every authoritarian character is both sadistic and masochistic. Which tendency will appear depends largely (but not entirely) on the situation. If he is in dominance status, he will tend to be cruel; if he is in subordinate status, he will tend to be masochistic. But because of these tendencies in himself, he will understand, and deep down within himself will agree with the cruelty of the superior person, even if he himself is the object of the cruelty. He will understand the bootlicker and the slave even if he himself is not the bootlicker or the slave. The same principles explain both the leader and the follower in the authoritarian group, both the slave-owner and the slave.[1]

One important distinction is necessary here. We must be careful not to identify all submissiveness or overdependent persons as authoritarian. The slave with a kind master, the dominated-over-protected person, the person who has low-self-esteem even though he is secure, the sheltered person or the cowed person, may all be submissive and dependent and *not* masochistic or authoritarian. With such people our analogy of the rabbits and the lions does not hold. If we must pursue an analogy, we should have to speak of a shepherd and his flock of sheep, rather than the jungle with its weak and its strong animals (see also Fromm, ibid., pp. 174 ff.). These passive followers, who are however, not basically authoritarian, must constitute a sizeable percentage of the population in both the "fascist" and "democratic" countries.

[1]See Jerome Weidman's story *Chutzbah*, about a man who is admired and envied by his neighbors for being "successful," ruthless, "strong," and clever, even though it is they who have been hurt and outwitted by him.

### The Possibility of Satisfaction

The authoritarian can because of his nature practically never be ultimately satisfied. He must go on and on and on. The overt need for power is of course insatiable because the only theoretical satisfaction would be to have complete power over everyone in the world and even then one could be threatened by the resentment of slaves, the lack of friends, the inability to trust anyone, and of course also by the biological exigencies of life—illness, old age, and death itself. The authoritarian must be perpetually and insatiably ambitious. This means also that he can never be happy except for a time. For the democratic person this is not true. He can be happy because his most basic needs are satisfied. Moreover, the satisfactions he seeks are attainable, whereas the satisfactions the authoritarian seeks are unattainable, even theoretically.

We can see further how this must be so if we recall that the authoritarian seeks power as a means to unconscious ends. His basic ungratified needs are for safety, belongingness, and for love. And since authoritarian power rarely attains these ends but rather is more likely to achieve even further frustration of these needs, the need for power must usually be unsatisfiable.

And yet it is possible to differentiate between relatively "adjusted" and relatively maladjusted authoritarians. So long as nothing contradicts their world-view and so long as they have power enough to protect themselves, they may be relatively contented. Certainly such a man will at least be *more* contented than if he had no power at all.[2]

### Guilt Feelings and Conflicts

In Western civilization, there are strong cultural forces that foster both authoritarian and democratic characters, e.g., capitalism, nationalism, militarism, authoritarian education, the patriarchial family, etc., versus the Christian ideal, humanitarianism, socialism, cooperative movements, etc. Intra-psychic conflict is therefore practically inevitable for the average authoritarian (unless he has been brought up under a consistently authoritarian culture from his earliest days). As might be expected he tends to reinterpret all the pressures at odds with his philosophy, forcing into the democratic forms an authoritarian content. (See for instance, how often the Christian ideal has been corrupted and perverted into its very opposite by various churches and other organized groups.)

[2]See, for excellent illustrations, the novel *What Makes Sammy Run*, by B. Schulberg, the moving picture *Citizen Kane*, and the play *You Can't Take It With You*.

Such reinterpretation is, even when it is relatively successful, a Procrustean task, not to be achieved without great effort, strain and repression.[3] I have found in most of my cases (not all) strong guilt feelings, sometimes quite conscious. These guilt feelings, as we should expect, are an additional source of the hostility feelings and impulses that are characteristic of the authoritarian character in this country.

## Other Characteristics

This description could clearly be carried on and on indefinitely. Because of limitation upon space, we need do no more than mention certain other tendencies of the authoritarian character; for fuller discussion, the reader is referred to Fromm's book, as well as to Hitler's *Mein Kampf*, still the best source book available.

1. The abyss between males and females. The tendency to dominate women because they are weaker, and to assign to them a lesser role. With this goes the tendency to divide all women into Madonnas and prostitutes, the former being good but non-sexual, the latter being sexual but bad. Another aspect of this tendency is the exaltation of masculinity and its sharp redefinition in terms of power, hardness, cruelty, etc., and the use of sex and "love" as a power mechanism.

2. The development of homosexuality.

3. The soldier-ideal. Ambivalent attitudes toward death.

4. The role of humiliation in an authoritarian world. Its function as a validation of status.

5. The antagonism to education particularly of the "inferior" ones.

6. The tendency to avoid responsibility for one's own fate.

7. The concept of *ecstatic* submission, of *eager* giving up of independence to some stronger protector.

8. The authoritarian's achievement of a pseudo-security through compulsive routine, order, discipline, fixity, and other compulsive-obsessive mechanisms.

## Closing Notes

Is it possible to change the authoritarian person? We can say "yes" with the utmost assurance, for this change has been wrought many times by psychoanalysis and by shorter therapies as part of their routine

[3]For an example, see Koestler, *Darkness at Noon*.

psychotherapeutic business. But this is only a partially practicable answer, for these people come to be cured, not of authoritarianism but almost always of specific neurotic or psychosomatic symptoms. Where there is no will or desire to become well, cure is very difficult.

There remains the final question, "Is the authoritarian ultimately right or wrong?" If we confine ourselves to purely psychological considerations the answer is easy. The conditions which the authoritarian attributes to human nature in general are in point of fact found only in a small proportion of our population. The only individuals who ultimately fulfill their conditions are those we call psychopathic personalities. Of no other human beings can it be said that they are completely selfish, completely ruthless, completely without conscience, completely without basic ties or self imposed obligations to other human beings.

## Editor's Introduction
## to Paper 7

Maslow's "Theory of Human Motivation" appeared in the *Psychological Review* in 1943 and in the years that followed became something of a psychological classic. It puts forward the thesis that human needs are hierarchically arranged, from lower to higher, and that the lower ones must be fairly well satisfied before the higher ones can appear. It also argues that certain human needs, formerly thought to be secondary and derivative, are in fact primary and basic. Here, too, is where Maslow made his first public mention of "self-actualization," although his idea of what the concept involved was not yet very fully formed.

# 7

# A Theory of Human Motivation

## A. H. Maslow

### I. Introduction

In a previous paper (13) various propositions were presented which would have to be included in any theory of human motivation that could lay claim to being definitive. These conclusions may be briefly summarized as follows:

1. The integrated wholeness of the organism must be one of the foundation stones of motivation theory.

2. The hunger drive (or any other physiological drive) was rejected as a centering point or model for a definitive theory of motivation. Any drive that is somatically based and localizable was shown to be atypical rather than typical in human motivation.

3. Such a theory should stress and center itself upon ultimate or basic goals rather than partial or superficial ones, upon ends rather than means to these ends. Such a stress would imply a more central place for unconscious than for conscious motivations.

4. There are usually available various cultural paths to the same goal. Therefore conscious, specific, local-cultural desires are not as fundamental in motivation theory as the more basic, unconscious goals.

5. Any motivated behavior, either preparatory or consummatory, must be understood to be a channel through which many basic needs may be simultaneously expressed or satisfied. Typically an act has *more* than one motivation.

6. Practically all organismic states are to be understood as motivated and as motivating.

7. Human needs arrange themselves in hierarchies of prepotency. That

From *Psychological Review*, 1943, **50**, 370–396. Copyright 1943 by the American Psychological Association, and reproduced by permission.

is to say, the appearance of one need usually rests on the prior satisfaction of another, more prepotent need. Man is a perpetually wanting animal. Also no need or drive can be treated as if it were isolated or discrete; every drive is related to the state of satisfaction or dissatisfaction of other drives.

8. *Lists* of drives will get us nowhere for various theoretical and practical reasons. Furthermore any classification of motivations must deal with the problem of levels of specificity or generalization of the motives to be classified.

9. Classifications of motivations must be based upon goals rather than upon instigating drives or motivated behavior.

10. Motivation theory should be human-centered rather than animal-centered.

11. The situation or the field in which the organism reacts must be taken into account but the field alone can rarely serve as an exclusive explanation for behavior. Furthermore the field itself must be interpreted in terms of the organism. Field theory cannot be a substitute for motivation theory.

12. Not only the integration of the organism must be taken into account, but also the possibility of isolated, specific, partial or segmental reactions.

It has since become necessary to add to these another affirmation.

13. Motivation theory is not synonymous with behavior theory. The motivations are only one class of determinants of behavior. While behavior is almost always motivated, it is also almost always biologically, culturally and situationally determined as well.

The present paper is an attempt to formulate a positive theory of motivation which will satisfy these theoretical demands and at the same time conform to the known facts, clinical and observational as well as experimental. It derives most directly, however, from clinical experience. This theory is, I think, in the functionalist tradition of James and Dewey, and is fused with the holism of Wertheimer (19), Goldstein (6), and Gestalt Psychology, and with the dynamicism of Freud (4) and Adler (1). This fusion or synthesis may arbitrarily be called a "general-dynamic" theory.

It is far easier to perceive and to criticize the aspects in motivation theory than to remedy them. Mostly this is because of the very serious lack of sound data in this area. I conceive this lack of sound facts to be due primarily to the absence of a valid theory of motivation. The present theory then must be considered to be a suggested program or framework for future research and must stand or fall, not so much on facts available or evidence presented, as upon researches yet to be done, researches suggested perhaps, by the questions raised in this paper.

## II. The Basic Needs

*The "Physiological" Needs.* The needs that are usually taken as the starting point for motivation theory are the so-called physiological drives. Two recent lines of research make it necessary to revise our customary notions about these needs, first, the development of the concept of homeostasis, and second, the finding that appetites (preferential choices among foods) are a fairly efficient indication of actual needs or lacks in the body.

Homeostasis refers to the body's automatic efforts to maintain a constant, normal state of the blood stream. Cannon (2) has described this process for (1) the water content of the blood, (2) salt content, (3) sugar content, (4) protein content, (5) fat content, (6) calcium content, (7) oxygen content, (8) constant hydrogen-ion level (acid-base balance) and (9) constant temperature of the blood. Obviously this list can be extended to include other minerals, the hormones, vitamins, etc.

Young in a recent article (21) has summarized the work on appetite in its relation to body needs. If the body lacks some chemical, the individual will tend to develop a specific appetite or partial hunger for that food element.

Thus it seems impossible as well as useless to make any list of fundamental physiological needs for they can come to almost any number one might wish, depending on the degree of specificity of description. We can not identify all physiological needs as homeostatic. That sexual desire, sleepiness, sheer activity and maternal behavior in animals, are homeostatic, has not yet been demonstrated. Furthermore, this list would not include the various sensory pleasures (tastes, smells, tickling, stroking) which are probably physiological and which may become the goals of motivated behavior.

In a previous paper (13) it has been pointed out that these physiological drives or needs are to be considered unusual rather than typical because they are isolable, and because they are localizable somatically. That is to say, they are relatively independent of each other, of other motivations and of the organism as a whole, and secondly, in many cases, it is possible to demonstrate a localized, underlying somatic base for the drive. This is true less generally than has been thought (exceptions are fatigue, sleepiness, maternal responses) but it is still true in the classic instances of hunger, sex, and thirst.

It should be pointed out again that any of the physiological needs and the consummatory behavior involved with them serve as channels for all sorts of other needs as well. That is to say, the person who thinks he is hungry may actually be seeking more for comfort, or dependence, than for vitamins or proteins. Conversely, it is possible to satisfy the hunger need in part by other activities such as drinking water or smoking cigarettes. In other words, relatively isolable as these physiological needs are, they are not completely so.

Undoubtedly these physiological needs are the most prepotent of all needs. What this means specifically is, that in the human being who is missing everything in life in an extreme fashion, it is most likely that the major motivation would be the physiological needs rather than any others. A person who is lacking food, safety, love, and esteem would most probably hunger for food more strongly than for anything else.

If all the needs are unsatisfied, and the organism is then dominated by the physiological needs, all other needs may become simply non-existent or be pushed into the background. It is then fair to characterize the whole organism by saying simply that it is hungry, for consciousness is almost completely preempted by hunger. All capacities are put into the service of hunger-satisfaction, and the organization of these capacities is almost entirely determined by the one purpose of satisfying hunger. The receptors and effectors, the intelligence, memory, habits, all may now be defined simply as hunger-gratifying tools. Capacities that are not useful for this purpose lie dormant, or are pushed into the background. The urge to write poetry, the desire to acquire an automobile, the interest in American history, the desire for a new pair of shoes are, in the extreme case, forgotten or become of secondary importance. For the man who is extremely and dangerously hungry, no other interests exist but food. He dreams food, he remembers food, he thinks about food, he emotes only about food, he perceives only food and he wants only food. The more subtle determinants that ordinarily fuse with the physiological drives in organizing even feeding, drinking or sexual behavior, may now be so completely overwhelmed as to allow us to speak at this time (but *only* at this time) of pure hunger drive and behavior, with the one unqualified aim of relief.

Another peculiar characteristic of the human organism when it is dominated by a certain need is that the whole philosophy of the future tends also to change. For our chronically and extremely hungry man, Utopia can be defined very simply as a place where there is plenty of food. He tends to think that, if only he is guaranteed food for the rest of his life, he will be perfectly happy and will never want anything more. Life itself tends to be defined in terms of eating. Anything else will be defined as unimportant. Freedom, love, community feeling, respect, philosophy, may all be waved aside as fripperies which are useless since they fail to fill the stomach. Such a man may fairly be said to live by bread alone.

It cannot possibly be denied that such things are true but their *generality* can be denied. Emergency conditions are, almost by definition, rare in the normally functioning peaceful society. That this truism can be forgotten is due mainly to two reasons. First, rats have few motivations other than physiological ones, and since so much of the research upon motivation has been made with these animals, it is easy to carry the rat-picture over to the human being. Secondly, it is too often not realized that culture itself is an adaptive tool, one of whose main functions is to make the physiological emergencies come less and less often. In most of the known societies, chronic extreme hunger of the emergency type is rare, rather than common. In any case, this is still true in the United States. The average American citizen is experiencing appetite rather than hunger when he says "I am hungry." He is apt to experience sheer life-and-death hunger only by accident and then only a few times through his entire life.

Obviously a good way to obscure the "higher" motivations, and to get a lopsided view of human capacities and human nature, is to make the organism extremely and chronically hungry or thirsty. Anyone who attempts to make an emergency picture into a typical one, and who will measure all of man's goals and desires by his behavior during extreme physiological deprivation is certainly being blind to many things. It is quite true that man lives by bread alone—when there is no bread. But what happens to man's desires when there *is* plenty of bread and when his belly is chronically filled?

*At once other (and "higher") needs emerge* and these, rather than physiological hungers, dominate the organism. And when these in turn are satisfied, again new (and still "higher") needs emerge and so on. This is what we mean by saying that the basic human needs are organized into a hierarchy of relative prepotency.

One main implication of this phrasing is that gratification becomes as important a concept as deprivation in motivation theory, for it releases the organism from the domination of a relatively more physiological need, permitting thereby the emergence of other more social goals. The physiological needs, along with their partial goals, when chronically gratified cease to exist as active determinants or organizers of behavior. They now exist only in a potential fashion in the sense that they may emerge again to dominate the organism if they are thwarted. But a want that is satisfied is no longer a want. The organism is dominated and its behavior organized only by unsatisfied needs. If hunger is satisfied, it becomes unimportant in the current dynamics of the individual.

This statement is somewhat qualified by a hypothesis to be discussed more fully later, namely that it is precisely those individuals in whom a certain need has always been satisfied who are best equipped to tolerate deprivation of that need in the future, and that furthermore, those who have been deprived in the past will react differently to current satisfactions than the one who has never been deprived.

*The Safety Needs.* If the physiological needs are relatively well gratified, there then emerges a new set of needs, which we may categorize roughly as the safety needs. All that has been said of the physiological needs is equally true, although in lesser degree, of these desires. The organism may equally well be wholly dominated by them. They may serve as the almost exclusive organizers of behavior, recruiting all the capacities of the organism in their service, and we may then fairly describe the whole organism as a safety-seeking mechanism. Again we may say of the receptors, the effectors, of the intellect and the other capacities that they are primarily safety-seeking tools. Again, as in the hungry man, we find that the dominating goal is a strong determinant not only of his current world-outlook and philosophy but also of his philosophy of the future. Practically everything looks less important than safety, (even sometimes the physiological needs, which, being satisfied, are now underestimated). A man, in this state, if it is extreme enough and chronic enough, may be characterized as living almost for safety alone.

Although in this paper we are interested primarily in the needs of the adult, we can approach an understanding of his safety needs perhaps more efficiently by observation of infants and children, in whom these needs are much more simple and obvious. One reason for the clearer appearance of the threat or danger reaction in infants, is that they do not inhibit this reaction at all, whereas adults in our society have been taught to inhibit it at all costs. Thus even when adults do feel their safety to be threatened we may not be able to see this on the surface. Infants will react in a total fashion and as if they were endangered, if they are disturbed or dropped suddenly, startled by loud noises, flashing light, or other unusual sensory stimulation, by rough handling, by general loss of support in the mother's arms, or by inadequate support.[1]

In infants we can also see a much more direct reaction to bodily illnesses of various kinds. Sometimes these illnesses seem to be immediately and *per se* threatening and seem to make the child feel unsafe. For instance, vomiting, colic or other sharp pains seem to make the child look at the whole world in a different way. At such a moment of pain, it may be postulated that, for the child, the appearance of the whole world suddenly changes from sunniness to darkness, so to speak, and becomes a place in which anything at all might happen, in which previously stable things have suddenly become unstable. Thus a child who because of some bad food is taken ill may, for a day or two, develop fear, nightmares, and a need for protection and reassurance never seen in him before his illness.

Another indication of the child's need for safety is his preference for some kind of undisrupted routine or rhythm. He seems to want a predictable, orderly world. For instance, injustice, unfairness, or inconsistency in the parents seems to make a child feel anxious and unsafe. This attitude may be not so much because of the injustice *per se* or any particular pains involved, but rather because this treatment threatens to make

[1]As the child grows up, sheer knowledge and familiarity as well as better motor development make these "dangers" less and less dangerous and more and more manageable. Throughout life it may be said that one of the main conative functions of education is this neutralizing of apparent dangers through knowledge, *e.g.*, I am not afraid of thunder because I know something about it.

the world look unreliable, or unsafe, or unpredictable. Young children seem to thrive better under a system which has at least a skeletal outline of rigidity, in which there is a schedule of a kind, some sort of routine, something that can be counted upon, not only for the present but also far into the future. Perhaps one could express this more accurately by saying that the child needs an organized world rather than an unorganized or unstructured one.

The central role of the parents and the normal family setup are indisputable. Quarreling, physical assault, separation, divorce or death within the family may be particularly terrifying. Also parental outbursts of rage or threats of punishment directed to the child, calling him names, speaking to him harshly, shaking him, handling him roughly, or actual physical punishment sometimes elicit such total panic and terror in the child that we must assume more is involved than the physical pain alone. While it is true that in some children this terror may represent also a fear of loss of parental love, it can also occur in completely rejected children, who seem to cling to the hating parents more for sheer safety and protection than because of hope of love.

Confronting the average child with new, unfamiliar, strange, unmanageable stimuli or situations will too frequently elicit the danger or terror reaction, as for example, getting lost or even being separated from the parents for a short time, being confronted with new faces, new situations or new tasks, the sight of strange, unfamiliar or uncontrollable objects, illness or death. Particularly at such times, the child's frantic clinging to his parents is eloquent testimony to their role as protectors (quite apart from their roles as food-givers and love-givers).

From these and similar observations, we may generalize and say that the average child in our society generally prefers a safe, orderly, predictable, organized world, which he can count on, and in which unexpected, unmanageable or other dangerous things do not happen, and in which, in any case, he has all-powerful parents who protect and shield him from harm.

That these reactions may so easily be observed in children is in a way a proof of the fact that children in our society feel too unsafe (or, in a word, are badly brought up). Children who are reared in an unthreatening, loving family do *not* ordinarily react as we have described above (17). In such children the danger reactions are apt to come mostly to objects or situations that adults too would consider dangerous.[2]

---

[2] A "test battery" for safety might be confronting the child with a small exploding firecracker, or with a bewhiskered face, having the mother leave the room, putting him upon a high ladder, a hypodermic injection, having a mouse crawl up to him, etc. Of course I cannot seriously recommend the deliberate use of such "tests" for they might very well harm the child being tested. But these and similar situations come up by the score in the child's ordinary day-to-day living and may be observed. There is no reason why these stimuli should not be used with, for example, young chimpanzees.

The healthy, normal, fortunate adult in our culture is largely satisfied in his safety needs. The peaceful, smoothly running, "good" society ordinarily makes its members feel safe enough from wild animals, extremes of temperature, criminals, assault and murder, tyranny, etc. Therefore, in a very real sense, he no longer has any safety needs as active motivators. Just as a sated man no longer feels hungry, a safe man no longer feels endangered. If we wish to see these needs directly and clearly we must turn to neurotic or near-neurotic individuals, and to the economic and social underdogs. In between these extremes, we can perceive the expressions of safety needs only in such phenomena as, for instance, the common preference for a job with tenure and protection, the desire for a savings account, and for insurance of various kinds (medical, dental, unemployment, disability, old age).

Other broader aspects of the attempt to seek safety and stability in the world are seen in the very common preference for familiar rather than unfamiliar things, or for the known rather than the unknown. The tendency to have some religion or world-philosophy that organizes the universe and the men in it into some sort of satisfactorily coherent, meaningful whole is also in part motivated by safety-seeking. Here too we may list science and philosophy in general as partially motivated by the safety needs (we shall see later that there are also other motivations to scientific, philosophical or religious endeavor).

Otherwise the need for safety is seen as an active and dominant mobilizer of the organism's resources only in emergencies, e.g., war, disease, natural catastrophes, crime waves, societal disorganization, neurosis, brain injury, chronically bad situation.

Some neurotic adults in our society are, in many ways, like the unsafe child in their desire for safety, although in the former it takes on a somewhat special appearance. Their reaction is often to unknown, psychological dangers in a world that is perceived to be hostile, overwhelming and threatening. Such a person behaves as if a great catastrophe were almost always impending, i.e., he is usually responding as if to an emergency. His safety needs often find specific expression in a search for a protector, or a stronger person on whom he may depend, or perhaps, a Fuehrer.

The neurotic individual may be described in a slightly different way with some usefulness as a grown-up person who retains his childish attitudes toward the world. That is to say, a neurotic adult may be said to behave "as if" he were actually afraid of a spanking, or of his mother's disapproval, or of being abandoned by his parents, or having his food taken away from him. It is as if his childish attitudes of fear and threat reaction to a dangerous world had gone underground, and untouched by the growing up and learning processes, were now ready to be called out by any stimulus that would make a child feel endangered and threatened.[3]

The neurosis in which the search for safety takes its clearest form is in the compulsive-obsessive neurosis. Compulsive-obsessives try frantically to order and stabilize the world so that no unmanageable, unexpected or unfamiliar dangers will ever appear (14). They hedge themselves about with all sorts of ceremonials, rules and formulas so that every possible contingency may be provided for and so that no new contingencies may appear. They are much like the brain injured cases, described by Goldstein (6), who manage to maintain their equilibrium by avoiding everything unfamiliar and strange and by ordering their restricted world in such a neat, disciplined, orderly fashion that everything in the world can be counted upon. They try to arrange the world so that anything unexpected (dangers) cannot possibly occur. If, through no fault of their own, something unexpected does occur, they go into a panic reaction as if this unexpected occurrence constituted a grave danger. What we can see only as a none-too-strong preference in the healthy person, *e.g.,* preference for the familiar, becomes a life-and-death necessity in abnormal cases.

*The Love Needs.* If both the physiological and the safety needs are fairly well gratified, then there will emerge the love and affection and belongingness needs, and the whole cycle already described will repeat itself with this new center. Now the person will feel keenly, as never before, the absence of friends, or a sweetheart, or a wife, or children. He will hunger for affectionate relations with people in general, namely, for a place in his group, and he will strive with great intensity to achieve this goal. He will want to attain such a place more than anything else in the world and may even forget that once, when he was hungry, he sneered at love.

In our society the thwarting of these needs is the most commonly found core in cases of maladjustment and more severe psychopathology. Love and affection, as well as their possible expression in sexuality, are generally looked upon with ambivalence and are customarily hedged about with many restrictions and inhibitions. Practically all theorists of psychopathology have stressed thwarting of the love needs as basic in the picture of maladjustment. Many clinical studies have therefore been made of this need and we know more about it perhaps than any of the other needs except the physiological ones (14).

One thing that must be stressed at this point is that love is not synonymous with sex. Sex may be studied as a purely physiological need.

[3]Not all neurotic individuals feel unsafe. Neurosis may have at its core a thwarting of the affection and esteem needs in a person who is generally safe.

Ordinarily sexual behavior is multi-determined, that is to say, determined not only by sexual but also by other needs, chief among which are the love and affection needs. Also not to be overlooked is the fact that the love needs involve both giving *and* receiving love.[4]

*The Esteem Needs.* All people in our society (with a few pathological exceptions) have a need or desire for a stable, firmly based, (usually) high evaluation of themselves, for self-respect, or self-esteem, and for the esteem of others. By firmly based self-esteem, we mean that which is soundly based upon real capacity, achievement and respect from others. These needs may be classified into two subsidiary sets. These are, first, the desire for strength, for achievement, for adequacy, for confidence in the face of the world, and for independence and freedom.[5] Secondly, we have what we may call the desire for reputation or prestige (defining it as respect or esteem from other people), recognition, attention, importance or appreciation.[6] These needs have been relatively stressed by Alfred Adler and his followers, and have been relatively neglected by Freud and the psychoanalysts. More and more today however there is appearing widespread appreciation of their central importance.

Satisfaction of the self-esteem need leads to feelings of self-confidence, worth, strength, capability and adequacy of being useful and necessary in the world. But thwarting of these needs produces feelings of inferiority, of weakness and of helplessness. These feelings in turn give rise to either basic discouragement or else compensatory or neurotic trends. An appreciation of the necessity of basic self-confidence and an understanding of how helpless people are without it, can be easily gained from a study of severe traumatic neurosis (8).[7]

*The Need for Self-Actualization.* Even if all these needs are satisfied, we may still often (if not always) expect that a new discontent and restlessness will soon develop, unless the individual is doing what he is fitted for. A musician must make music, an artist must paint, a poet must write, if he is to be ultimately happy. What a man *can* be, he *must* be. This need we may call self-actualization.

[4]For further details see (12) and (16, Chap. 5).

[5]Whether or not this particular desire is universal we do not know. The crucial question, especially important today, is "Will men who are enslaved and dominated inevitably feel dissatisfied and rebellious?" We may assume on the basis of commonly known clinical data that a man who has known true freedom (not paid for by giving up safety and security but rather built on the basis of adequate safety and security) will not willingly or easily allow his freedom to be taken away from him. But we do not know that this is true for the person born into slavery. The events of the next decade should give us our answer. See discussion of this problem in (5).

[6]Perhaps the desire for prestige and respect from others is subsidiary to the desire for self-esteem or confidence in oneself. Observation of children seems to indicate that this is so, but clinical data give no clear support for such a conclusion.

[7]For more extensive discussion of normal self-esteem, as well as for reports of various researches, see (11).

This term, first coined by Kurt Goldstein, is being used in this paper in a much more specific and limited fashion. It refers to the desire for self-fulfillment, namely, to the tendency for him to become actualized in what he is potentially. This tendency might be phrased as the desire to become more and more what one is, to become everything that one is capable of becoming.

The specific form that these needs will take will of course vary greatly from person to person. In one individual it may take the form of the desire to be an ideal mother, in another it may be expressed athletically, and in still another it may be expressed in painting pictures or in inventions. It is not necessarily a creative urge although in people who have any capacities for creation it will take this form.

The clear emergence of these needs rests upon prior satisfaction of the physiological, safety, love and esteem needs. We shall call people who are satisfied in these needs, basically satisfied people, and it is from these that we may expect the fullest (and healthiest) creativeness.[8] Since, in our society, basically satisfied people are the exception, we do not know much about self-actualization, either experimentally or clinically. It remains a challenging problem for research.

*The Preconditions for the Basic Need Satisfactions.* There are certain conditions which are immediate prerequisites for the basic need satisfactions. Danger to these is reacted to almost as if it were a direct danger to the basic needs themselves. Such conditions as freedom to speak, freedom to do what one wishes so long as no harm is done to others, freedom to express one's self, freedom to investigate and seek for information, freedom to defend one's self, justice, fairness, honesty, orderliness in the group are examples of such preconditions for basic need satisfactions. Thwarting in these freedoms will be reacted to with a threat or emergency response. These conditions are not ends in themselves but they are *almost* so since they are so closely related to the basic needs, which are apparently the only ends in themselves. These conditions are defended because without them the basic satisfactions are quite impossible, or at least, very severely endangered.

If we remember that the cognitive capacities (perceptual, intellectual, learning) are a set of adjustive tools, which have, among other functions, that of satisfaction of our basic needs, then it is clear that

---

[8]Clearly creative behavior, like painting, is like any other behavior in having multiple determinants. It may be in "innately creative" people whether they are satisfied or not, happy or unhappy, hungry or sated. Also it is clear that creative activity may be compensatory, ameliorative or purely economic. It is my impression (as yet unconfirmed) that it is possible to distinguish the artistic and intellectual products of basically satisfied people from those of basically unsatisfied people by inspection alone. In any case, here too we must distinguish, in a dynamic fashion, the overt behavior itself from its various motivations or purposes.

any danger to them, any deprivation or blocking of their free use, must also be indirectly threatening to the basic needs themselves. Such a statement is a partial solution of the general problems of curiosity, the search for knowledge, truth and wisdom, and the ever-persistent urge to solve the cosmic mysteries.

We must therefore introduce another hypothesis and speak of degrees of closeness to the basic needs, for we have already pointed out that *any* conscious desires (partial goals) are more or less important as they are more or less close to the basic needs. The same statement may be made for various behavior acts. An act is psychologically important if it contributes directly to satisfaction of basic needs. The less directly it so contributes, or the weaker this contribution is, the less important this act must be conceived to be from the point of view of dynamic psychology. A similar statement may be made for the various defense or coping mechanisms. Some are very directly related to the protection or attainment of the basic needs, others are only weakly and distantly related. Indeed if we wished, we could speak of more basic and less basic defense mechanisms, and then affirm that danger to the more basic defenses is more threatening than danger to less basic defenses (always remembering that this is so only because of their relationship to the basic needs).

*The Desires to Know and to Understand.* So far, we have mentioned the cognitive needs only in passing. Acquiring knowledge and systematizing the universe have been considered as, in part, techniques for the achievement of basic safety in the world, or, for the intelligent man, expressions of self-actualization. Also freedom in inquiry and expression have been discussed as preconditions of satisfactions of the basic needs. True though these formulations may be, they do not constitute definitive answers to the question as to the motivation role of curiosity, learning, philosophizing, experimenting, etc. They are, at best, no more than partial answers.

This question is especially difficult because we know so little about the facts. Curiosity, exploration, desire for the facts, desire to know may certainly be observed easily enough. The fact that they often are pursued even at great cost to the individual's safety testifies to the partial character of our previous discussion. In addition, the writer must admit that, though he has sufficient clinical evidence to postulate the desire to know as a very strong drive in intelligent people, no data are available for unintelligent people. It may then be largely a function of relatively high intelligence. Rather tentatively, then, and largely in the hope of stimulating discussion and research, we shall postulate a basic desire to know, to be aware of reality, to get the facts, to satisfy curiosity, or as Wertheimer phrases it, to see rather than to be blind.

This postulation, however, is not enough. Even after we know, we are impelled to know more and more minutely and microscopically on the one hand, and on the other, more and more extensively in the direction of a world philosophy, religion, etc. The facts that we acquire, if they are isolated or atomistic, inevitably get theorized about, and either analyzed or organized or both. This process has been phrased by some as the search for "meaning." We shall then postulate a desire to understand, to systematize, to organize, to analyze, to look for relations and meanings.

Once these desires are accepted for discussion, we see that they too form themselves into a small hierarchy in which the desire to know is prepotent over the desire to understand. All the characteristics of hierarchy of prepotency that we have described above, seem to hold for this one as well.

We must guard ourselves against the too easy tendency to separate these desires from the basic needs we have discussed above, *i.e.*, to make a sharp dichotomy between "cognitive" and "conative" needs. The desire to know and to understand are themselves conative, *i.e.*, have a striving character, and are as much personality needs as the "basic needs" we have already discussed (19).

### III. Further Characteristics of the Basic Needs

*The Degree of Fixity of the Hierarchy of Basic Needs.* We have spoken so far as if this hierarchy were a fixed order but actually it is not nearly as rigid as we may have implied. It is true that most of the people with whom we have worked have seemed to have these basic needs in about the order that has been indicated. However, there have been a number of exceptions.

(1) There are some people in whom, for instance, self-esteem seems to be more important than love. This most common reversal in the hierarchy is usually due to the development of the notion that the person who is most likely to be loved is a strong or powerful person, one who inspires respect or fear, and who is self confident or aggressive. Therefore such people who lack love and seek it, may try hard to put on a front of aggressive, confident behavior. But essentially they seek high self-esteem and its behavior expressions more as a means-to-an-end than for its own sake; they seek self-assertion for the sake of love rather than for self-esteem itself.

(2) There are other, apparently innately creative people in whom the drive to creativeness seems to be more important than any other counter-determinant. Their creativeness might appear not as self-

actualization released by basic satisfaction, but in spite of lack of basic satisfaction.

(3) In certain people the level of aspiration may be permanently deadened or lowered. That is to say, the less prepotent goals may simply be lost, and may disappear forever, so that the person who has experienced life at a very low level, *i.e.*, chronic unemployment, may continue to be satisfied for the rest of his life if only he can get enough food.

(4) The so-called "psychopathic personality" is another example of permanent loss of the love needs. These are people who, according to the best data available (9), have been starved for love in the earliest months of their lives and have simply lost forever the desire and the ability to give and to receive affection (as animals lose sucking or pecking reflexes that are not exercised soon enough after birth).

(5) Another cause of reversal of the hierarchy is that when a need has been satisfied for a long time, this need may be underevaluated. People who have never experienced chronic hunger are apt to underestimate its effects and to look upon food as a rather unimportant thing. If they are dominated by a higher need, this higher need will seem to be the most important of all. It then becomes possible, and indeed does actually happen, that they may, for the sake of this higher need, put themselves into the position of being deprived in a more basic need. We may expect that after a long-time deprivation of the more basic need there will be a tendency to reevaluate both needs so that the more prepotent need will actually become consciously prepotent for the individual who may have given it up very lightly. Thus, a man who has given up his job rather than lose his self-respect, and who then starves for six months or so, may be willing to take his job back even at the price of losing his self-respect.

(6) Another partial explanation of *apparent* reversals is seen in the fact that we have been talking about the hierarchy of prepotency in terms of consciously felt wants or desires rather than of behavior. Looking at behavior itself may give us the wrong impression. What we have claimed is that the person will *want* the more basic of two needs when deprived in both. There is no necessary implication here that he will act upon his desires. Let us say again that there are many determinants of behavior other than the needs and desires.

(7) Perhaps more important than all these exceptions are the ones that involve ideals, high social standards, high values and the like. With such values people become martyrs; they will give up everything for the sake of a particular ideal, or value. These people may be understood, at least in part, by reference to one basic concept (or hypothesis) which may be called "increased frustration-tolerance through early gratification." People who have been satisfied in their basic needs throughout their lives, particularly in their earlier years, seem to develop exceptional

power to withstand present or future thwarting of these needs simply because they have strong, healthy character structure as a result of basic satisfaction. They are the "strong" people who can easily weather disagreement or opposition, who can swim against the stream of public opinion and who can stand up for the truth at great personal cost. It is just the ones who have loved and been well loved, and who have had many deep friendships who can hold out against hatred, rejection or persecution.

I say all this in spite of the fact that there is a certain amount of sheer habituation which is also involved in any full discussion of frustration tolerance. For instance, it is likely that those persons who have been accustomed to relative starvation for a long time, are partially enabled thereby to withstand food deprivation. What sort of balance must be made between these two tendencies, of habituation on the one hand, and of past satisfaction breeding present frustration tolerance on the other hand, remains to be worked out by further research. Meanwhile we may assume that they are both operative, side by side, since they do not contradict each other. In respect to this phenomenon of increased frustration tolerance, it seems probable that the most important gratifications come in the first two years of life. That is to say, people who have been made secure and strong in the earliest years, tend to remain secure and strong thereafter in the face of whatever threatens.

*Degrees of Relative Satisfaction.* So far, our theoretical discussion may have given the impression that these five sets of needs are somehow in a step-wise, all-or-none relationship to each other. We have spoken in such terms as the following: "If one need is satisfied, then another emerges." This statement might give the false impression that a need must be satisfied 100 per cent before the next need emerges. In actual fact, most members of our society who are normal, are partially satisfied in all their basic needs and partially unsatisfied in all their basic needs at the same time. A more realistic description of the hierarchy would be in terms of decreasing percentages of satisfaction as we go up the hierarchy of prepotency. For instance, if I may assign arbitrary figures for the sake of illustration, it is as if the average citizen is satisfied perhaps 85 per cent in his physiological needs, 70 per cent in his safety needs, 50 per cent in his love needs, 40 per cent in his self-esteem needs, and 10 per cent in his self-actualization needs.

As for the concept of emergence of a new need after satisfaction of the prepotent need, this emergence is not a sudden, saltatory phenomenon but rather a gradual emergence by slow degrees from nothingness. For instance, if prepotent need A is satisfied only 10 per cent then need B may not be visible at all. However, as this need A becomes satisfied 25 per cent, need B may emerge 5 per cent, as need A becomes satisfied 75 per cent need B may emerge 90 per cent, and so on.

*Unconscious Character of Needs.*   These needs are neither necessarily conscious nor unconscious. On the whole, however, in the average person, they are more often unconscious rather than conscious. It is not necessary at this point to overhaul the tremendous mass of evidence which indicates the crucial importance of unconscious motivation. It would by now be expected, on a priori grounds alone, that unconscious motivations would on the whole be rather more important than the conscious motivations. What we have called the basic needs are very often largely unconscious although they may, with suitable techniques, and with sophisticated people become conscious.

*Cultural Specificity and Generality of Needs.*   This classification of basic needs makes some attempt to take account of the relative unity behind the superficial differences in specific desires from one culture to another. Certainly in any particular culture an individual's conscious motivational content will usually be extremely different from the conscious motivational content of an individual in another society. However, it is the common experience of anthropologists that people, even in different societies, are much more alike than we would think from our first contact with them, and that as we know them better we seem to find more and more of this commonness. We then recognize the most startling differences to be superficial rather than basic, *e.g.,* differences in style of hairdress, clothes, tastes in food, etc. Our classification of basic needs is in part an attempt to account for this unity behind the apparent diversity from culture to culture. No claim is made that it is ultimate or universal for all cultures. The claim is made only that it is relatively *more* ultimate, more universal, more basic, than the superficial conscious desires from culture to culture, and makes a somewhat closer approach to common-human characteristics. Basic needs are *more* common-human than superficial desires or behaviors.

*Multiple Motivations of Behavior.*   These needs must be understood *not* to be *exclusive* or single determiners of certain kinds of behavior. An example may be found in any behavior that seems to be physiologically motivated, such as eating, or sexual play or the like. The clinical psychologists have long since found that any behavior may be a channel through which flow various determinants. Or to say it in another way, most behavior is multi-motivated. Within the sphere of motivational determinants any behavior tends to be determined by several or *all* of the basic needs simultaneously rather than by only one of them. The latter would be more an exception than the former. Eating may be partially for the sake of filling the stomach, and partially for the sake of comfort and amelioration of other needs. One may make love not only for pure sexual release, but also to convince one's self of one's masculinity, or to make a conquest, to feel powerful, or to win more basic affection.

As an illustration, I may point out that it would be possible (theoretically if not practically) to analyze a single act of an individual and see in it the expression of his physiological needs, his safety needs, his love needs, his esteem needs and self-actualization. This contrasts sharply with the more naive brand of trait psychology in which one trait or one motive accounts for a certain kind of act, *i.e.*, an aggressive act is traced solely to a trait of aggressiveness.

*Multiple Determinants of Behavior.* Not all behavior is determined by the basic needs. We might even say that not all behavior is motivated. There are many determinants of behavior other than motives.[9] For instance, one other important class of determinants is the so-called "field" determinants. Theoretically, at least, behavior may be determined completely by the field, or even by specific isolated external stimuli, as in association of ideas, or certain conditioned reflexes. If in response to the stimulus word "table," I immediately perceive a memory image of a table, this response certainly has nothing to do with my basic needs.

Secondly, we may call attention again to the concept of "degree of closeness to the basic needs" or "degree of motivation." Some behavior is highly motivated, other behavior is only weakly motivated. Some is not motivated at all (but all behavior is determined).

Another important point[10] is that there is a basic difference between expressive behavior and coping behavior (functional striving, purposive goal seeking). An expressive behavior does not try to do anything; it is simply a reflection of the personality. A stupid man behaves stupidly, not because he wants to, or tries to, or is motivated to, but simply because he *is* what he is. The same is true when I speak in a bass voice rather than tenor or soprano. The random movements of a healthy child, the smile on the face of a happy man even when he is alone, the springiness of the healthy man's walk, and the erectness of his carriage are other examples of expressive, non-functional behavior. Also the *style* in which a man carries out almost all his behavior, motivated as well as unmotivated, is often expressive.

We may then ask, is all behavior expressive or reflective of the character structure? The answer is "No." Rote, habitual, automatized, or conventional behavior may or may not be expressive. The same is true for most "stimulus-bound" behaviors.

It is finally necessary to stress that expressiveness of behavior, and goal-directedness of behavior are not mutually exclusive categories. Average behavior is usually both.

---

[9] I am aware that many psychologists and psychoanalysts use the term "motivated" and "determined" synonymously, *e.g.*, Freud. But I consider this an obfuscating usage. Sharp distinctions are necessary for clarity of thought, and precision in experimentation.

[10] To be discussed fully in a subsequent publication.

*Goals as Centering Principle in Motivation Theory.* It will be observed that the basic principle in our classification has been neither the instigation nor the motivated behavior but rather the functions, effects, purposes, or goals of the behavior. It has been proven sufficiently by various people that this is the most suitable point for centering in any motivation theory.[11]

*Animal- and Human-Centering.* This theory starts with the human being rather than any lower and presumably "simpler" animal. Too many of the findings that have been made in animals have been proven to be true for animals but not for the human being. There is no reason whatsoever why we should start with animals in order to study human motivation. The logic or rather illogic behind this general fallacy of "pseudo-simplicity" has been exposed often enough by philosophers and logicians as well as by scientists in each of the various fields. It is no more necessary to study animals before one can study man than it is to study mathematics before one can study geology or psychology or biology.

We may also reject the old, naive, behaviorism which assumed that it was somehow necessary, or at least more "scientific" to judge human beings by animal standards. One consequence of this belief was that the whole notion of purpose and goal was excluded from motivational psychology simply because one could not ask a white rat about his purposes. Tolman (18) has long since proven in animal studies themselves that this exclusion was not necessary.

*Motivation and the Theory of Psychopathogenesis.* The conscious motivational content of everyday life has, according to the foregoing, been conceived to be relatively important or unimportant accordingly as it is more or less closely related to the basic goals. A desire for an ice cream cone might actually be an indirect expression of a desire for love. If it is, then this desire for the ice cream cone becomes extremely important motivation. If however the ice cream is simply something to cool the mouth with, or a casual appetitive reaction, then the desire is relatively unimportant. Everyday conscious desires are to be regarded as symptoms, as *surface indicators of more basic needs.* If we were to take these superficial desires at their face value we would find ourselves in a state of complete confusion which could never be resolved, since we would be dealing seriously with symptoms rather than with what lay behind the symptoms.

Thwarting of unimportant desires produces no psychopathological results; thwarting of a basically important need does produce such results. Any theory of psychopathogenesis must then be based on a sound theory of motivation. A conflict or a frustration is not necessarily

[11]The interested reader is referred to the very excellent discussion of this point in Murray's *Explorations in Personality* (15).

pathogenic. It becomes so only when it threatens or thwarts the basic needs, or partial needs that are closely related to the basic needs (10).

*The Role of Gratified Needs.* It has been pointed out above several times that our needs usually emerge only when more prepotent needs have been gratified. Thus gratification has an important role in motivation theory. Apart from this, however, needs cease to play an active determining or organizing role as soon as they are gratified.

What this means is that, *e.g.*, a basically satisfied person no longer has the needs for esteem, love, safety, etc. The only sense in which he might be said to have them is in the almost metaphysical sense that a sated man has hunger, or a filled bottle has emptiness. If we are interested in what *actually* motivates us, and not in what has, will, or might motivate us, then a satisfied need is not a motivator. It must be considered for all practical purposes simply not to exist, to have disappeared. This point should be emphasized because it has been either overlooked or contradicted in every theory of motivation I know.[12] The perfectly healthy, normal, fortunate man has no sex needs or hunger needs, or needs for safety, or for love, or for prestige, or self-esteem, except in stray moments of quickly passing threat. If we were to say otherwise, we should also have to aver that every man had all the pathological reflexes, *e.g.*, Babinski, etc., because if his nervous system were damaged, these would appear.

It is such considerations as these that suggest the bold postulation that a man who is thwarted in any of his basic needs may fairly be envisaged simply as a sick man. This is a fair parallel to our designation as "sick" of the man who lacks vitamins or minerals. Who is to say that a lack of love is less important than a lack of vitamins? Since we know the pathogenic effects of love starvation, who is to say that we are invoking value-questions in an unscientific or illegitimate way, any more than the physician does who diagnoses and treats pellagra or scurvy? If I were permitted this usage, I should then say simply that a healthy man is primarily motivated by his needs to develop and actualize his fullest potentialities and capacities. If a man has any other basic needs in any active, chronic sense, then he is simply an unhealthy man. He is as surely sick as if he had suddenly developed a strong salt-hunger or calcium hunger.[13]

[12]Note that acceptance of this theory necessitates basic revision of the Freudian theory.

[13]If we were to use the word "sick" in this way, we should then also have to face squarely the relations of man to his society. One clear implication of our definition would be that (1) since a man is to be called sick who is basically thwarted, and (2) since such basic thwarting is made possible ultimately only by forces outside the individual, then (3) sickness in the individual must come ultimately from a sickness in the society. The "good" or healthy society would then be defined as one that permitted man's highest purposes to emerge by satisfying all his prepotent basic needs.

If this statement seems unusual or paradoxical the reader may be assured that this is only one among many such paradoxes that will appear as we revise our ways of looking at man's deeper motivations. When we ask what man wants of life, we deal with his very essence.

## IV. Summary

(1) There are at least five sets of goals, which we may call basic needs. These are briefly physiological, safety, love, esteem, and self-actualization. In addition, we are motivated by the desire to achieve or maintain the various conditions upon which these basic satisfactions rest and by certain more intellectual desires.

(2) These basic goals are related to each other, being arranged in a hierarchy of prepotency. This means that the most prepotent goal will monopolize consciousness and will tend of itself to organize the recruitment of the various capacities of the organism. The less prepotent needs are minimized, even forgotten or denied. But when a need is fairly well satisfied, the next prepotent ("higher") need emerges, in turn to dominate the conscious life and to serve as the center of organization of behavior, since gratified needs are not active motivators.

Thus man is a perpetually wanting animal. Ordinarily the satisfaction of these wants is not altogether mutually exclusive, but only tends to be. The average member of our society is most often partially satisfied and partially unsatisfied in all of his wants. The hierarchy principle is usually empirically observed in terms of increasing percentages of non-satisfaction as we go up the hierarchy. Reversals of the average order of the hierarchy are sometimes observed. Also it has been observed that an individual may permanently lose the higher wants in the hierarchy under special conditions. There are not only ordinarily multiple motivations for usual behavior, but in addition many determinants other than motives.

(3) Any thwarting or possibility of thwarting of these basic human goals, or danger to the defenses which protect them, or to the conditions upon which they rest, is considered to be a psychological threat. With a few exceptions, all psychopathology may be partially traced to such threats. A basically thwarted man may actually be defined as a "sick" man, if we wish.

(4) It is such basic threats which bring about the general emergency reactions.

(5) Certain other basic problems have not been dealt with because of limitations of space. Among these are (a) the problem of values in any definitive motivation theory, (b) the relation between appetites,

desires, needs and what is "good" for the organism, (c) the etiology of the basic needs and their possible derivation in early childhood, (d) redefinition of motivational concepts, i.e., drive, desire, wish, need, goal, (e) implication of our theory for hedonistic theory, (f) the nature of the uncompleted act, of success and failure, and of aspiration-level, (g) the role of association, habit and conditioning, (h) relation to the theory of inter-personal relations, (i) implications for psychotherapy, (j) implications for theory of society, (k) the theory of selfishness, (l) the relation between needs and cultural patterns, (m) the relation between this theory and Allport's theory of functional autonomy. These as well as certain other less important questions must be considered as motivation theory attempts to become definitive.

### References

1. Adler, A. *Social interest.* London: Faber & Faber, 1938.
2. Cannon, W. B. *Wisdom of the body.* New York: Norton, 1932.
3. Freud, A. *The ego and the mechanisms of defense.* London: Hogarth, 1937.
4. Freud, S. *New introductory lectures on psychoanalysis.* New York: Norton, 1933.
5. Fromm, E. *Escape from freedom.* New York: Farrar and Rinehart, 1941.
6. Goldstein, K. *The organism.* New York: American Book Co., 1939.
7. Horney, K. *The neurotic personality of our time.* New York: Norton, 1937.
8. Kardiner, A. *The traumatic neuroses of war.* New York: Hoeber, 1941.
9. Levy, D. M. Primary affect hunger. *Amer. J. Psychiat.*, 1937, **94**, 643–652.
10. Maslow, A. H. Conflict, frustration, and the theory of threat. *J. abnorm. (soc.) Psychol.*, 1943, **38**, 81–86.
11. ———. Dominance, personality and social behavior in women. *J. soc. Psychol.*, 1939, **10**, 3–39.
12. ———. The dynamics of psychological security-insecurity. *Character & Pers.*, 1942, **10**, 331–344.
13. ———. A preface to motivation theory. *Psychosomatic Med.*, 1943, **5**, 85–92.
14. ———, & Mittelmann, B. *Principles of abnormal psychology.* New York: Harper & Bros., 1941.
15. Murray, H. A., *et al. Explorations in personality.* New York: Oxford University Press, 1938.
16. Plant, J. *Personality and the cultural pattern.* New York: Commonwealth Fund, 1937.
17. Shirley, M. Children's adjustments to a strange situation. *J. abnorm. (soc.) Psychol.*, 1942, **37**, 201–217.
18. Tolman, E. C. *Purposive behavior in animals and men.* New York: Century, 1932.
19. Wertheimer, M. Unpublished lectures at the New School for Social Research.
20. Young, P. T. *Motivation of behavior.* New York: John Wiley & Sons, 1936.
21. ———. The experimental analysis of appetite. *Psychol. Bull.*, 1941, **38**, 129–164.

*Editor's Introduction
to Paper 8*

This final paper, which first appeared in 1950 as part of a published symposium on human values, marks the culmination of the development that we have been following. It seeks to make three quite distinct points: (1) that there are real, observable, flesh-and-blood persons in the world who can be described as "self-actualizing"; (2) that these self-actualizing persons are the most psychologically healthy specimens of humanity to be found; and (3) that it is they who best reveal what human nature truly is. Beyond this, the paper needs no commentary—it speaks for itself.

# 8

# Self-Actualizing People:
# A Study of
# Psychological Health

*A. H. Maslow*

## Personal Foreword

The study to be reported here is unusual in various ways. It was not planned as an ordinary research; it was not a social venture but a private one, motivated by my own curiosity and pointed toward the solution of various personal, moral, ethical, and scientific problems. I sought only to convince and to teach myself (as is quite proper in a personal quest) rather than to prove or to demonstrate to others. For this reason, it has no "design."

Quite unexpectedly, however, these studies have proved to be so enlightening, and even startling, to me (and to a few others), that it seems fair that some sort of report should be made to others in spite of this and other shortcomings.

At first I had thought that I could present the lessons I had learned, without reference to their technically questionable source, simply by a series of discrete and independent "theoretical" papers. Some of these have appeared, [23] [26] and more will in the future. But even these papers suggested that it would be more honest to indicate the "data" from which they sprang, for, in actuality, I considered them empirical reports rather than theoretical constructions.

Finally, I consider the problem of psychological health to be so pressing that *any* leads, *any* bits of data, however moot, are endowed with a certain temporary value. This kind of research is in principle so

From *Personality Symposia:* Symposium #1 on Values, 1950, pp. 11–34. Reprinted by permission of Grune & Stratton, Inc.

difficult—involving as it does a kind of lifting oneself by one's axiological bootstraps—that, if we were to wait for conventionally reliable data, we should have to wait forever. It seems that the only manly thing to do is not to fear mistakes, to plunge in, to do the best that one can, hoping to learn enough from blunders to correct them eventually. At present the only alternative is simply to refuse to work with the problem. Accordingly, for whatever use can be made of it, the following report is presented with due apologies to those who insist upon conventional reliability, validity, sampling, etc.

## Subjects and Methods

The subjects were selected from among personal acquaintances and friends, and from among public and historical figures. In addition, three thousand college students were screened, but yielded only one immediately usable subject and a dozen or so possible future subjects. It was hoped that figures created by novelists or dramatists could be used for demonstration purposes, but none were found that were usable in our culture and our time (in itself a thought-provoking finding).

The "first clinical definition," on the basis of which subjects were finally chosen or rejected, had a positive as well as a merely negative side. The negative criterion was an absence of neurosis, psychopathic personality, psychosis, or strong tendencies in these directions. Possible psychosomatic illness called forth closer scrutiny and screening. Wherever possible, Rorschach tests were given, but turned out to be far more useful in revealing concealed psychopathology than in selecting healthy people. The positive criterion for selection was positive evidence of self-actualization (SA), as yet a difficult syndrome to describe accurately. For the purposes of this discussion, it may be loosely described as the full use and exploitation of talents, capacities, potentialities, etc. Such people seem to be fulfilling themselves and to be doing the best that they are capable of doing. They are people who have developed or are developing to the full stature of which they are capable.[11][21][24][25][26]

This connotes also either gratification past or present of the basic emotional needs for safety, belongingness, love, respect, and self-respect and of the cognitive needs for knowledge and for understanding or, in a few cases, "conquest" of these needs. This is to say that all subjects felt safe and unanxious, accepted, loved and loving, respectworthy and respected, and that they had worked out their philosophical, religious, or axiological bearings. It is still an open question as to whether this "basic gratification" is a sufficient or only a prerequisite condition of self-actualization. It may be that self-actualization means basic gratification plus at least minimum talent, capacity, or "richness."

In general, the technique of selection used was that of *iteration*, previously used in studies of the personality syndromes of self-esteem and of security.[22] This consists briefly in starting with the personal or cultural nontechnical state of belief, collating the various extant usages and definitions of the syndrome, and then defining it more carefully, still in terms of actual usage (what might be called the "lexicographical stage") with, however, the elimination of the logical and factual inconsistencies customarily found in folk definitions.

On the basis of the "corrected folk definition," the first groups of subjects are selected, a group who are high in the quality and a group who are low in it. These people are studied as carefully as possible in the clinical style, and, on the basis of this empirical study, the original "corrected folk definition" is further changed and corrected as required by the data now in hand. This gives the "first clinical definition." On the basis of this new definition, the original group of subjects is reselected, some being retained, some being dropped, and some new ones being added. This second-level group of subjects is then, in its turn, clinically and, if possible, experimentally and statistically, studied, which, in turn, causes modification, correction, and enrichment of the first clinical definition, with which, in turn, a new group of subjects is selected, and so on. In this way an originally vague and unscientific folk concept can become more and more exact, more and more operational in character, and therefore more scientific.

Of course, external, theoretical, and practical considerations may intrude into this spiral-like process of self-correction. For instance, early in this study, it was found that folk usage was so unrealistically demanding that no living human being could possibly fit the definition. We had to stop excluding a possible subject on the basis of single foibles, mistakes, or foolishness; or, to put it in another way, we could not use perfection as a basis for selection, since no subject was perfect.

Another such problem was presented by the fact that in all cases it was impossible to get full and satisfactory information of the kind usually demanded in clinical work. Possible subjects, when informed of the purpose of the research, became self-conscious, froze up, laughed off the whole effort, or broke off the relationship. As a result, since this early experience, all subjects have been studied indirectly—indeed, almost surreptitiously.

Since living people were studied, whose names could not be divulged, two desiderata or even requirements of ordinary scientific work became impossible to achieve: namely, repeatability of the investigation and public availability of the data upon which conclusions were made.

These difficulties are partly overcome by the inclusion of public and historical figures, and by the supplementary study of young people and children who could conceivably be used publicly.

The subjects have been divided into the following categories:

*Cases:*

3 fairly sure and 1 probable contemporaries

2 fairly sure historical figures (Lincoln in his last years and Thomas Jefferson)

6 highly probable public and historical figures (Einstein, Eleanor Roosevelt, Jane Addams, William James, and Spinoza)

*Partial Cases:*

5 contemporaries who fairly certainly fall short somewhat but who can yet be used for study

5 historical figures who probably or certainly fall short but who can yet be used for study: Walt Whitman, Henry Thoreau, Beethoven, F. D. Roosevelt, Freud

*Potential or Possible Cases:*

16 younger people who seem to be developing in the direction of self-actualization, and G. W. Carver, Eugene V. Debs, Albert Schweitzer, Thomas Eakins, Fritz Kreisler, Goethe

## Gathering and Presentation of the Data

"Data" here consist not so much of the usual gathering of specific and discrete facts as in the slow development of a global or holistic impression of the sort that we form of our friends and acquaintances. It was rarely possible to "set up" a situation, to ask pointed questions, or to do any testing with my older subjects (although this *was* possible and was done with younger subjects). Contacts were fortuitous and of the ordinary social sort. Friends and relations were questioned where this was possible.

Because of this and also because of the small number of subjects, as well as the incompleteness of the data for many subjects, any quantitative presentation is impossible; only composite "impressions" can be offered for whatever they may be worth (and of course they are worth much less than controlled objective observation, since the investigator is never quite certain about what is description and what is projection).

The holistic analysis of these total impressions yields, as the most important and useful whole-characteristics of self-actualizing people, for further clinical and experimental study, the following:

*1. More Efficient Perception of Reality and*
*More Comfortable Relations with It*

The first form in which this capacity was noticed was as an unusual ability to detect the spurious, the fake, and the dishonest in personality, and, in general, to judge people correctly and efficiently. In an informal check experiment with a group of college students, a clear tendency was discerned for the more secure (the more healthy) to judge their professors more accurately than did the less secure students.

As the study progressed, it slowly became apparent that this efficiency extended to many other areas of life—indeed, *all* areas that were tested. In art and music, in things of the intellect, in scientific matters, in politics and public affairs, they seemed as a group to be able to see concealed or confused realities more swiftly and more correctly than others. Thus, an informal experiment indicated that their predictions of the future from whatever facts were in hand at the time seemed to be more often correct because less based upon wish, desire, anxiety, fear, or upon generalized, character-determined optimism or pessimism.

At first this was phrased as good taste or good judgment, the implication being relative and not absolute. But for many reasons (some to be detailed below), it has become progressively more clear that this had better be called perception (not taste) of something that was absolutely "there" (reality, not a set of opinions).[29][31] It is hoped that this conclusion—or hypothesis—can soon be put to the experimental test.

If this is so, thus it would be impossible to overstress the importance of the implications of this phenomenon. Recently Money-Kyrle,[27] an English psychoanalyst, has indicated that he believes it possible to call a neurotic person not only *relatively* but *absolutely* inefficient, simply because he does not perceive the real world as accurately or as efficiently as does the healthy person. The neurotic is not only emotionally sick—he is cognitively *wrong!* If health and neurosis are, respectively, correct and incorrect perceptions of reality, propositions of fact and propositions of value merge in this area, and, in principle, value-propositions should then be empirically demonstrable rather than merely matters of taste or exhortation. For those who have wrestled with this problem, it will be clear that we may have here a partial basis for a true science of values, and consequently of ethics, social relations, politics, religion, etc.

It is doubtful that maladjustment or even extreme neurosis would disturb perception enough to affect acuity of perception of light, or touch, or odor. But it is probable that this effect can be demonstrated in spheres of perception removed from the merely physiological, e.g., *Einstellung* experiments,[34] etc. It should also follow that the effects of wish, desire, prejudice upon perception, as in many recent experiments, should be very much less in healthy people than in sick. A priori considerations encourage the hypothesis that this superiority in the perception of reality eventuates in a superior ability to reason, to perceive the truth, to come to conclusions, to be logical, and to be cognitively efficient in general.[17][35]

One particularly impressive and instructive aspect of this better relationship with reality has been described in another place.[23] It was found that self-actualizing people distinguished far more easily than most the fresh, concrete, and idiosyncratic from the generic, abstract, and "rubricized." The consequence is that they live more in the "real" world of nature than in the man-made set of concepts, expectations, beliefs, and stereotypes which most people confuse with the world. They are therefore far more apt to perceive what is "there" rather than their own wishes, hopes, fears, anxieties, their own theories and beliefs, or those of their cultural group.

The relationship with the unknown seems to be of exceptional promise as another bridge between academic and clinical psychology. Our healthy subjects are uniformly unthreatened and unfrightened by the unknown, being therein quite different from average men. They accept it, are comfortable with it, and often are even *more* attracted by it than by the known. To use Frenkel-Brunswik's phrase, they can tolerate the ambiguous.[7]

These latter, it is true, are the intellectuals, the researchers, and the scientists, so that perhaps the major determinant here is intellectual power. And yet we all know how many scientists with high I.Q., through timidity, conventionality, anxiety, or other character defects, occupy themselves exclusively with what is known, with polishing it, arranging and rearranging it, classifying it, and otherwise puttering with it instead of discovering, as they are supposed to do.[5][30][31]

Since, for healthy people, the unknown is not frightening, they do not have to spend any time laying the ghost, whistling past the cemetery, or otherwise protecting themselves against imagined dangers. They do not neglect the unknown, or deny it, or run away from it, or try to make believe it is really known; nor do they organize, dichotomize, or rubricize it prematurely. They do not cling to the familiar (nor is their quest for truth a catastrophic need for certainty, safety, definiteness, and order, such as we see in an exaggerated form in Goldstein's brain-injured[11] or in the compulsive-obsessive neurotic). They can be, when the objective total situation calls for it, comfortably disorderly, anarchic, chaotic, vague, doubtful, uncertain, indefinite, approximate, inexact, or inaccurate (all at certain moments in science, art, or life in general, quite desirable).

Thus it comes about that doubt, tentativeness, uncertainty with the consequent necessity for abeyance of decision, which is for most a torture, can be for some a pleasantly stimulating challenge, a high spot in life rather than a low.

*2. Acceptance (Self, Others, Nature)*

A good many personal qualities, which can be perceived on the surface and which seem at first to be various and unconnected, may be understood as manifestations or derivatives of a more fundamental single attitude, namely, of a relative lack of overriding guilt, of crippling shame, and of extreme or severe anxiety. This is in direct contrast with the neurotic person, who in every instance may be described as crippled by guilt and/or shame and/or anxiety. Even the normal member of our culture feels unnecessarily guilty or ashamed about too many things and has anxieties in too many unnecessary situations. Our healthy individuals find it possible to accept themselves and their own nature without chagrin or complaint or, for that matter, even without thinking about the matter very much.

They can accept their own human nature with all its shortcomings, with all its discrepancies from the ideal image, without feeling real concern. It would convey the wrong impression to say that they are self-satisfied. What we must say rather is that they can take the frailties and sins, weaknesses and evils of human nature in the same unquestioning spirit that one takes or accepts the characteristics of nature. One does not complain about water because it is wet, or about rocks because they are hard, or about trees because they are green. As the child looks out upon the world with wide, uncritical, innocent eyes, simply noting and observing what is the case, without either arguing the matter or demanding that it be otherwise, so does the self-actualizing person look upon human nature in himself and in others. This is of course not the same as resignation in the Eastern sense, but resignation too can be observed in our subjects especially in the face of illness and death.

Be it observed that this amounts to saying in another form what we have already described; namely, that the self-actualized person sees reality more clearly: our subjects see human nature as it *is* and not as they would prefer it to be. Their eyes see what is before them without being strained through spectacles of various sorts to distort or shape or color the reality.[5] [23]

The first and most obvious level of acceptance is the so-called animal level. These self-actualizing people tend to be good and lusty animals, hearty in their appetites and enjoying themselves mightily without regret or shame or apology. They seem to have a uniformly good appetite for food; they seem to sleep well; they seem to enjoy their sexual lives without unnecessary inhibition, and so on for all the relatively physiological impulses. They are able to "accept" themselves not only on these low levels, but at all levels as well; e.g., love, safety, belongingness, honor, self-respect. All of these are accepted without question as worthwhile simply because they are part of human nature and because these people are inclined to accept the work of nature rather than to argue with her for not having constructed things to a different pattern. This shows itself in a relative lack of the disgusts and aversions seen in average people, and especially in neurotics, e.g., food annoyances, disgust with body products, body odors, and body functions.

Closely related to self-acceptance and to acceptance of others is (a) their lack of defensiveness, protective coloration, or pose, and (b) their distaste for such artificialities in others. Cant, guile, hypocrisy, "front," "face," playing a game, trying to impress in conventional ways—these are all absent in themselves to an unusual degree. Since they can live comfortably even with their own shortcomings, these finally come to be perceived, especially in later life, as not shortcomings at all, but simply as neutral personal characteristics.

This is not an absolute lack of guilt, shame, sadness, anxiety, defensiveness; it is a lack of unnecessary (because unrealistic) guilt, etc. The animal processes, e.g., sex, urination, pregnancy, menstruation, growing old, etc., are part of reality and so must be accepted. Thus, no healthy woman feels guilty or defensive about being female or about any of the female processes.

What healthy people *do* feel guilty about (or ashamed, anxious, sad, or defensive) are (a) improvable shortcomings, e.g., laziness, thoughtlessness, loss of temper, hurting others; (b) stubborn remnants of psychological ill health, e.g., prejudice, jealousy, envy; (c) habits, which, though relatively independent of character structure, may yet be very strong; or (d) shortcomings of the species or of the culture or of the group with which they have identified. The general formula seems to be that healthy people will feel bad about discrepancies between what is and what might very well be or ought to be.[1] [10] [12]

### 3. Spontaneity

Self-actualizing people can all be described as relatively spontaneous in behavior and far more spontaneous than that in their inner life, thoughts, impulses, etc. Their behavior is marked by simplicity and naturalness, and by lack of artificiality or straining for effect. This does not necessarily mean consistently unconventional behavior. If we were to take an actual count of the number of times that the self-actualizing person behaved in an unconventional manner, the tally would not be high. His unconventionality is not superficial but essential or internal. It is his impulses, thought, consciousness that are so unusually unconventional, spontaneous, and natural. Apparently recognizing that the world of people in which he lives could not understand or accept this, and since he has no wish to hurt them or to fight with them over every triviality, he will go through the ceremonies and rituals of convention with a good-humored shrug and with the best possible grace. Thus I have seen a man accept an "honor" he laughed at and even despised in private, rather than make an issue of it and hurt the people who thought they were pleasing him.

That this "conventionality" is a cloak which rests very lightly upon his shoulders and is easily cast aside can be seen from the fact that the self-actualizing person practically never allows convention to hamper him or inhibit him from doing anything that he considers very important or basic. It is at such moments that his essential lack of conventionality appears and not as with the average Bohemian or authority-rebel who makes great issues of trivial things and who will fight against some unimportant regulation as if it were a world issue.

This same inner attitude can also be seen in those moments when the person becomes keenly absorbed in something that is close to one of his main interests. He can then be seen quite casually to drop off all sorts of rules of behavior to which at other times he conforms, as if he were conventional voluntarily and by design.

Finally this external habit of behavior can be voluntarily dropped when in the company of people who do not demand or expect routine behavior. That this relative control of behavior is felt as something of a burden is seen by our subjects' preference for such company as allows them to be more free, natural, and spontaneous and which relieves them of what they find sometimes to be effortful conduct.

One consequence or correlate of this characteristic is that these people have codes of ethics which are relatively autonomous and individual rather than conventional. The unthinking observer might sometimes believe them to be "unethical," since they can break not only conventions but laws when the situation seems to demand it. But the very opposite is the case. They are the most ethical of people, even though their ethics are not necessarily the same as those of the people around them. It is this kind of observation which leads us to understand very assuredly that the ordinary "ethical" behavior of the average person is largely conventional behavior rather than truly ethical behavior, i.e., behavior based on fundamentally accepted principles.

Because of this alienation from ordinary conventions, and from the ordinarily accepted hypocrisies, lies, and inconsistencies of social life, they sometimes feel like spies, or aliens in a foreign land, and sometimes *behave* so.

I should not give the impression that they try to hide what they are like. Sometimes they let themselves go deliberately, out of momentary irritation with customary rigidity or with conventional blindness. They may, for instance, be trying to teach someone, or they may be trying to protect someone from hurt or injustice, or they may sometimes find emotions bubbling up from within them which are so pleasant or even ecstatic that it seems almost sacrilegious to suppress them. In such instances I have observed that they are not anxious or guilty or ashamed of the impression that they make on the onlooker. It is their claim that they usually behave in a conventional fashion simply because no great issues are involved or because they know people will be hurt or embarrassed by any other kind of behavior.

Their ease of penetration to reality, their closer approach to an animal-like or child-like acceptance and spontaneity imply a superior awareness of their own impulses, desires, opinions, and subjective reactions in general.[9] [27] [30] [31] Clinical study of this capacity confirms beyond a doubt the opinion, e.g., of Fromm,[9] [10] that the average "normal," "well-adjusted" person often hasn't the slightest idea of what he is, of what he wants, of what his own opinions are.

It was such findings as these that led ultimately to the discovery of a most profound difference between self-actualizing people and others, namely, that the motivational life of self-actualizing people is not only quantitatively different, but also qualitatively different, from that of ordinary people.[25] [26] It seems probable that we must construct a profoundly different psychology of motivation for self-actualizing people, i.e., expression—or growth-motivation—rather than deficiency-motivation. Indeed, it may turn out to be more fruitful to consider the concept of "motivation" to apply *only* to non-self-actualizers. Our subjects no longer "strive" in the ordinary sense but rather "develop." They attempt to grow to perfection and to develop more and more fully in their own style. The motivation of ordinary men is a striving for the basic need gratification which they lack. But self-actualizing people in fact lack none of these gratifications. And yet they have impulses. They work, they try, and they are ambitious, even though in an unusual sense. For them motivation is just character-growth, character-expression, maturation and development—in a word, self-actualization. Could these self-actualizing people be more human, more revealing of the "original nature" of the species, closer to the "species-type" in the taxonomical sense? Ought a biological species to be judged by its crippled, warped, only partially developed specimens, or by examples that have been overdomesticated, caged, and trained?

### 4. Problem-Centering

Our subjects are in general strongly focused on problems outside themselves. In current terminology they are problem-centered rather than ego-centered. They generally are not problems for themselves, and are not generally much concerned about themselves, i.e., as contrasted with the ordinary introspectiveness that one finds in insecure people. These individuals customarily have some mission in life, some task to fulfill, some problem outside of themselves which enlists much of their energies.[2]

This is not necessarily a task that they would prefer or choose for themselves; it may be a task that they feel is their responsibility, duty, or obligation. This is why we use the phrase "a task that they must do" rather than the phrase "a task that they want to do." In general these tasks are nonpersonal or "unselfish," concerned rather with the good of mankind in general, or of a nation in general or of a few individuals in the subject's family.

With a few exceptions, we can say that our subjects are ordinarily concerned with basic issues and eternal questions of the type that we have learned to call by the names philosophical or ethical. Such people live customarily in the widest possible frame of reference. They seem never to get so close to the trees that they fail to see the forest. They work within a framework of values which are broad and not petty, universal and not local, and in terms of a century rather than the moment. In a word, these people are all, in one sense or another, philosophers, however homely.

Of course, such an attitude carries with it dozens of implications for every area of daily living. For instance, one of the main "presenting symptoms" originally worked with ("bigness," lack of smallness, triviality, pettiness) can be subsumed under this more general heading. This impression of being above small things, of having a larger horizon, a wider breadth of vision, of living in the widest frame of reference, *sub specie aeternitatis*, is of the utmost social and interpersonal importance; it seems to impart a certain serenity and lack of worry over immediate concerns, which makes life easier not only for themselves but for all who are associated with them.

### 5. The Quality of Detachment; the Need for Privacy

For all my subjects it is true that they can be solitary, without harm to themselves and without discomfort. Furthermore, it is true for almost all of them that they positively *like* solitude and privacy to a definitely greater degree than the average person. The dichotomy "introvert-extrovert" applies hardly at all to these people and will not be used here. The term that seems to be most useful is "detachment."

It is often possible for them to remain above the battle, to remain unruffled, undisturbed by that which produces turmoil in others. They find it easy to be aloof, reserved, and also calm and serene; thus, it becomes possible for them to take personal misfortunes without reacting violently, as the ordinary person does. They seem to be able to retain their dignity even in undignified surroundings and situations. Perhaps this comes in part from their tendency to stick by their own interpretation of a situation, rather than to rely upon what other people feel or think about the matter.

This quality of detachment may have some connection with certain other qualities as well. For one thing it is possible to call my subjects more objective (in *all* senses of that word) than average people. We have seen that they are more problem-centered than ego-centered. This is true even when the problem concerns themselves, their own wishes, motives, hopes, or aspirations. Consequently, they have the ability to concentrate, to a degree not usual for ordinary men. Intense concentration produces as a by-product such phenomena as "absent-mindedness," the ability to forget and to be oblivious of other surroundings. An example is the ability to sleep soundly, to have undisturbed appetite, to be able to smile and laugh through a period of problems, worry, and responsibility.

In social relations with most people, detachment creates certain troubles and problems. It is really interpreted by "normal" people as coldness, snobbishness, lack of affection, unfriendliness, or even hostility.

By contrast, the ordinary friendship relationship is more clinging, more demanding, more desirous of reassurance, compliment, support, warmth, and exclusiveness. It is true that self-actualizing people don't "need" others in the ordinary sense. But since this being needed, or being missed, is the usual earmark of friendship, it is evident that detachment will not easily be accepted by average people.

*6. Autonomy, Independence of Culture and Environment*

One characteristic of self-actualizing people which to a certain extent crosscuts much of what we have already described is their relative independence of the physical and social environment. Since they are propelled by growth-motivation, rather than deficiency-motivation, self-actualizing people are not dependent for their main satisfactions on the real world, or other people, or culture, or means-to-ends, or, in general, on extrinsic satisfactions. Rather they are dependent for their own development and continued growth upon their own potentialities and latent resources. Just as the tree needs sunshine, and water, and food, so do most people need love, safety, and the other basic need gratifications which can come only from without. But once these external satisfiers are obtained, once these inner deficiencies are satiated by outside satisfiers, the true problem of individual human development begins, i.e., self-actualization.

This independence of environment means a relative stability in the face of hard knocks, blows, deprivations, frustrations, and the like.

These people can maintain a relative serenity and happiness in the midst of circumstances that would drive other people to suicide. They have also been described as "self-contained."

Deficiency-motivated people *must* have other people available, since most of their main need gratifications (love, safety, respect, prestige, belongingness) can come only from other human beings. But growth-motivated people may actually be hampered by others. The determinants of satisfaction and of the good life are for them now inner-individual and *not* social. They have become strong enough to be independent of the good opinion of other people, or even of their affection. The honors, the status, the rewards, the prestige, and the love they can bestow must have become less important than self-development and inner growth.[13] [29] [30] [32] [34] [37] We must remember that the best technique we know, even though not the only one, for getting to this point of independence from love and respect, is to have been given plenty of this very same love and respect in the past.[24]

### 7. Continued Freshness of Appreciation

Self-actualized people have the wonderful capacity to appreciate again and again, freshly and naively, the basic goods of life, with awe, pleasure, wonder, and even ecstasy, however stale these experiences may have become to others. Thus, for such a person, every sunset is as beautiful as the first one, any flower may be of breath-taking loveliness, even after he has seen a million flowers. The thousandth baby he sees is just as miraculous a product as the first one he saw. He remains as convinced of his luck in marriage thirty years after his marriage and is as surprised by his wife's beauty when she is sixty as he was forty years before. For such people even the casual workday, moment-to-moment business of living can be thrilling, exciting, and ecstatic. These intense feelings do not come all the time; they come occasionally rather than usually, but at the most unexpected moments. The person may cross the river on the ferry ten times, and at the eleventh crossing have a strong recurrence of the same feelings, reaction of beauty and excitement, as when he crossed the river for the first time.[6]

There are some differences in choice of beautiful objects. Some subjects go primarily to nature; for others it is primarily children; and for a few subjects, it has been primarily great music. But it may certainly be said that they derive ecstasy, inspiration, and strength from the basic experiences of life. No one of them, for instance, will get this basic sort of reaction from going to a night club or getting a lot of money or having a good time at a party.

Perhaps one special experience may be added. For several of my subjects the sexual pleasures and particularly the orgasm provided not passing pleasure alone, but some kind of basic strengthening and revivifying that some people derive from music or nature. I shall say more about this in the section on the mystic experience.

It is probable that this acute richness of subjective experience is an aspect of closeness of relationship to the concrete and fresh *per se* reality discussed above. Perhaps what we call staleness in experience is a consequence of ticketing off a rich perception into one or another category or rubric as it proves to be no longer advantageous, or useful, or threatening, or otherwise ego-involved.[23]

### 8. The "Mystic Experience," the "Oceanic Feeling"

Those subjective expressions which have been called the mystic experience and described so well by William James[14] are a fairly common experience for our subjects. The strong emotions described in the previous section sometimes get strong enough, chaotic and widespread enough, to be called mystic experiences.

My interest and attention in this subject were first enlisted by several of my subjects who described their sexual orgasms in vaguely familiar terms, which later I remembered had been used by various writers to describe what *they* called the mystic experience. There were the same feelings of limitless horizons opening up to the vision, of the feeling of being simultaneously more powerful and also more helpless than one ever was before, the feeling of great ecstasy and wonder and awe, the loss of placing in time and space with, finally, the conviction that something extremely important and valuable had happened, so that the subject is to some extent transformed and strengthened even in his daily life by such experiences.[13] [29] [34]

It is quite important to dissociate this experience from any theological or supernatural reference, even though for thousands of years they have been linked. None of our subjects spontaneously made any such tie-up, although in later conversation some semireligious conclusions were drawn by a few, e.g., "life must have a meaning," etc. Because this experience is a natural experience, well within the jurisdiction of science, it is probably better to use Freud's term for it, i.e., the oceanic feeling.

We may also learn from our subjects that such experiences can occur in a lesser degree of intensity. The theological literature had generally assumed an absolute, qualitative difference between the mystic experience and all others. As soon as it is divorced from supernatural reference, and studied as a natural phenomenon, it becomes possible to place the mystic experience on a quantitative continuum from intense to mild. We discover then that the *mild* mystic experience occurs in many, perhaps even most, individuals, and that in the favored individual it occurs dozens of times a day.

Apparently, the acute mystic experience is a tremendous intensification of *any* of the experiences in which there is loss of self or transcendence of it, e.g., problem-centering, intense concentration, "muga" behavior as described by Benedict,[4] intense sensuous experience, self-forgetful and intense enjoyment of music or art.

### 9. Gemeinschaftsgefühl

This word, invented by Alfred Adler,[1] is the only one available which describes well the "flavor" of the feelings for mankind expressed by self-actualizing subjects. They have for human beings in general a deep feeling of identification, sympathy, and affection, in spite of the occasional anger, impatience, or disgust described below. Because of this they have a genuine desire to help the human race. It is as if they are all members of a single family. One's feelings toward his brothers would be on the whole affectionate, even if these brothers were foolish, weak, or even if they were sometimes nasty. They would still be more easily forgiven than strangers.

If one's view is not general enough and if it is not spread over a long enough period of time, then one may not see this feeling of identification with mankind. The self-actualizing person is, after all, very different from other people in thought, impulse, behavior, emotion. When it comes down to it, in certain basic ways he is like an alien in a strange land. Very few really understand him however much they may like him. He is often saddened, exasperated, and even enraged by the shortcomings of the average person, and, while they are to him ordinarily no more than a nuisance, they sometimes become bitter tragedy. However far apart he is from them at times, he nevertheless feels a basic underlying kinship with these creatures whom he must regard with, if not condescension, at least the knowledge that he can do many things better than they can, that he can see things that they cannot see, that the truth which is so clear to him is for most people veiled and hidden. This is what Adler called the "older-brotherly" attitude.

### 10. Interpersonal Relations

Self-actualizing people have deeper and more profound interpersonal relations than any other adults (although not necessarily deeper than those of children). They are capable of more fusion, greater love, more perfect identification, more obliteration of the ego boundaries than other people would consider possible. There are, however, certain special characteristics of these relationships. In the first place, it is my observation that the opposite members in these relationships are ordinarily (about 2/3 of the cases) also self-actualizing persons. There is high selectiveness here considering the small proportion of such people in the general population.

One consequence of this phenomenon and of certain others as well is that self-actualizing people have these especially deep ties with rather few individuals. Their circle of friends is rather small. The ones whom they love profoundly are few in number. Partly this is for the reason that being very close to someone in this self-actualizing style seems to require a good deal of time. Devotion is not a matter of a moment. One subject expressed it so: "I haven't got time for many friends. Nobody has, that is, if they are to be *real* friends." The only possible exception in my group was one woman who seemed to be especially equipped socially. It was almost as if her appointed task in life was to have close and warm and beautiful relations with all the members of her family and their families as well as all her friends and theirs. Perhaps this was because she was an uneducated woman who had no formal "task" or "career." This exclusiveness of devotion can and does exist side by side with a widespreading *Gemeinschaftsgefühl,* benevolence, affection, and friendliness (as qualified above); these people *tend* to be kind or at least patient to almost everyone. They have an especially tender love for children and are easily touched by them. In a very real even though special sense, they love or rather have compassion for all mankind.

This "love" does not imply lack of discrimination. The fact is that they can speak realistically and harshly of those who deserve it, and especially of the hypocritical, the pretentious, the pompous, the self-inflated. But the face-to-face relationships, even with these people, do not show signs of realistically low evaluations. One explanatory statement was about as follows: "Most people after all do not amount to much, but they *could* have. They make all sorts of foolish mistakes and wind up being miserable and not knowing how they got that way when their intentions were good. Those who are not nice are usually paying for it in deep unhappiness. They should be pitied rather than attacked."

Perhaps the briefest possible description is to say that their hostile reactions to others are (a) deserved, and (b) for the good of the person attacked or for someone else's good. This is to say, with Fromm, that their hostility is not character-based but is reactive or situational.[9]

All the subjects for whom I have data show in common another characteristic which is appropriate to mention here, namely, that they attract at least some admirers, "friends," or even disciples or worshipers.

The relation between the individual and his train of admirers is apt to be rather one-sided. The admirers are apt to demand more than our individual is willing to give. And, furthermore, these devotions are apt to be rather embarrassing, distressing, and even distasteful to the self-actualizing person, since they often go beyond ordinary bounds. The usual picture is of our subject being kind and pleasant when forced into these relationships but ordinarily trying to avoid them as gracefully as possible.

### 11. The Democratic Character Structure

All my subjects without exception may be said to be democratic people in the deepest possible sense. I say this on the basis of a previous analysis of authoritarian and democratic character structures[20] which is too elaborate to present here; it is possible only to describe some aspects of this behavior in short space. These people have all the obvious or superficial democratic characteristics. They can be, and are, friendly with anyone of suitable character, regardless of class, education, political belief, race, or color. As a matter of fact, it often seems as if they are not even aware of these differences, which are for the average person so obvious and so important.

They have not only this most obvious quality, but their democratic feeling goes deeper as well. For instance, they find it possible to learn from anybody who has something to teach them—no matter what other characteristics he may have. In such a learning relationship, they do not try to maintain any outward "dignity" or to maintain status or age prestige or the like. It should even be said that my subjects share a quality that could be called "humility" of a certain type. They are all quite aware of their own worth, so that there is no humbleness of the cringing or of the designing and calculating type. They are equally aware of how little they know in comparison with what *could* be known and what is known by others. Because of this it is possible for them without pose to be honestly respectful, and even humble, before people who can teach them something which they do not know or who have a skill they do not possess. They give this honest respect to a carpenter who is a good carpenter or, for that matter, to anybody who is a master of his own tools or his own craft.

The careful distinction must be made between this democratic feeling and a lack of discrimination in taste, of an undiscriminating equality of any one human being with any other. These individuals, themselves elite, select for their friends elite, but this is an elite of character, capacity, and talent, rather than of birth, race, blood, name, family, age, youth, fame, or power.

Most profound, but also most vague, is the hard-to-get-at tendency to give a certain quantum of respect to *any* human being just because he is a human individual; our subjects seem not to wish to go beyond a certain minimum point, even with scoundrels, of demeaning, of derogating, or robbing of dignity.

### 12. Means and Ends

I have found none of my subjects to be chronically unsure about the difference between right and wrong in his actual living. Whether or not they could verbalize the matter, they rarely showed in their day-to-day living the chaos, the confusion, the inconsistency, or the conflict that is so common in the average person's ethical dealings. This may be phrased also in such terms as: these individuals are strongly ethical, they have definite moral standards, they do right and do not do wrong. Needless to say, their notions of right and wrong are often not the conventional ones.

One way of expressing the quality I am trying to describe was suggested by Dr. David Levy, who pointed out that a few centuries ago these would all have been described as "men who walk in the path of God" or as the "Godly Man." So far as religion is concerned, none of my subjects are orthodoxly religious, but on the other hand I know of only one who describes himself as an atheist (four of the total group studied). All the others for whom I have information hesitate to call themselves atheists. They say that they believe in a God but describe this God more as a metaphysical concept than as a personal figure. Whether or not they could be called religious people as a group must then depend entirely on the concept or definition of religion that we choose to use. If religion is defined only in social-behavioral terms, then these are all "religious" people, the atheists included. But if we use the term religion more conservatively so as to include and stress the supernatural element (certainly the more common usage), then our answer must be quite different, for then almost none of them are religious.

Self-actualizing people most of the time behave as though, for them, means and ends are clearly distinguishable. In general, they are fixed on ends rather than on means, and means are quite definitely subordinated to these ends. This, however, is an oversimple statement. Our subjects make the situation more complex by often regarding as ends-in-themselves many experiences and activities which are, for other people, only means-to-ends. Our subjects are somewhat more likely to appreciate for its own sake, and in an absolute way, the "doing itself"; they can often enjoy for its own sake the getting-to-some-place as well as the arriving. It is occasionally possible for them to make out of the most trivial and routine activity an intrinsically enjoyable game or dance or play. Wertheimer pointed out that some children are so creative that they can transform hackneyed routine, mechanical and rote experiences, e.g., as in one of his experiments, transporting books from one set of shelves to another, into a structured and amusing game of a sort by doing this according to a certain system or with a certain rhythm.

### 13. Philosophical, Unhostile Sense of Humor

One very early finding that was quite easy to make, because it was common to all my subjects, was that their sense of humor is not of the ordinary type. They do not consider funny what the average man considers to be funny. Thus they do not laugh at hostile humor (making people laugh by hurting someone) or superiority humor (laughing at someone else's inferiority) or authority-rebellion humor (the unfunny smutty joke).

Characteristically what they consider humor is more closely allied to philosophy than to anything else. It may also be called the humor of the real, because it consists in large part in poking fun at human beings in general when they are foolish, or forget their place in the universe, or try to be big when they are actually small. This can take the form of poking fun at themselves, but this is not done in any masochistic or clown-like way. Lincoln's humor can serve as a suitable example. Probably Lincoln never made a joke which hurt anybody else; it is also likely that many or even most of his jokes had something to say, had a function beyond just producing a laugh. (They often seemed to be education in a more palatable form akin to parables or fables.)

On a simple quantitative basis, our subjects may be said to be humorous less often than the average of the population. Punning, joking, witty remarks, gay repartee, or persiflage of the ordinary sort is much less often seen than the rather thoughtful, philosophical humor which elicits a smile more usually than a laugh, which is intrinsic to the situation rather than added to it, which is spontaneous rather than planned, and which very often can never be repeated. It should not be surprising that the average man, accustomed as he is to joke books and belly laughs, considers our subjects to be rather on the sober and serious side.

### 14. Creativeness

This is a universal characteristic of all the people studied or observed. There is no exception. Each one shows in one way or another a special kind of creativeness or originality or inventiveness which has certain peculiar characteristics. These special characteristics can be understood more fully in the light of discussion later in this paper. For one thing, it is different from "special-talent creativeness" of the Mozart type. We may as well face the fact that the so-called "geniuses" display ability which we do not understand. All we can say of them is that they seem to be specially endowed with a drive and a capacity which may have rather little relationship to the rest of the personality and with which, from all evidence, the individuals seem to be born. Such talent we have no concern with here, since it doesn't rest upon psychic health or basic satisfaction. The creativeness of the self-actualized man seems rather to be akin to the naive and universal creativeness of unspoiled children. It seems to be more a fundamental characteristic of common human nature—a potentiality given to all human beings at birth. Most human beings lose this as they become acculturated, but some few individuals seem either to retain this fresh and naive direct way of looking at life or, else, if they have lost it, as most people do, to recover it later in life.

This creativeness appears in some of our subjects not in the usual forms of writing books, composing music, or producing artistic objects, but rather may be much more humble. It is as if this special type of creativeness, being an expression of healthy personality, is projected out upon the world or touches whatever activity the person is engaged in. In this sense there can be creative shoemakers or carpenters or clerks. Whatever one does can be done with a certain attitude, a certain spirit which arises out of the nature of the character of the person performing the act. One can even *see* creatively, as the child does.

This quality is differentiated out here for the sake of discussion, as if it were something separate from the characteristics which precede it and follow it; but this is not actually the case. Perhaps when we speak of creativeness here we are simply describing from another point of view, namely, from the point of view of consequences, what we have described above as a greater freshness, penetration, and efficiency of perception. These people seem to see the true and the real more easily. It is because of this that they seem to other more limited men creative.

Furthermore, as we have seen, these individuals are less inhibited, less constricted, less bound, in a word, less acculturated. In more positive terms, they are more spontaneous, more natural, "more human." This too would have as one of its consequences what would seem to other people to be creativeness. If we assume, as we may from our study of children, that all people were once spontaneous, and, perhaps in their deepest roots, still are, but that these people have in addition to their deep spontaneity a superficial but powerful set of inhibitions, then this spontaneity must be checked so as not to appear very often. If there were no choking-off forces, then we might expect that every human being would show this special type of creativeness.

### The Imperfections of Self-Actualizing People

The ordinary mistake that is made by novelists, poets, and essayists about the good human being is to make him to be like him. The individual's own wishes for perfection and his guilt and shame about shortcomings are projected upon various kinds of people from whom the average man demands much more than he himself gives. Thus teachers and ministers are ordinarily conceived to be rather joyless people who have no mundane desires and who have no weaknesses. It is my belief that most of the novelists who have attempted to portray good (healthy) people did this sort of thing, making them into stuffed shirts or marionettes or unreal projections of unreal ideals, rather than into the robust, hearty, lusty individuals they really are. Our subjects show many of the lesser human failings—if they are in fact failings. (They too are equipped with silly, wasteful, or thoughtless habits. They can be boring, stubborn, irritating. They are by no means free from a rather superficial vanity, pride, partiality to their own productions, family, friends, and children.)

Our subjects are occasionally capable of an extraordinary and unexpected ruthlessness. It must be remembered that they are very strong people. This makes it possible for them to display a surgical coldness when this is called for, beyond the power of the average man. The man who found that a long-trusted acquaintance was dishonest cut himself off from this friendship sharply and abruptly and without any pangs whatsoever. Another woman who was married to someone she did not love, when she decided on divorce, did it with a decisiveness that looked almost like ruthlessness. Some of them recover so quickly from the death of people close to them as to seem heartless.

Not only are these people strong but they are also independent of the opinions of other people. One woman, extremely irritated by the stuffy conventionalism of some individuals she was introduced to at a gathering, went far out of her way to shock these people by her language and behavior. One might say that it was all right for her to react to irritation in this way, but another result was that these people were completely hostile not only to the woman but to the friends in whose home this meeting took place. While our subject wanted to *alienate* these people, the host and hostess definitely did not.

We may mention one more example which arises primarily from the absorption of our subjects in an impersonal world. In their concentration, in their fascinated interest, in their intense concentration on some phenomenon or question, they may become absent-minded or humorless and forget their ordinary social politeness. In such circumstances, they are apt to show themselves more clearly as essentially not interested in chatting, gay conversation, party-going, or the like. They may use language or behavior which may be very distressing, shocking, insulting, or hurtful to others. Other undesirable (at least from the point of view of others) consequences of detachment have been listed above.

Even their kindness can lead them into mistakes, e.g., marrying out of pity, getting too closely involved with neurotics, bores, unhappy people, and then being sorry for it, allowing scoundrels to impose on them for awhile, giving more than they demand so that occasionally they encourage parasites and psychopaths, etc.

Finally, it has already been pointed out that these people are *not* free of guilt, anxiety, sadness, self-castigation, internal strife, and conflict. The fact that these arise out of *non-neurotic sources* is of little consequence to most people today (even to most psychologists), who are therefore apt to think them *un*healthy for this reason.

## The Values of Self-Actualization

A firm foundation for a value-system is automatically furnished to the self-actualizer by his philosophic acceptance of the nature of his self, of human nature, of much of social life, and of nature and physical reality. These "acceptance-values" account for a high percentage of the total of his individual value-judgments from day to day. What he approves of, disapproves of, is loyal to, opposes, or proposes, what pleases him or displeases him, can often be understood as surface derivations of this source trait of acceptance.

Not only is this foundation automatically (and universally) supplied to *all* SA's by their intrinsic dynamics (so that in at least this respect fully developed human nature may be universal and cross-cultural); other determiners are supplied as well by these same dynamics. Among these are (a) his peculiarly comfortable relationships with reality, (b) his *Gemeinschaftsgefühl*, (c) his basically satisfied condition, from which flow, as epiphenomena, various consequences of surplus, of wealth, of overflowing abundance, (d) his characteristic relations to means and ends, etc. (see above).

One most important consequence of this attitude toward the world—as well as a validation of it—is the fact that conflict and struggle, ambivalence and uncertainty over choice, lessen or disappear in many areas of life. Apparently morality is largely an epiphenomenon of nonacceptance or dissatisfaction. Many "problems" are seen to be gratuitous and fade out of existence in the atmosphere of pagan acceptance. It is not so much that the problem is solved as that it becomes clearly seen that it never was an intrinsic problem in the first place, but only a sick-man-created one, e.g., card-playing, dancing, wearing short dresses, exposing the head (in some churches) or *not* exposing the head (in others), drinking wine, or eating some meats and not others, or eating them on some days but not on others. Not only are such trivialities deflated; the process also goes on at a more important level, e.g., the relations between the sexes, attitudes toward the structure of the body and toward its functioning, and attitudes toward death itself.

The pursuit of this finding to more profound levels has suggested to the writer that much else of what passes for morals, ethics, and values may be the gratuitous epiphenomena of the pervasive psychopathology of the "average." Many conflicts, frustrations, and threats (which force the kind of choice in which value is expressed) evaporate or resolve for the self-actualizing person in the same way as do, let us say, conflicts over dancing. For him the seemingly irreconcilable battle of the sexes becomes no conflict at all but rather a delightful collaboration. The "antagonistic" interests of adults and children turn out to be not so antagonistic after all. Just as with sex and age differences, so also is it with natural differences, class and caste differences, political differences, role differences, religious differences, etc. As we know, these are each fertile breeding grounds for anxiety, fear, hostility, aggression, defensiveness, and jealousy. But it begins to appear that they *need not be*, for our subjects' reaction to differences is much less often of this undesirable type.

To take the teacher-student relationship as a specific paradigm, our teacher-subjects behaved in a very unneurotic way simply by interpreting the whole situation differently, i.e., as a pleasant collaboration rather than as a clash of wills, of authority, of dignity, etc. The replacement of artificial dignity—which is easily threatened—with the natural simplicity which is *not* easily threatened, the giving up of the attempt to be omniscient and omnipotent, the absence of student-threatening authoritarianism, the refusal to regard the students as competing with each other or with the teacher, the refusal to assume the "professor" stereotype and the insistence on remaining as realistically human as, say, a plumber or a carpenter—all of these created a classroom atmosphere in which suspicion, wariness, defensiveness, hostility, and anxiety disappeared. So also do similar threat-responses tend to disappear in marriages, in families, and in other interpersonal situations when threat itself is reduced.

It is possible to generalize even further, for it seems possible that most or perhaps even all value dichotomies or polarities tend to disappear or resolve in self-actualizing people. These people are neither selfish nor unselfish in the ordinary sense; they are both (or neither).

They are neither rationalists nor intuitionalists, neither classical nor romantic, neither self-interested nor other-interested, neither introverts nor extroverts, etc. Rather they are both. Or, to be accurate, in them these dichotomies simply do not apply.

The principles and the values of the desperate man and of the psychologically healthy man must be different perceptions (interpretations) of the physical world, the social world, and the private psychological world, whose organization and economy are in part the responsibility of the person's value system. For the basically deprived man the world is a dangerous place, a jungle, an enemy territory populated by (a) those whom he can dominate and (b) those who can dominate him. His value system is of necessity, like that of any jungle denizen, dominated and organized by the "lower" needs, especially the creature needs and the safety needs. The basically satisfied person is in a different case. He can afford out of his abundance to take these needs and their satisfaction for granted and can devote himself to higher gratifications. This is to say that their value systems are different—in fact, *must* be different.

The topmost portion of the value system of the SA person is entirely unique and idiosyncratic-character-structure-expressive. This must be true by definition, for self-actualization is actualization of a self, and no two selves are altogether alike. There is only one Renoir, one Brahms, one Spinoza. Our subjects had very much in common, as we have seen, and yet, at the same time, were more completely individualized, more unmistakably themselves, less easily confounded with others than any average control group could possibly be. That is to say, they are simultaneously very much alike and very much unlike each other. They are more completely "individual" than any group that has ever been described and yet are also more completely socialized, more identified with humanity, than any other group yet described.

## Bibliography

1. Adler, A. *Social interest*. New York: Putnam, 1939.
2. Angyal, A. *Foundations for a science of personality*. New York: Commonwealth Fund, 1941.
3. Benedict, R. Unpublished lectures on synergy in society. Bryn Mawr, ca. 1942.
4. ———— *The chrysanthemum and the sword*. Boston: Houghton Mifflin, 1946.
5. Bergson, H. *Creative evolution*. New York: Modern Library, 1944.
6. Eastman, M. *The enjoyment of poetry*. New York: Scribner, 1928.
7. Frenkel-Brunswik, E. Intolerance of ambiguity as an emotional and perceptual personality variable. *J. Personality*, 1949, **18**, 108–143.
8. Freud, S. *Collected papers*. London: Hogarth Press, 1924, Vol LL.
9. Fromm, E. *Escape from freedom*. New York: Farrar and Rinehart, 1941.
10. ———— *Man for himself*. New York: Rinehart, 1947.
11. Goldstein, K. *The organism*. New York: American Book Company, 1939.
12. Horney, K. *Our inner conflicts*. New York: Norton, 1945.
13. Huxley, A. *The perennial philosophy*. New York: Harper, 1944.

14. James, W. *The varieties of religious experience*. New York: Modern Library, 1943.
15. Johnson, W. *People in quandaries*. New York: Harper, 1946.
16. King, C. D. The meaning of normal. *J. Biolo. Med.*, 1945, **17,** 493.
17. Köhler, W. *The place of values in a world of facts*. New York: Liveright, 1938.
18. Korzybski, A. *Science and sanity*. (3rd ed.) Lakeville, Conn.: International Non-Aristotelaian Library Publishing Co., 1948.
19. Maier, N. R. F. The role of frustration in social movements. *Psychol. Rev.*, 1942, **49,** 586–599.
20. Maslow, A. H. The authoritarian character structure. *J. Soc. Psychol.*, 1943, **18,** 401–411.
21. ———— A theory of human motivation. *Psychol. Rev.*, 1943, **50,** 370–396.
22. ———— Dynamics of personality organization, I and II. *Psychol. Rev.*, 1943, **50,** 514–539, 541–558.
23. ———— Cognition of the particular and of the generic. *Psychol. Rev.*, 1948, **55,** 20–40.
24. ———— Higher and lower needs. *J. Psychol.*, 1948, **25,** 433–436.
25. ———— Our maligned animal nature. *J. Psychol.*, 1949, **28,** 273–278.
26. ———— The expressive component of behavior. *Psychol. Rev.*, 1949, **56,** 261–272.
27. Money-Kyrle, R. E. Towards a common aim—a psycho-analytical contribution to ethics. *Brit. J. Med. Psychol.*, 1944, **29,** 105–117.
28. ———— Some aspects of political ethics from the psycho-analytical point of view. *Int. J. Psychoanal.*, 1944, **25,** 166–171.
29. Northrop, F. S. C. *The meeting of East and West*. New York: Macmillan, 1946.
30. Rand, A. *The fountainhead*. Indianapolis: Bobbs-Merrill, 1943.
31. Reik, T. *Listening with the third ear*. New York: Farrar and Straus, 1948.
32. Rogers, C. *Counseling and psychotherapy*. Boston: Houghton Mifflin, 1942.
33. Rokeach, M. Generalized mental rigidity as a factor in ethnocentrism. *J. Abnorm. & Social Psychol.*, 1948, **43,** 259–278.
34. Taylor, E. *Richer by Asia*. Boston: Houghton Mifflin, 1947.
35. Wertheimer, M. Some problems in the theory of ethics. *Social Research*, 1935, **2,** 353–367.
36. Whitehead, A. *The aims of education*. New York: Mentor Books, 1949.
37. Wolfe, T. *You can't go home again*. New York: Harper, 1949.

# Index